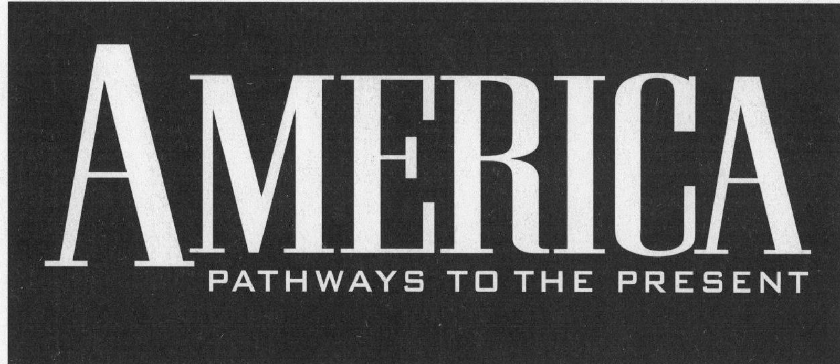

CHAPTER TESTS

WITH TEST BANK CD-ROM

Prentice Hall

Needham, Massachusetts

Upper Saddle River, New Jersey

PRENTICE HALL

Printed in the United States of America

ISBN 0-13-435894-5

4 5 6 7 8 9 03 02 01 00

Table of Contents

UNIT 6 The United States on the Brink of Change, 1890–1920

UNIT 7 Boom Times to Hard Times, 1919–1938

UNIT 8 Hot and Cold War, 1939–1960

UNIT 9 The Upheaval of the Sixties, 1960–1975

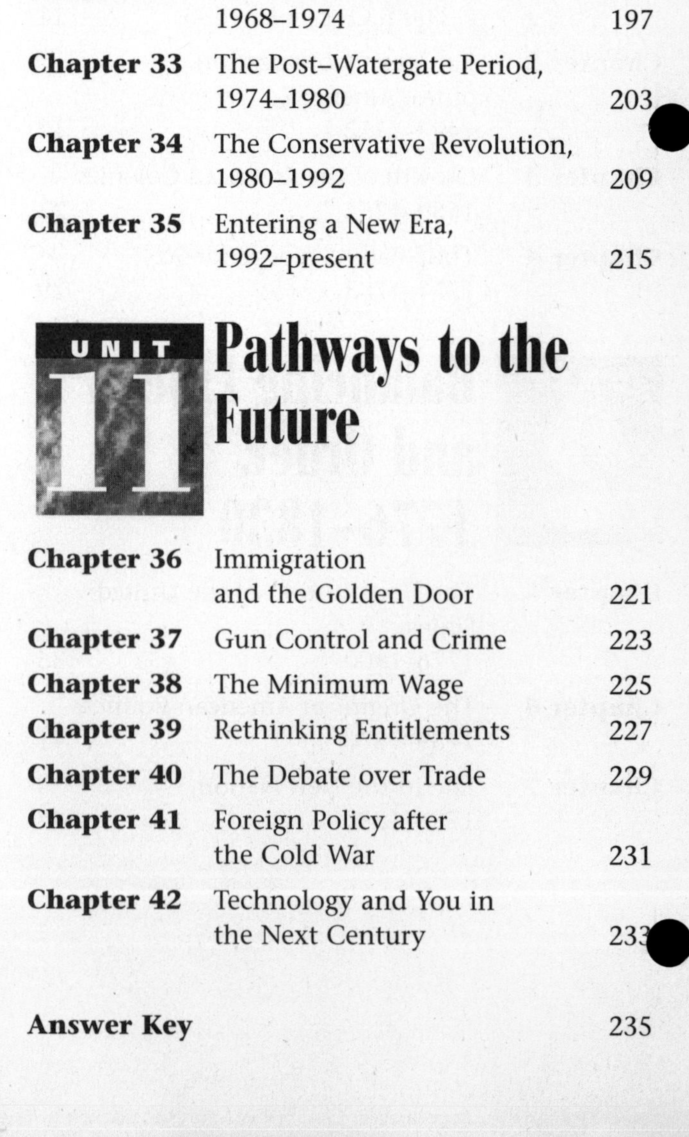

UNIT 10 Continuity and Change, 1968–present

UNIT 11 Pathways to the Future

PRENTICE HALL
AMERICA: PATHWAYS TO THE PRESENT
© 2000

A Perfect Curriculum Fit

The third edition has two volumes—the Survey and Modern American History. The at-a-glance chart below shows the correlation of the two volumes.

SURVEY EDITION	MODERN AMERICAN HISTORY
Unit 1	**Themes in American History**
Chapter 1: The Atlantic World	Government
Chapter 2: European Colonization of the Americas	Geography
Chapter 3: Growth of the American Colonies	Culture
Chapter 4: The Road to Independence	Economics
	Diversity
Unit 2	Foreign Relations
Chapter 5: The Constitution of the United States	Science and Technology
Chapter 6: The Origins of American Politics	
Chapter 7: Life in the New Nation	
Unit 3	**Unit 1: Building a Powerful Nation**
Chapter 8: The Market Revolution	Chapter 1: American History to the Civil War
Chapter 9: Religion and Reform	Section 1: Exploration and the Colonial Era
Chapter 10: Beyond the Mississippi	Section 2: The American Revolution
	Section 3: The Constitution
Unit 4	Section 4: The United States, 1789-1830
Chapter 11: The Coming of the Civil War	Section 5: The United States, 1830-1860
Chapter 12: The Civil War	Chapter 2: The Civil War
Chapter 13: Reconstruction	Chapter 3: Reconstruction
Unit 5	
Chapter 14: The Expansion of American Industry	Chapter 4: The Expansion of American Industry
Chapter 15: Looking to the West	Chapter 5: Looking to the West
Chapter 16: Politics, Immigration, and Urban Life	Chapter 6: Politics, Immigration, and Urban Life
Chapter 17: Daily Life in the Gilded Age	Chapter 7: Daily Life in the Gilded Age

SAME CONTENT FOR BOTH EDITIONS FROM UNIT 6	SAME CONTENT FOR BOTH EDITIONS FROM UNIT 2
Unit 6	**Unit 2: The United States on the Brink of Change**
Chapter 18: Becoming a World Power	Chapter 8: Becoming a World Power
Chapter 19: The Era of Progressive Reform	Chapter 9: The Era of Progressive Reform
Chapter 20: The World War I Era	Chapter 10: The World War I Era
Unit 7	**Unit 3: Boom Times to Hard Times**
Chapter 21: The Twenties	Chapter 11: The Twenties
Chapter 22: Crash and Depression	Chapter 12: Crash and Depression
Chapter 23: The New Deal	Chapter 13: The New Deal
Unit 8	**Unit 4: Hot and Cold War**
Chapter 24: World War II	Chapter 14: World War II
Chapter 25: World War II at Home	Chapter 15: World War II at Home
Chapter 26: The Cold War	Chapter 16: The Cold War
Chapter 27: The Postwar Years at Home	Chapter 17: The Postwar Years at Home
Unit 9	**Unit 5: The Upheaval of the Sixties**
Chapter 28: The Kennedy and Johnson Years	Chapter 18: The Kennedy and Johnson Years
Chapter 29: The Civil Rights Movement	Chapter 19: The Civil Rights Movement
Chapter 30: Other Social Movements	Chapter 20: Other Social Movements
Chapter 31: The Vietnam War and American Society	Chapter 21: The Vietnam War and American Society
Unit 10	**Unit 6: Continuity and Change**
Chapter 32: The Nixon Years	Chapter 22: The Nixon Years
Chapter 33: The Post-Watergate Period	Chapter 23: The Post-Watergate Period
Chapter 34: The Conservative Revolution	Chapter 24: The Conservative Revolution
Chapter 35: Entering a New Era	Chapter 25: Entering a New Era
Unit 11	**Unit 7: Pathways to the Future**
Chapter 36: Immigration and the Golden Door	Chapter 26: Immigration and the Golden Door
Chapter 37: Gun Control and Crime	Chapter 27: Gun Control and Crime
Chapter 38: The Minimum Wage	Chapter 28: The Minimum Wage
Chapter 39: Rethinking Entitlements	Chapter 29: Rethinking Entitlements
Chapter 40: The Debate over Trade	Chapter 30: The Debate over Trade
Chapter 41: Foreign Policy after the Cold War	Chapter 31: Foreign Policy after the Cold War
Chapter 42: Technology and You in the Next Century	Chapter 32: Technology and You in the Next Century
Epilogue: Why Study History? A Nation Looks Ahead	Epilogue: Why Study History? A Nation Looks Ahead

About the *Chapter Tests*

This booklet contains chapter tests for *America: Pathways to the Present*. For each chapter, there are two different reproducible tests—Test A and Test B. Each test contains five parts: Key Terms, People, and Places; Identifying Main Ideas; Critical Thinking; Interpreting a Chart/Graph, Political Cartoon or other visual document; and Analyzing a Document.

The tests employ a variety of questioning strategies that require students to use higher order thinking skills as well as comprehension skills. The tests include enhanced multiple-choice questions so you can meet the needs of all your students.

About the *Test Bank CD-ROM*

The Test Bank CD-ROM provides all the chapter tests **plus** additional unit-level tests *for America: Pathways to the Present.* This program gives you great flexibility in creating quizzes, chapter and unit tests, midterms, and finals tailored to your individual classroom needs. The *Test Bank* also allows you to create tests to meet state and local curriculum requirements and to build the appropriate content, skills, and critical thinking into your testing program. It allows you to edit existing questions, create your own test questions, scramble the sequence for multiple versions of the same test, and generate customized answer keys.

The dual-platform Test Bank CD-ROM allows both Windows and Macintosh users to access the *Test Bank* on a single CD-ROM. For technical support, call our toll free HELP hotline at **1-800-234-5TEC.**

About the *Prentice Hall Dial-A-Test®* *Service*

If you do not have access to a computer or would like the convenience of designing your own tests without typing a word, you may want to take advantage of our free Dial-A-Test® Service. Available to all users of *America: Pathways to the Present,* Dial-A-Test® is simple to use.

HERE'S HOW IT WORKS

1. **Choose the questions you want** from the ready-made Chapter Test Questions.
2. **Enter the numbers of the questions** in the order you want on a Dial-A-Test® Order Form (see page ix for a master that you may photocopy). Be sure to include the chapter number on the form. For example, in the case of test question 17, taken from Chapter 1 Test A, mark the order form with the designation 1A,17.

3. **Use a separate Dial-A-Test® order form** for each original test you request.
4. **If you would like another version** of your original test with the questions scrambled, or put in another sequence, simply check the line labeled *Alternate Version I* on the order form. For a third version, check the line labeled *Alternate Version II.* Please note that Prentice Hall reserves the right to limit the number of tests and versions you can request at any one time, especially during the busier times of the year when midterms and finals are given.

5. **Choose the method** by which you would like to order your original test and/or multiple versions of your original test. To order by telephone, call toll free 1-800-468-8378 between 9:00 A.M. and 4:30 P.M. Eastern Standard Time and read the test question numbers to our Dial-A-Test® operator. Give the customer service representative the following reference number 0-13-437483-5. To order by mail, send your completed Dial-A-Test® order form to the address listed below. Now you may also FAX your order to 1-614-771-7365.

6. **You may order** up to 100 questions per test by telephone on our toll-free 800 number or up to 200 questions per test by mail.

7. **Please allow a minimum of two weeks** for shipping, especially if you are ordering by mail. Although we process your order within 48 hours of your call or the receipt of your form by mail, mailing may take up to two weeks. Thus we ask you to plan accordingly and expect to receive your original test, any alternate test versions that you requested, and complete answer keys within a reasonable amount of time.

8. **Tests are available all year.** You can order tests before the school year begins, during vacation, or as you need them.

9. **For additional order forms** or to ask questions regarding this service, please write to the following address:

Dial-A-Test®
Prentice Hall School Division
4350 Equity Drive
Columbus, OH 43228

-ORDER FORM-
CTS

DIAL-A-TEST®
PRENTICE HALL SCHOOL DIVISION
CUSTOMIZED TESTING SERVICE
TOLL-FREE NUMBER 800-468-8378 (H O-T-T-E-S-T)

-ORDER FORM-
CTS

You may **call** the PH Dial-A-Test® toll-free number during our business hours (9:00 A.M.-4:30 P.M. EST). Now you may also FAX your order to 1-614-771-7365 anytime.

DIAL-A-TEST®
PRENTICE HALL SCHOOL DIVISION
4350 EQUITY DRIVE
COLUMBUS, OH 43228

FOR PH USE DATE REC. DATE SENT
__ PHONE __ MAIL __ FAX ________ ________

EXACT TEXT TITLE/VOL. *America: Pathways to the Present*
© DATE 2000 **CODE** 0-13-437483-5

CUSTOMER INFORMATION
NAME ____________
SCHOOL ____________
ADDRESS ____________
CITY ____________ STATE ____ ZIP ____
PHONE ____________ EXT. ____

DATE BY WHICH TEST IS NEEDED ________

TEST USAGE (CHECK ONE)
__ SAMPLE __ QUIZ __ CHAPTER TEST
__ UNIT TEST __ SEMESTER TEST __ FINAL EXAM

VERSIONS (SEE page viii, point 4.)
__ 1. Original
__ 2. Alternate Version I
__ 3. Alternate Version II

TEST IDENTIFICATION (This information will appear at the top of your test.)
____
____
____
____

EXAMPLE: Mr. Hernandez
American History, Period 5
Chapter Test

1 ____	26 ____	51 ____	76 ____	101 ____	126 ____	151 ____	176 ____
2 ____	27 ____	52 ____	77 ____	102 ____	127 ____	152 ____	177 ____
3 ____	28 ____	53 ____	78 ____	103 ____	128 ____	153 ____	178 ____
4 ____	29 ____	54 ____	79 ____	104 ____	129 ____	154 ____	179 ____
5 ____	30 ____	55 ____	80 ____	105 ____	130 ____	155 ____	180 ____
6 ____	31 ____	56 ____	81 ____	106 ____	131 ____	156 ____	181 ____
7 ____	32 ____	57 ____	82 ____	107 ____	132 ____	157 ____	182 ____
8 ____	33 ____	58 ____	83 ____	108 ____	133 ____	158 ____	183 ____
9 ____	34 ____	59 ____	84 ____	109 ____	134 ____	159 ____	184 ____
10 ____	35 ____	60 ____	85 ____	110 ____	135 ____	160 ____	185 ____
11 ____	36 ____	61 ____	86 ____	111 ____	136 ____	161 ____	186 ____
12 ____	37 ____	62 ____	87 ____	112 ____	137 ____	162 ____	187 ____
13 ____	38 ____	63 ____	88 ____	113 ____	138 ____	163 ____	188 ____
14 ____	39 ____	64 ____	89 ____	114 ____	139 ____	164 ____	189 ____
15 ____	40 ____	65 ____	90 ____	115 ____	140 ____	165 ____	190 ____
16 ____	41 ____	66 ____	91 ____	116 ____	141 ____	166 ____	191 ____
17 ____	42 ____	67 ____	92 ____	117 ____	142 ____	167 ____	192 ____
18 ____	43 ____	68 ____	93 ____	118 ____	143 ____	168 ____	193 ____
19 ____	44 ____	69 ____	94 ____	119 ____	144 ____	169 ____	194 ____
20 ____	45 ____	70 ____	95 ____	120 ____	145 ____	170 ____	195 ____
21 ____	46 ____	71 ____	96 ____	121 ____	146 ____	171 ____	196 ____
22 ____	47 ____	72 ____	97 ____	122 ____	147 ____	172 ____	197 ____
23 ____	48 ____	73 ____	98 ____	123 ____	148 ____	173 ____	198 ____
24 ____	49 ____	74 ____	99 ____	124 ____	149 ____	174 ____	199 ____
25 ____	50 ____	75 ____	100 ____	125 ____	150 ____	175 ____	200 ____

Teaching Resources & Classroom Assessment At Your Fingertips

Only Prentice Hall gives you the ability to streamline the way you plan and assess lessons all on one dual-platform CD-ROM.

Choice. *ResourcePro™* gives you access to material by chapter or by type of resource and lets you print it directly from the CD-ROM.

Manageability. This user-friendly CD-ROM allows you to view Teaching Resources and Literature database instantly. Using the search function, you can find resources by word, terms, and topics.

Planning Flexibility. Using Planning Express, you can choose a predesigned lesson plan or create your own. Planning Express is flexible enough to suit your individual teaching style or block scheduling needs.

Assessment. Customize assessment for all your lessons by accessing all chapter tests and additional unit tests on the Test Bank. You can edit existing questions and generate customized answer keys.

NAME ____________ CLASS ________ DATE ________

TEST FORM A

The Atlantic World (c. 700 B.C.- c. A.D. 1600)

CHAPTER 1

A. Identifying Key Terms, People, and Places

Match the descriptions in Column I with the terms in Column II. Write the letter of the correct answer in the blank provided. You will not use all the terms. *(20 points)*

Column I

____ **1.** term used to describe the people who move their homes regularly in search of food

____ **2.** a group of families descended from a common ancestor

____ **3.** a political and economic system developed for protection in Europe

____ **4.** someone who rules over a kingdom

____ **5.** an era of enormous creativity and rapid change begun in Italy in the 1300s

____ **6.** term used to describe an item in short supply

____ **7.** an agreement that divided non-Christian lands between Spain and Portugal

____ **8.** the Protestant revolt against Church authority

____ **9.** the historical era also known as the "medieval period"

____ **10.** a farm product grown strictly for sale

Column II

a. Reformation

b. cash crop

c. scarce

d. Treaty of Tordesillas

e. nomadic

f. Middle Ages

g. Renaissance

h. monarch

i. clan

j. feudalism

k. barter

l. savanna

m. Columbian Exchange

B. Identifying Main Ideas

Write the letter of the correct ending in the blank provided. (*32 points*)

____ **11.** In Native American cultures, the social structure was determined by
a. a group of elected officials. **b.** the women.
c. kinship groups. **d.** the youngest members of a clan.

____ **12.** Native Americans passed down their traditions from generation to generation through
a. barter. **b.** oral history.
c. written records. **d.** trade routes.

____ **13.** Europeans fought the Crusades
a. to establish new trade routes to the Indies.
b. to put limitations on European trade.
c. to take control of Jerusalem from Muslim Turks.
d. to convert Muslims to Christianity.

CHAPTER 1

_____ **14.** In Europe, the Black Death of the 1300s brought on
a. rapid population growth.
b. rapid growth of cities.
c. death to one third of the entire population.
d. an end to belief in the Church's authority.

_____ **15.** In the late 1400s in Africa, the empire of Songhai
a. thrived as a major trading power.
b. cut off all business with European traders.
c. began to decline as a result of corrupt government.
d. was destroyed by Arab invaders.

_____ **16.** Slavery in Africa differed from slavery as it developed in the Americas in that
a. women and children were not enslaved.
b. only complete families were enslaved.
c. enslavement lasted only seven years.
d. slaves could move up in society and out of slavery.

_____ **17.** Spain decided to back Columbus's voyage to the west in the hopes that it would
a. help to finally defeat the Muslims.
b. make Columbus rich and famous.
c. gain Spain a trading advantage over Portugal.
d. bring an end to feudalism in Europe.

_____ **18.** By the end of his life, Columbus had proved himself to be
a. a seaman of great navigational skills.
b. a successful governor of Hispaniola.
c. a veteran of two voyages to the Americas.
d. a man of great prestige at the Spanish court.

C. Critical Thinking

Answer the following questions on the back of this paper or on a separate sheet of paper. (*24 points*)

19. Recognizing Ideologies How would you contrast the beliefs of Europeans, Native Americans, and West Africans regarding land ownership?

20. Testing Conclusions Historian Alfred W. Crosby once remarked, "The Columbian exchange of peoples, plants, products, and diseases, and ideas [was] the most important event in human history since the end of the Ice Age..." What evidence would you use to support Crosby's statement?

CHAPTER 1

D. Interpreting a Chart

Use the chart below to answer questions 21-22. Write your answers on the back of this paper or on a separate sheet of paper. (*12 points*)

21. Name three diseases that the Columbian Exchange transmitted to the Americas.

22. Which crops went from the Americas to Europe, Africa, and Asia?

a. maize and beans

b. measles and typhus

c. wheat and rice

d. horses and pigs

E. Analyzing a Document

In the excerpt from a letter below, Columbus described his dealings with the first Native Americans he met. Read the excerpt and then answer the questions about it on the back of this paper or on a separate sheet of paper. (*12 points*)

> ...I seized by force several Indians on the first island, in order that they might learn from us, and in like manner tell us about those things in these lands of which they themselves had knowledge; and the plan succeeded, for in a short time we understood them and they us, sometimes by gestures and signs, sometimes by words; and it was a great advantage to us.

The Letter of Columbus on the Discovery of America (New York: Lenox Library, 1892)

23. What indication does this excerpt give about Columbus's attitude towards the Native Americans?

24. What do you think the Native Americans' reactions to Columbus might have been?

NAME ______________________ CLASS ____________ DATE ____________

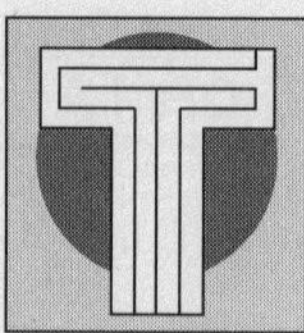

TEST FORM B

The Atlantic World (c. 700 B.C.- c. A.D. 1600)

CHAPTER 1

A. Identifying Key Terms, People, and Places

Complete each sentence in Column I by writing the letter of the correct term from Column II in each blank. You will not use all the terms. (*20 points*)

Column I

_____ **1.** Among Native Americans, family relationships, called _____ determined social status.

_____ **2.** Native Americans carried out _____ along trade routes crisscrossing the land.

_____ **3.** The _____ were the wars European Christians fought against the Turks.

_____ **4.** Merchants, traders, and artisans created a new _____ in medieval Europe.

_____ **5.** This term is used for someone who rules a kingdom.

_____ **6.** The _____ was an era of rebirth beginning in Italy in the 1300s.

_____ **7.** The _____ was a revolt against Church authority beginning in the 1500s.

_____ **8.** _____ is the name that describes an African region of tropical grasslands and scattered trees.

_____ **9.** Spain and Portugal established large farming operations called _____.

_____ **10.** Farm products grown strictly for sale are called _____.

Column II

a. monarch
b. Reformation
c. Columbian Exchange
d. kinship
e. nomadic
f. barter
g. savanna
h. Crusades
i. plantations
j. middle class
k. Renaissance
l. cash crops
m. feudalism

B. Identifying Main Ideas

Write the letter of the correct answer in the blank provided. (*32 points*)

_____ **11.** In what woodland environment of North America did the Senaca, Lenape, and Iroquois develop their ways of life?
a. Southwest
b. Northeast
c. Plains
d. Northwest Coast

_____ **12.** Which of the following did Native Americans believe could not be sold?
a. obsidian
b. shells
c. land
d. copper

_____ 13. Why did Europeans develop the system of feudalism?
- **a.** to drive the Turkish Muslims from Jerusalem
- **b.** to develop a web of trade routes
- **c.** to spread Christianity to other parts of the world
- **d.** to protect people from attacking and looting

_____ 14. Which development in the 1400s created a communications revolution in Europe?
- **a.** the printing press
- **b.** Dutch painting
- **c.** humanism
- **d.** seafaring technology

_____ 15. Which one of the following best describes the main types of vegetation regions in West Africa?
- **a.** mountain oaks and desert mesquites
- **b.** dryland, roots, and pine nuts
- **c.** rain forests, savanna, and desert
- **d.** woodlands and swamps

_____ 16. Which of the following provided West Africans with the types of support that modern governments provide today?
- **a.** nomadic peoples
- **b.** lineage groups
- **c.** the Iroquois League
- **d.** Inuits and Aleuts

_____ 17. Which of the following is true of the Columbus legend?
- **a.** He was the only voyager who believed the earth was round.
- **b.** He was the first person ever to reach the Americas.
- **c.** He was the first European to set foot on American soil.
- **d.** He developed a genius for navigation.

_____ 18. The Treaty of Tordesillas of 1494 settled
- **a.** Columbus's dispute over the governorship of Hispaniola.
- **b.** a dispute over using Africans as slaves.
- **c.** the dispute between Spain and Portugal over claims to new lands.
- **d.** a dispute over Europeans' capturing Native Americans as slaves.

C. Critical Thinking

Answer the following questions on the back of this paper or on a separate sheet of paper. (*24 points*)

19. Making Comparisons How were the trading systems of Native Americans, Europeans, and West Africans alike in the 1400s? How did these systems differ?

20. Predicting Consequences How might history have been different if European diseases had not affected Native Americans?

CHAPTER 1

D. Interpreting the Chart

Use the chart below to answer questions 21-22. Write your answers on the back of this paper or on a separate sheet of paper. (*12 points*)

21. Name four types of animals that the Columbian Exchange brought to the Americas.

22. As part of the Columbian Exchange, which crops went from Europe, Africa and Asia to the Americas?

a. measles and typhus
b. peanuts and potatoes
c. wheat and rice
d. beans and peanuts

E. Analyzing a Document

In the excerpt from a letter below, Columbus described his dealings with the first Native Americans he met. Read the excerpt and then answer the questions about it on the back of this paper or on a separate sheet of paper. (*12 points*)

> ...I seized by force several Indians on the first island, in order that they might learn from us, and in like manner tell us about those things in these lands of which they themselves had knowledge; and the plan succeeded, for in a short time we understood them and they us, sometimes by gestures and signs, sometimes by words; and it was a great advantage to us.

The Letter of Columbus on the Discovery of America (New York: Lenox Library, 1892)

23. Why did Columbus want to capture Native Americans?

24. How did the two groups overcome their language barrier so that they could communicate with each other?

NAME ______________________ CLASS ____________ DATE ____________

TEST FORM A

CHAPTER 2

European Colonization of the Americas (1492-1752)

A. Identifying Key Terms, People, and Places

Complete each sentence in Column I by writing the letter of the correct term from Column II in each blank. You will not use all the terms. (*20 points*)

Column I

_____ 1. A Spanish conqueror who came to fight in the Americas was called a(n) _____.

_____ **2.** A(n) _____ is a narrow strip of land that joins two larger land areas.

_____ **3.** The 1680 uprising of Native Americans against the Spanish in New Mexico is known as the _____ .

_____ **4.** An organization funded by investors to establish colonies is called a _____.

_____ **5.** A(n) _____ was someone who was contracted to work for a master for a set period of time.

_____ **6.** The _____ was an agreement drawn up by the Pilgrims to unite themselves as a colony.

_____ **7.** The _____ were held to determine if certain Puritans were dealing with the devil.

_____ **8.** The name _____ was given to certain Native American leaders.

_____ **9.** New York was a colony with _____, or a great variety of people.

_____ **10.** A colony over which an individual or group had been granted full governing rights was called a _____ .

Column II

a. joint-stock company

b. Salem witch trials

c. conquistador

d. proprietary colony

e. indentured servant

f. isthmus

g. Great Migration

h. Pequot War

i. diversity

j. mestizo

k. royal colony

l. Pueblo Revolt

m. Mayflower Compact

n. Bacon's Rebellion

o. sachem

B. Identifying Main Ideas

Write the letter of the correct answer in the blank provided. (*32 points*)

_____ **11.** Which of the following best identifies the major economic activities of the Spanish colonies?

a. growing tobacco and building ships
b. mining, farming, and ranching
c. fur trapping and fur trading
d. searching for the seven golden cities

TEST FORM A (continued)

CHAPTER 2

_____ 12. A major goal of the encomienda system was to
a. force Native Americans to work for Spanish colonists.
b. drive Native Americans off their land.
c. help Europeans adapt to Native American culture.
d. prevent the development of social classes in the Americas.

_____ 13. Which of the following best describes the Northwest Passage?
a. John Cabot's sailing across the Atlantic Ocean from England
b. Ferdinand Magellan's circumnavigating the world
c. a water route across North America
d. The Puritans' route from England to Massachusetts

_____ 14. Which of the following caused Jamestown's near failure?
a. the discovery of gold and silver in the colony
b. John Smith's leadership
c. the failure of the tobacco crop
d. the swampy site chosen for its settlement

_____ 15. Which of the following did most to shape the growth of New France?
a. the search for gold
b. the fur trade
c. the establishment of farming communities
d. the enslavement of Native Americans

_____ 16. Which of the following was a driving force in Puritan settlements?
a. a love of luxury and wealth
b. a desire to live without religion
c. a passion for social order
d. a desire to return to England

_____ 17. Why did the English drive the Dutch from New York?
a. England wanted a base from which to fight the Spanish.
b. The Dutch had been persecuting English settlers.
c. England and Holland had gone to war in Europe.
d. England envied New York's prosperity under the Dutch.

_____ 18. Which three colonies were founded in an attempt to escape religious persecution?
a. New York, New Jersey, and Georgia
b. Massachusetts, Pennsylvania, and Maryland
c. North Carolina, South Carolina, and Virginia
d. New York, Virginia, and Georgia

C. Critical Thinking

Answer the following questions on the back of this paper or on a separate sheet of paper. (*24 points*)

19. **Recognizing Causes** Identify two reasons why the British wanted to establish colonies in the Americas.

20. **Recognizing Ideologies** How would you compare the beliefs of the Puritans about religious tolerance with those of William Penn?

D. Interpreting a Graph

Use the graph below to answer questions 21-22. Write your answers on the lines provided. (*12 points*)

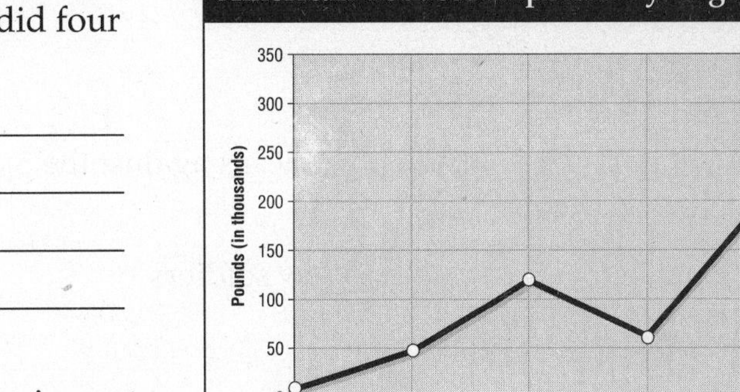

21. How much more American tobacco did England import in 1620 than it did four years earlier?

____

____

____

____

22. During which period did tobacco imports decrease?

____

____

E. Analyzing a Document

On the right is the cover of a pamphlet advertising for colonists to come to Virginia. You will note that the letters *f* and *s* are similar on it. Study it and then answer the questions about it on this paper or on a separate sheet of paper. (*12 points*)

23. What does the document tell you about from where people were being sought to colonize Virginia?

24. How did it try to attract people to become colonists?

NAME ______________________ CLASS ______________ DATE ______________

TEST FORM B

European Colonization of the Americas (1492-1752)

CHAPTER 2

A. Identifying Key Terms, People, and Places

Match the descriptions in Column I with the terms in Column II. Write the letter of the correct answer in the blank provided. You will not use all the terms. *(20 points)*

Column I

_____ **1.** Spanish term for conqueror

_____ **2.** a 1680 uprising of Native Americans against the Spanish in New Mexico

_____ **3.** a Spanish fort occupied by a few soldiers

_____ **4.** a lawmaking assembly

_____ **5.** an uprising of Virginia settlers demanding a greater voice in their government

_____ **6.** an agreement by the Pilgrims to unite themselves under laws they pledged to obey

_____ **7.** the idea that people of different faiths should live together in peace

_____ **8.** a name given to certain Native American leaders

_____ **9.** a colony over which an individual or group had full governing rights

_____ **10.** a safe place

Column II

a. legislature
b. religious tolerance
c. haven
d. Pequot War
e. mission
f. conquistador
g. royal colony
h. presidio
i. proprietary colony
j. Pueblo Revolt
k. Great Migration
l. charter
m. sachem
n. Mayflower Compact
o. Bacon's Rebellion

B. Identifying Main Ideas

Write the letter of the correct answer in the blank provided. *(32 points)*

_____ **11.** The Spanish encouraged settlement in Florida
- **a.** to establish trade routes across the Pacific Ocean.
- **b.** to mine the mountainous areas there.
- **c.** to safeguard Spanish fleets with defensive bases.
- **d.** to end the spread of English settlement.

_____ **12.** Spain wanted to establish missions to
- **a.** convert Native Americans to Spanish religion and customs.
- **b.** reduce the Spanish population.
- **c.** provide work for hidalgos.
- **d.** help Spanish settlers to adapt to Native American culture.

CHAPTER 2

_____ **13.** English explorers like Cabot, Frobisher, and Hudson were searching for
- **a.** the seven golden cities.
- **b.** the Great Migration.
- **c.** a Northwest Passage.
- **d.** a land route to California.

_____ **14.** The Virginia colony survived largely because the English colonists
- **a.** were well cared for by the Virginia Company.
- **b.** developed lasting friendships with Native Americans.
- **c.** worked cooperatively for the good of the colony.
- **d.** began growing tobacco for sale.

_____ **15.** New France was shaped mainly by
- **a.** raising cash crops.
- **b.** the fur trade.
- **c.** enslaving Native Americans.
- **d.** the search for gold.

_____ **16.** The Puritans migrated to New England to
- **a.** escape religious persecution.
- **b.** establish Catholic missions.
- **c.** maintain the practices of the Anglican Church.
- **d.** start tobacco plantations.

_____ **17.** The population of the Middle Colonies was known for its
- **a.** lack of farming skills.
- **b.** hatred of the other colonies.
- **c.** diversity.
- **d.** lack of religion.

_____ **18.** Both Pennsylvania and Maryland were established to
- **a.** offer a haven for certain religious groups.
- **b.** provide freedom for enslaved Africans.
- **c.** train Native Americans in the colonists' ways.
- **d.** provide new homes for the New York Dutch.

C. Critical Thinking

Answer the following questions on the back of this paper or on a separate sheet of paper. (*24 points*)

19. Making Comparisons How would you contrast the impact that the French fur traders and the English settlers of New England had on Native American groups?

20. Recognizing Ideologies How did Anne Hutchinson's ideology differ from that of the Puritan authorities?

CHAPTER 2

D. Interpreting a Graph

Use the graph below to answer questions 21-22. Write your answers on the lines provided. (*12 points*)

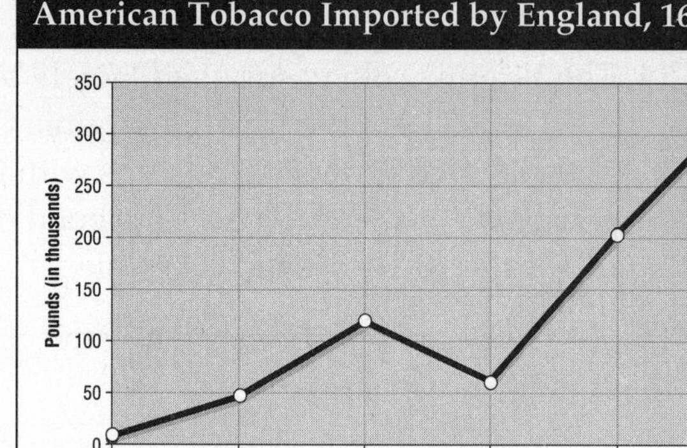

21. By how many pounds did tobacco imports decrease between 1620 and 1622?

______

______

______

______

22. During which two two-year periods did tobacco imports grow the most? By how much?

______

______

E. Analyzing a Document

On the right is the cover of a pamphlet advertising for colonists to come to Virginia. You will note that the letters *f* and *s* are similar on it. Study it and then answer the questions about it on the back of this paper or on a separate sheet of paper. (*12 points*)

23. What reasons does the document give for coming to settle in Virginia?

24. What type of work does it suggest that settlers will do in Virginia?

NAME ______________________ CLASS ____________ DATE ____________

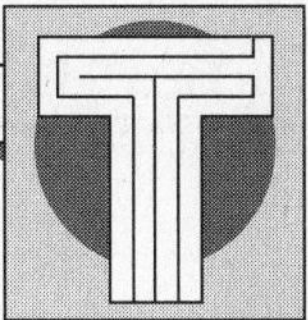

TEST FORM A

CHAPTER 3

Growth of the American Colonies (1689-1754)

A. Identifying Key Terms, People, and Places

Complete each of the following sentences by circling the correct term or name in parentheses. (*20 points*)

1. The theory of (*mercantilism, salutary neglect*) held that a country should try to gain as much gold and silver as it could in order to become wealthy and powerful.
2. (*Balance of trade, Triangular trade*) is the difference in value between a country's imports and exports.
3. A tax levied on a crop or a product is called a (*mutiny, duty*).
4. Men and women who were among the wealthy in colonial society were said to be members of the (*immigrants, gentry*).
5. An (*apprentice, almanac*) is a person placed under a legal contract to work for another person in exchange for learning a trade.
6. The main staple crop in colonial Virginia was (*tobacco, rice*).
7. A household that can make everything it needs to maintain itself is said to be (*self-sufficient, itinerant*).
8. Enslaved Africans were transported to the Americas from Africa via the (*Great Migration, Middle Passage*).
9. An example of an uprising by slaves seeking to free themselves in the mid-1700s is the (*Stono Rebellion, Great Awakening*).
10. The difference of opinion about religious matters that caused several colonial churches to splinter is referred to as (*tolerance, dissent*).

B. Identifying Main Ideas

Write the letter of the correct ending in the blank provided. (*32 points*)

_____ **11.** England prized its North American colonies because
- **a.** they provided England with natural resources of gold and silver.
- **b.** they provided soldiers for the British Army to fight in European wars.
- **c.** they supplied England with food and raw materials and bought English goods.
- **d.** they manufactured goods for England.

_____ **12.** The British policy of salutary neglect
- **a.** prevented the colonies from developing diverse economies.
- **b.** sent many royal officers to run the colonies.
- **c.** enforced strict laws such as the Navigation Act.
- **d.** allowed the colonies economic freedom.

_____ **13.** Which of these is an accurate statement about the British colonies?
a. Children benefited from an excellent system of public education.
b. Politics and society were dominated by landowning men.
c. Society provided equal opportunities for all groups.
d. Society could not be divided into clear social levels.

_____ **14.** The desire in the colonies to increase the production of staple crops like tobacco and rice led to
a. a decrease in the use of indentured servants as a labor force.
b. an increase in the number of slaves brought from Africa.
c. the establishment of the Navigation Act.
d. a lessening of the flow of immigrants to the colonies.

_____ **15.** Olaudah Equiano is remembered for
a. developing a new method of cultivating rice.
b. writing a vivid account the Middle Passage.
c. leading a famous slave revolt.
d. making a daring escape from slavery.

_____ **16.** In colonial South Carolina and Georgia, most slaves worked
a. in cities. **b.** on fishing ships.
c. in factories. **d.** on farms.

_____ **17.** In the early 1750s, colonists in western Pennsylvania and Virginia competed with the Native Americans and French for control of
a. the low country.
b. the forks of the Ohio River.
c. the Fall Line.
d. Canada.

_____ **18.** The Great Awakening is best described as
a. the conversion of thousands of Native Americans to Christianity.
b. the shift of many New Englanders to the Quaker faith.
c. a total rejection of Puritan ideas.
d. a series of religious revivals in the British colonies.

C. Critical Thinking

Answer the following questions on the back of this paper or on a separate sheet of paper. (*24 points*)

19. Identifying Central Issues In what ways did colonial legislatures dominate colonial governments?

20. Testing Conclusions Your textbook states that "The status of women in colonial society was determined by the men in their lives." What facts can you cite to support this conclusion?

D. Interpreting a Map

Use the map on the right to answer questions 21-22. Write your answers on the back of this paper or on a separate sheet of paper. (*12 points*)

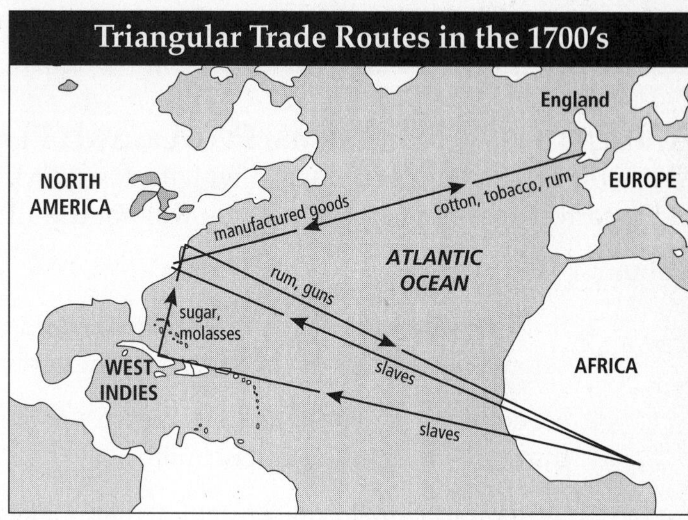

21. Name the three continents involved in the triangular trade.

22. In what ways did the colonies and Britain benefit from triangular trade?

E. Analyzing a Document

The stanzas below come from a poem written by a young Englishman named James Revel. As punishment for a crime, Revel was transported to Virginia and forced to work as an indentured servant. Read the excerpt, then answer the questions about it on the back of this paper or on a separate sheet of paper. (*12 points*)

> Thus twelve long tedious years did pass away,
> And but two more by law I had to stay:
> When Death did for my cruel Master call,
> But that was no relief to us at all.
>
> The Widow would not the Plantation hold,
> So we and that were both for to be sold,
> A lawyer rich who at James-Town did dwell,
> Came down to view it and lik'd it very well.
>
> He bought the Negroes who for life were slaves,
> But no transported Fellons would he have,
> So we were put like Sheep into a fold,
> There unto the best bidder to be sold.

from "The Poor Unhappy Transported Felon's Sorrowful Account of His Fourteen Years Transportation at Virginia in America," by James Ravel, Virginia Magazine of History and Biography 56, 1948.

23. For how many years was Ravel sentenced to work as an indentured servant?

24. How was Ravel's situation different from that of slaves?

NAME ______________________ CLASS ______________ DATE ______________

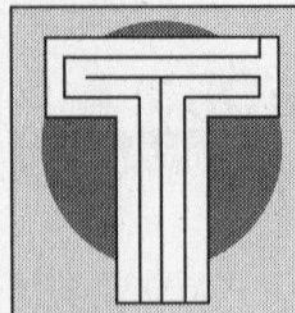

TEST FORM B

Growth of the American Colonies, 1689-1754

CHAPTER 3

A. Identifying Key Terms, People, and Places

Match the descriptions in Column 1 with the terms in Column II. Write the letter of the correct answer in each blank. You will not use all the terms. (*20 points*)

Column I

_____ **1.** British policy of the early 1700s that allowed the American colonies great freedom in governing themselves

_____ **2.** economic system designed to increase a nation's wealth, largely through the accumulation of bullion

_____ **3.** farm product that is in constant demand, like rice or tobacco

_____ **4.** social rank of wealthy gentlemen like William Byrd II of Virginia

_____ **5.** book with information about calendars, weather predictions, proverbs and advice

_____ **6.** colonial household in which all family members worked to provide everything they needed to maintain themselves

_____ **7.** coastal plain region of South Carolina and Georgia

_____ **8.** way that enslaved Africans being brought by ship to the colonies occasionally resisted their fate

_____ **9.** people who enter a new country to settle

_____ **10.** revival of religious feeling that stirred colonial society in the mid-1700s

Column II

a. staple crop
b. Ohio Valley
c. low country
d. almanac
e. triangular trade
f. immigrants
g. Great Awakening
h. balance of trade
i. salutary neglect
j. mutiny
k. gentry
l. self-sufficient
m. mercantilism

B. Identifying Main Ideas

Write the letter of the correct answer in the blank provided. (*32 points*)

_____ **11.** Britain did not want the colonies to manufacture goods because
a. it did not want colonial farming to suffer.
b. it wanted to ship raw materials to the colonies and sell them there.
c. it wanted the profit from selling manufactured goods to the colonies.
d. it wanted to ship bullion to the colonies.

_____ **12.** Which one of the following helped the colonial legislatures come to dominate colonial government?
a. The king appointed colonial governors.
b. Governors could veto measures passed by colonial legislatures.
c. The legislatures set the salaries for royal officials.
d. Governors decided when colonial legislatures could meet.

_____ **13.** Which one of the following groups held a large number of the seats in the colonial assemblies?
a. tradespeople **b.** lawyers
c. small farmers **d.** women

_____ **14.** Which colonial region was most active in promoting public education?
a. the New England Colonies **b.** the Southern Colonies
c. the Middle Atlantic Colonies **d.** the Canadian Colonies.

_____ **15.** What major role did West Africans play in the European settlement of the Americas?
a. They supplied the labor needed to cultivate cash crops.
b. They supplied the firearms needed to control rebellious Native Americans.
c. They taught Europeans methods for farming tobacco.
d. They were the largest consumer of American products.

_____ **16.** What was the major work of enslaved African Americans in Virginia and Maryland?
a. growing rice
b. cultivating tobacco
c. cultivating indigo
d. shipbuilding

_____ **17.** Which of the following was a result of a land shortage in the British colonies?
a. The slave trade ended.
b. Colonists pushed westward into Native American lands.
c. Britain limited immigration to the colonies.
d. Colonists began to fear starvation and rebellion.

_____ **18.** What effect did the Great Awakening have on religious life in the colonies?
a. It enhanced the political and spiritual authority of ministers.
b. It reinforced the social order in the colonies.
c. It strengthened traditional Puritan teachings.
d. It helped make religion in the colonies more democratic.

C. Critical Thinking

Answer the following questions on the back of this paper or on a separate sheet of paper. (*24 points*)

19. Testing Conclusions Your textbook states that "life was better for most white colonists than it would have been in Europe." Give examples to support this.

20. Making Comparisons Compare the lives of enslaved Africans who lived in the New England, Middle, and Southern colonies in the 1700s. How were their lives different? How were they similar?

CHAPTER 3

CHAPTER 3

D. Interpreting a Map

Use the map on the right to answer questions 21-22. Write your answers on the back of this paper or on a separate sheet of paper. (*12 points*)

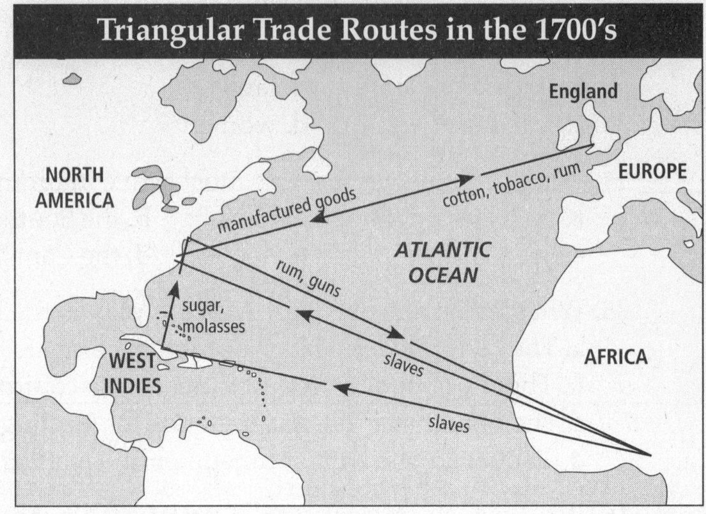

21. What areas were involved in the triangular trade?

22. What were two destinations of enslaved Africans and what crops were cultivated in each place?

E. Analyzing a Document

The stanzas below come from a poem written by a young Englishman named James Revel. As punishment for a crime, Revel was transported to Virginia and forced to work as an indentured servant. Read the excerpt, then answer the questions about it on the back of this paper or on a separate sheet of paper. (*12 points*)

> Thus twelve long tedious years did pass away,
> And but two more by law I had to stay:
> When Death did for my cruel Master call,
> But that was no relief to us at all.
>
> The Widow would not the Plantation hold,
> So we and that were both for to be sold,
> A lawyer rich who at James-Town did dwell,
> Came down to view it and lik'd it very well.
>
> He bought the Negroes who for life were slaves,
> But no transported Fellons would he have,
> So we were put like Sheep into a fold,
> There unto the best bidder to be sold.

from "The Poor Unhappy Transported Felon's Sorrowful Account of His Fourteen Years Transportation at Virginia in America," by James Ravel, Virginia Magazine of History and Biography 56, 1948.

23. How many more years did Ravel have to work until he was free?

24. What happened to Ravel when his "Master" died?

NAME ______________________ CLASS ____________ DATE ____________

TEST FORM A

CHAPTER 4

The Road to Independence (1754-1783)

A. Identifying Key Terms, People, and Places

Match the descriptions in Column I with the terms in Column II. Write the letter of the correct answer in the blank provided. You will not use all the terms. *(20 points)*

Column I

_____ **1.** a military struggle in which the British fought against the French and their Native American allies

_____ **2.** a 1754 plan to unite the colonies in a permanent union

_____ **3.** a military action that cuts off an enemy stronghold and starves it into surrendering

_____ **4.** a Native American uprising against the British in the Great Lakes region

_____ **5.** British law that taxed colonial newspapers and other printed materials

_____ **6.** statement of the reasons for the colonies to separate from Britain

_____ **7.** a person killed, wounded, or missing

_____ **8.** a foreign soldier hired to fight in a war

_____ **9.** a steady increase in prices over time

_____ **10.** the agreement that ended the Revolutionary War

Column II

a. Declaration of Independence
b. Battle of Bunker Hill
c. French and Indian War
d. Proclamation of 1763
e. siege
f. inflation
g. Albany Plan of Union
h. Treaty of Paris
i. militia
j. Olive Branch Petition
k. mercenary
l. Pontiac's Rebellion
m. casualty
n. Stamp Act

B. Identifying Main Ideas

Write the letter of the correct ending in the blank provided. *(32 points)*

_____ **11.** As a result of the French and Indian War,
a. Native Americans gained control of the Great Lakes region.
b. Britain lost control of lands east of the Mississippi River.
c. France turned Canada over to Britain.
d. France gained control of Florida.

_____ **12.** The French and Indian War led to
a. a massive migration to Canada.
b. a weakening of colonial loyalty to Britain.
c. the end of Britain's involvement in colonial affairs.
d. an increased colonial dependence on Britain.

_____ **13.** The Sugar Act and Stamp Act are examples of how the
a. British continued to leave the colonies alone.
b. British tried to raise money in the colonies.
c. colonists eagerly sacrificed to pay their war debts.
d. British tried to stimulate colonial economies.

_____ **14.** A direct result of the Intolerable Acts was the
a. colonial attack on French forts.
b. calling together of the First Continental Congress.
c. cancellation of the Townshend taxes.
d. breaking up of all colonial militias.

_____ **15.** The Revolutionary war began with the
a. Battle of Saratoga.
b. Battle of Trenton.
c. Battles of Lexington and Concord.
d. Battle of Bunker Hill.

_____ **16.** The idea of natural rights is best defined as
a. individuals' duties to their government.
b. the economic interests of the people.
c. a government's powers over its citizens.
d. rights belonging to all people because they are human.

_____ **17.** In their attitudes toward the Revolutionary War, John Adams estimated that colonists were split
a. one half Patriots and one half Loyalists.
b. one third Patriots, on third Loyalists, one third neutral.
c. two thirds Patriots and one third Loyalists.
d. two thirds Loyalists and one third Patriots.

_____ **18.** The Americans won the Revolutionary War mainly because
a. their armies were better trained and disciplined than the British.
b. British arms were inferior to American arms.
c. they had the determination to outlast the British.
d. the American navy was superior to the British navy.

C. Critical Thinking

Answer the following questions on the back of this paper or on a separate sheet of paper. *(24 points)*

19. Determining Relevance Why do you think Thomas Paine's *Common Sense* had so strong an effect on so many Americans?

20. Making Comparisons Compare American and British advantages and disadvantages during the Revolutionary War.

D. Interpreting a Political Cartoon

Use the cartoon below to answer questions 21-22. Write your answers on the back of this paper or on another sheet of paper. *(12 points)*

Britons within the Yankeean Plains,
Mind how Ye March & Trench

The American Rattle Snake

The serpent in the Congress's Reigns,
As well as in the French

21. Who does the rattlesnake represent?

22. The snake boasts that it has already defeated two British armies. What is meant by the snake's statement "…and room for more I've got behind"?

E. Analyzing a Document

The verses below come from a colonial poem entitled "A Lady's Adieu to Her Tea-Table." Read them and then answer the questions about the poem on the back of this paper or on a separate sheet of paper. (*12 points*)

> Farewell the Teaboard with your gaudy attire,
> Ye cups and saucers that I did admire;
> To my cream pot and tongs I now bid adieu;
> That pleasure's all fled that I once found in you…
> No more shall my teapot so generous be
> In filling the cups with this pernicious [evil] tea,
> For I'll fill it with water and drink out of same,
> Before I'll lose Liberty that dearest name…

23. What action of colonial protest does this poem reflect?

24. Why do you think this poem might have been written and distributed?

NAME ______________________ CLASS ______________ DATE ______________

CHAPTER 4

TEST FORM B

The Road to Independence (1754-1783)

A. Identifying Key Terms, People, and Places

Complete each sentence in Column I by writing the letter of the correct term from Column II in each blank. You will not use all the terms. *(20 points)*

Column I

_____ **1.** The _____ pitted the British and American colonists against the French and their Native American allies.

_____ **2.** A _____ is a group of armed citizens who serve as soldiers during an emergency.

_____ **3.** During _____, Native Americans in the Great Lakes region fought against the British.

_____ **4.** King George issued the _____ to close the region west of the Appalachians to colonial settlement.

_____ **5.** The _____ placed a tax on colonial newspapers and other printed materials.

_____ **6.** Thomas Paine wrote _____ to urge colonists to break from Britain.

_____ **7.** The four sections of the _____ explained why the colonies should cut their ties from Britain.

_____ **8.** A _____ is a foreign soldier hired to fight a war.

_____ **9.** The _____ was fought on Christmas night, 1776.

_____ **10.** A _____ is a naval action designed to isolate an area from outside contact.

Column II

a. *Common Sense*
b. boycott
c. Battle of Trenton
d. French and Indian War
e. profiteering
f. Pontiac's Rebellion
g. Battle of Bunker Hill
h. militia
i. Albany Plan of Union
j. Proclamation of 1763
k. mercenary
l. Stamp Act
m. Declaration of Independence
n. blockade

B. Identifying Main Ideas

Write the letter of the correct ending in the blank provided. *(32 points)*

_____ **11.** What was a major outcome of the French and Indian War?
a. The Native Americans surrendered the Great Lakes region.
b. The French surrendered all of Canada to the British.
c. The British promised independence to the colonies.
d. The British turned over all of Canada to the French.

_____ **12.** Which statement best describes British-American relations after the French and Indian War?
a. The British began to respect American culture.
b. The colonists began to question British authority.
c. The British began to treat Americans as equals.
d. The colonists became more dependent on Britain.

_____ **13.** Why did many colonists protest the Stamp Act?
a. The act enabled the British to censor all written materials in the colonies.
b. The act threatened to disrupt trading patterns with overseas markets.
c. The act increased the cost of British imports.
d. The act taxed the colonists without their consent.

_____ **14.** The First Continental Congress voted to
a. end the boycott of imports from Britain.
b. call for the formation of colonial militias.
c. imprison all British tax collectors.
d. adopt the Declaration of Independence.

_____ **15.** The political ideas of Thomas Jefferson were greatly influenced by
a. the Olive Branch Petition.
b. the Albany Plan of Union.
c. the Enlightenment.
d. the Battle of Yorktown.

_____ **16.** What was a major advantage of the American side in the Revolutionary War?
a. Patriot forces were fighting on their own territory.
b. British forces were not well equipped.
c. Americans had a well-supplied, stable, and effective fighting force.
d. The British people strongly supported their forces fighting in the colonies.

_____ **17.** The results of the Battle of Saratoga
a. destroyed morale among the American colonists.
b. encouraged Britain to end the Revolutionary War immediately.
c. convinced the French to ally themselves with the Americans.
d. forced the Americans to retreat from the area around Trenton.

_____ **18.** American victory in the Revolutionary War led to
a. expanded political and legal power for women.
b. the abolition of slavery in the Southern Colonies.
c. the strengthening of the Iroquois League.
d. the spread of the idea of liberty at home and abroad.

C. Critical Thinking

Answer the following questions on the back of this paper or on a separate sheet of paper. *(24 points)*

19. Identifying Central Ideas Explain the thinking behind the protest "no taxation without representation!"

20. Demonstrating Reasoned Judgment Former President Calvin Coolidge once said, "Nothing in the world can take the place of persistence….Persistence and determination are omnipotent [all-powerful]." Based on what you have learned about the Revolutionary War, do you agree or disagree with Coolidge? Explain.

CHAPTER 4

D. Interpreting a Political Cartoon

Use the cartoon below to answer questions 21-22. Write your answers on the back of this paper or on another sheet of paper. *(12 points)*

21. The cartoon is meant as a warning to what nation?

22. What impression does the cartoon give about the strength of the Americans?

E. Analyzing a Document

The verses below come from a colonial poem entitled "A Lady's Adieu to Her Tea-Table." Read them and then answer the questions about the poem on the back of this paper or on a separate sheet of paper. *(12 points)*

> Farewell the Teaboard with your gaudy attire,
> Ye cups and saucers that I did admire;
> To my cream pot and tongs I now bid adieu;
> That pleasure's all fled that I once found in you…
> No more shall my teapot so generous be
> In filling the cups with this pernicious [evil] tea,
> For I'll fill it with water and drink out of same,
> Before I'll lose Liberty that dearest name…

23. What is the writer giving up? Why?

24. What does she hope this action will win for her and the colonies?

NAME ______________________ CLASS ____________ DATE ____________

TEST FORM A

The Constitution of the United States (1776-1800)

CHAPTER 5

A. Identifying Key Terms, People, and Places

Match the descriptions in Column I with the terms in Column II. Write the letter of the correct answer in the blank provided. You will not use all the terms. (*20 points*)

Column I

_____ **1.** part of the government that makes laws

_____ **2.** government run by the people through their elected representatives

_____ **3.** plan of government that describes the different parts of the government and their duties and powers

_____ **4.** the power to prohibit an act from becoming a law

_____ **5.** the division of government into three branches

_____ **6.** government structure in which each branch has the ability to limit the power of the others

_____ **7.** group concerned only with its own interests

_____ **8.** official swearing-in ceremony

_____ **9.** head of the major departments of the executive branch

_____ **10.** something done or said that becomes a tradition to be followed

Column II

a. precedent
b. administration
c. executive branch
d. separation of powers
e. constitution
f. administration
g. faction
h. judicial branch
i. legislative branch
j. inauguration
k. veto
l. Cabinet
m. domestic affairs
n. checks and balances
o. republic

B. Identifying Main Ideas

Write the letter of the correct answer in the blank provided. (*32 points*)

_____ **11.** Which of the following was a weakness of the Articles of Confederation?
a. Only Congress had the power to tax.
b. There was no legislative branch of government.
c. State governments had no authority.
d. There was no national court system.

_____ **12.** How did the Nationalists regard Shays' Rebellion?
a. as proof that the states had too little power
b. as an example of how governments abuse their power
c. as proof that only a strong national government could prevent social disorder
d. as a demonstration of Americans' commitment to democracy

CHAPTER 5

_____ 13. What issue did the Great Compromise resolve?
- **a.** representation in the legislature
- **b.** abolition of slavery
- **c.** the veto power of the executive
- **d.** whether taxes were to be paid in specie or paper money

_____ 14. The Three-Fifths Compromise resolved the issue of
- **a.** how enslaved people were to be counted in the population.
- **b.** whether larger states could have more representatives in Congress.
- **c.** whether Congress would have one or two houses.
- **d.** how many representatives each state would have in the Senate.

_____ 15. Which of the following was designed to ensure that the President would not gain dictatorial powers over government?
- **a.** the system of checks and balances
- **b.** the Elastic Clause
- **c.** the Electoral College
- **d.** the Cabinet

_____ 16. The Antifederalists argued against the Constitution because they felt
- **a.** it gave too much power to the people.
- **b.** it created a weak executive branch.
- **c.** it made the national government too strong.
- **d.** the Articles of Confederation did not need to be reformed.

_____ 17. Which of the following was added to the Constitution to help gain the support of Antifederalists?
- **a.** the Bill of Rights
- **b.** the Great Compromise
- **c.** the national court system
- **d.** the Preamble

_____ 18. Which of the following was a major goal of George Washington as President?
- **a.** to go to war with Britain again
- **b.** to gain respect for the United States among nations
- **c.** to see that the Articles of Confederation were reformed
- **d.** to repay the French for their help during the American Revolution

C. Critical Thinking

Answer the following questions on the back of this paper or on a separate sheet of paper. (*24 points*)

19. Expressing Problems Clearly Describe the reasons why the Nationalists opposed the Articles of Confederation.

20. Identifying Central Issues At the Constitutional Convention, delegates debated whether or not slaves should be included when calculating a state's population. Why was this issue important, and how was the debate resolved?

D. Interpreting a Political Map

Use the map to answer questions 21-22. Write your answers on the lines provided. (*12 points*)

21. Which state had the most electoral votes in 1792? The least?

____

____

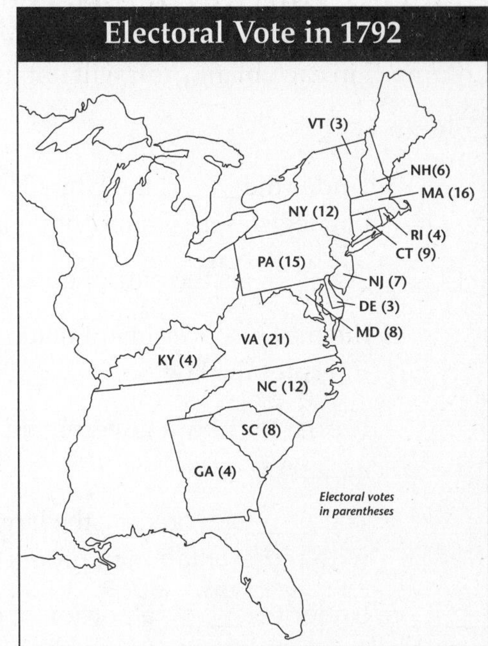

22. At the Constitutional Convention, why did Virginia favor a plan by which states with larger populations would have more voting power in Congress than states with smaller populations?

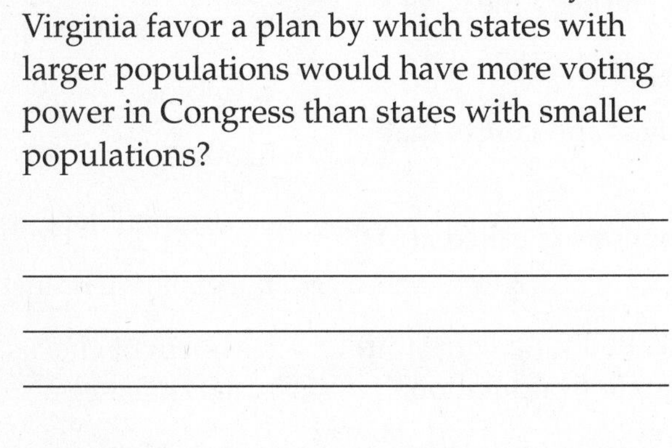

____

____

____

____

E. Analyzing a Document

The following are words Benjamin Franklin used to urge his fellow delegates to the Constitutional Convention to adopt the Constitution. Read them and then answer the questions about them on the back of this paper or on a separate sheet of paper. (*12 points*)

> ...When you assemble a number of men to have the advantage of their joint wisdom, you inevitably assemble with those men all their prejudices, their passions, their errors of opinion, their local interests and their selfish views. From such an assembly can a perfect production be expected? It therefore astonishes me, sir, to find this system approaching so near to perfection as it does... Thus I consent, sir, to this Constitution, because I expect no better, and because I am not sure that it is not the best. The opinions I have had of its errors I sacrifice to the common good.

Henry D. Gilpin, Ed., *The Papers of James Madison* (New York, 1841)

23. According to Franklin, what happens when a diverse group of people comes together?

24. Did Franklin believe the Constitution was perfect? Explain.

NAME ______________________ CLASS ____________ DATE ____________

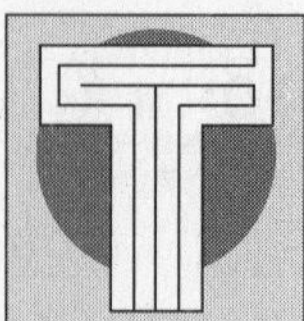

TEST FORM B

The Constitution of the United States (1776-1800)

CHAPTER 5

A. Identifying Key Terms, People, and Places

Complete each sentence in Column I by writing the letter of the correct term from Column II in each blank. You will not use all the terms. (*20 points*)

Column I

_____ **1.** Under the _____, the United States government consisted of a legislature which both passed and enforced the laws.

_____ **2.** The _____ is the part of government that makes laws.

_____ **3.**The part of government made up of judges and courts that interpret the law is the _____.

_____ **4.** A plan for how a government should operate is called a(n) _____.

_____ **5.** The _____, favored by the large states, called for a legislature with representation in proportion to a state's population.

_____ **6.** Under the _____, a portion of enslaved people were to be counted as part of a state's population.

_____ **7.** The power of the President to veto acts of Congress is an example of the _____.

_____ **8.** The candidate who receives the majority of votes in the _____ becomes President of the United States.

_____ **9.** The _____ guarantees that the individual freedoms of American citizens will be protected.

_____ **10.** The President appoints the _____ , the heads of the major departments of the executive branch.

Column II

a. Electoral College

b. judicial branch

c. Cabinet

d. administration

e. Virginia Plan

f. legislative branch

i. system of checks and balances

j. Three-Fifths Compromise

k. constitution

l. Great Compromise

m. Articles of Confederation

n. precedent

o. Bill of Rights

B. Identifying Main Ideas

Write the letter of the correct ending in the blank provided. (*32 points*)

_____ **11.** In the 1780s, the Nationalists organized to
a. create a unicameral legislature.
b. strengthen the power of the states.
c. promote the need for a stronger central government.
d. fight against taxation.

_____ 12. Shays' Rebellion grew out of
- a. protest against strong government under the Articles of Confederation.
- b. unrest among Massachusetts farmers over taxes.
- c. dissatisfaction with the outcome of the Annapolis Convention.
- d. the widespread desire for more power for state governments.

_____ 13. Delegates to the Constitutional Convention were initially supposed to
- a. throw out the Articles of Confederation and start all over.
- b. write new constitutions for the states they represented.
- c. amend the Articles of Confederation.
- d. determine whether slavery would be allowed to continue.

_____ 14. The system of checks and balances is designed to ensure that
- a. no one branch of government will gain too much power.
- b. the Senate will not be controlled too much by the people.
- c. the President will be elected directly by the people.
- d. state legislatures will share power with the Congress.

_____ 15. The concurrent powers in the federal system of government are those
- a. delegated to the national government.
- b. delegated to the state government.
- c. denied to national and state governments.
- d. held and exercised by both national and state governments.

_____ 16. The Antifederalists opposed the Constitution because they thought it
- a. gave the federal government too much power.
- b. provided no way to change the Constitution.
- c. gave the state governments too much power.
- d. created a weak federal court system.

_____ 17. Some Antifederalists agreed to support the Constitution after the Federalists added the
- a. Elastic Clause.
- b. Bill of Rights.
- c. Preamble.
- d. system of checks and balances.

_____ 18. President Washington hoped that citizens would view the new government as
- a. modest and practical.
- b. powerful and impressive.
- c. weak and nonthreatening.
- d. threatening and dictatorial.

C. Critical Thinking

Answer the following questions on the back of this paper or on a separate sheet of paper. (*24 points*)

19. Identifying Central Issues Explain why Antifederalists objected to the proposed Constitution.

20. Demonstrating Reasoned Judgement Why do you think Washington behaved so carefully during his Presidency?

CHAPTER 5

D. Interpreting a Political Map

Use the map to answer questions 21-22. Write your answers on the lines provided. (*12 points*)

21. How many representatives did New York have in the Senate? In the House of Representatives?

____

____

22. If you had been running for President in 1792, in which three states would you have campaigned hardest? Explain.

____

____

____

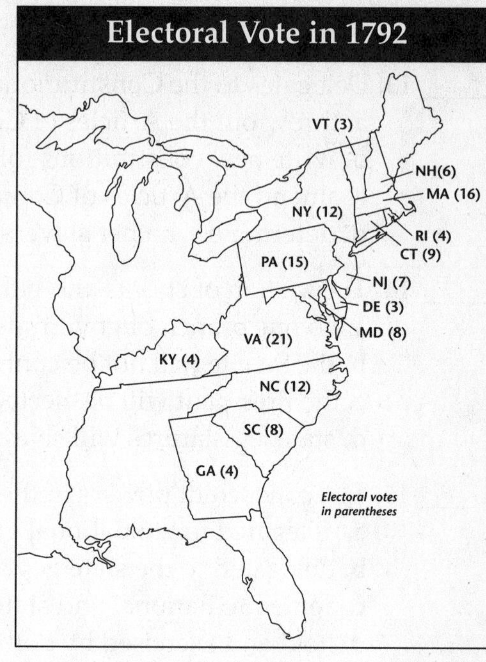

E. Analyzing a Document

The following are words Benjamin Franklin used to urge his fellow delegates to the Constitutional Convention to adopt the Constitution. Read them and then answer the questions about them on the back of this paper or on a separate sheet of paper. (*12 points*)

> ...When you assemble a number of men to have the advantage of their joint wisdom, you inevitably assemble with those men all their prejudices, their passions, their errors of opinion, their local interests and their selfish views. From such an assembly can a perfect production be expected? It therefore astonishes me, sir, to find this system approaching so near to perfection as it does...Thus I consent, sir, to this Constitution, because I expect no better, and because I am not sure that it is not the best. The opinions I have had of its errors I sacrifice to the common good.

Henry D. Gilpin, Ed., *The Papers of James Madison* (New York, 1841)

23. According to Franklin, what is the negative effect of assembling a group of wise men?

24. Why did Franklin support a Constitution that he felt was not perfect?

NAME ______________________ CLASS ______________ DATE ______________

TEST FORM A

CHAPTER 6

The Origins of American Politics (1789-1820)

A. Identifying Key Terms, People, and Places

Complete each sentence in Column I by writing the letter of the correct term from Column II in the blank. You will not use all the terms. (*20 points*)

Column I

_____ **1.** A tax on foreign goods imported into a country is called a(n) _____.

_____ **2.** A(n) _____ is a group of people who seek to win public office so they can govern according to their policies.

_____ **3.** The _____ held that a state could declare a federal law unconstitutional.

_____ **4.** The power of federal courts to decide if laws are in keeping with the Constitution is called _____ .

_____ **5.** The _____ greatly increased the size of the United States.

_____ **6.** A(n) _____ is a restriction on trade.

_____ **7.** The agreement that stripped Native Americans of the southern two thirds of Ohio was called the _____.

_____ **8.** William Henry Harrison fought the warriors of Tenskwatawa at the _____.

_____ **9.** The _____ was fought after the War of 1812 had already been ended by treaty.

_____ **10.** In 1820, the balance between slave and free states was maintained when Congress reached the _____.

Column II

a. Battle of Tippecanoe
b. Treaty of Greenville
c. embargo
d. Missouri Compromise
e. *Marbury* v. *Madison*
f. judicial review
g. tariff
h. Battle of New Orleans
i. XYZ Affair
j. impressment
k. political party
l. Louisiana Purchase
m. Treaty of Ghent
n. Virginia and Kentucky Resolutions

B. Identifying Main Ideas

Write the letter of the correct ending in the blank provided. (*32 points*)

_____ **11.** Alexander Hamilton supported
a. declaring tariffs illegal.
b. establishing the nation's capital in Philadelphia.
c. having the federal government take on the states' debts.
d. ending the tax on whiskey.

TEST FORM A *(continued)*

_____ **12.** Unlike the Federalists, Jeffersonian Republicans
a. were pro-British in disputes between France and Britain.
b. objected to the interference of the national government in the economy.
c. supported most forms of taxation.
d. favored the creation of a national bank.

_____ **13.** As President, John Adams supported
a. decreasing the size of the army.
b. the Virginia and Kentucky resolutions.
c. the Whiskey Rebellion.
d. the Alien and Sedition Acts.

_____ **14.** Jefferson's election as President in 1800 demonstrated that
a. the country could peacefully transfer power from one party to another.
b. the Constitution needed to be reformed.
c. there was no need for a two-party system.
d. Washington was no longer seen as a hero.

_____ **15.** John Marshall is remembered for
a. killing Alexander Hamilton in a duel.
b. serving as Chief Justice of the Supreme Court for 34 years.
c. negotiating treaties that gained new lands for the United States.
d. serving many terms in the House of Representatives.

_____ **16.** A major goal of the Lewis and Clark expedition was to
a. gather information about natural resources west of the Mississippi.
b. gain control over the Native Americans living west of the Mississippi.
c. drive the Spanish out of the lands of the Southwest.
d. drive the French out of fur trading forts along the Mississippi.

_____ **17.** To deal with the United States, Native American leader Tecumseh called for
a. accepting white culture and living in peace.
b. blending Indian and American cultures.
c. returning to Indian religious traditions.
d. taking military action against the expansion of the United States.

_____ **18.** The War of 1812 ended with
a. a clear victory for the United States.
b. a clear victory for Britain.
c. the removal of all British claims to land in North America.
d. a return to the pre-war boundaries between United States and British territories.

C. Critical Thinking

Answer the following questions on the back of this paper or on a separate sheet of paper. (*24 points*)

19. Making Comparisons How did the Federalists and Jeffersonian Republicans differ in their opinion of how the Constitution should be interpreted?

20. Recognizing Cause and Effect Describe the practice of impressment and explain how it helped to bring on the War of 1812.

D. Interpreting a Graph

Use the graph to answer questions 21-22. Write your answers on the back of this paper or on a separate sheet of paper. (*12 points*)

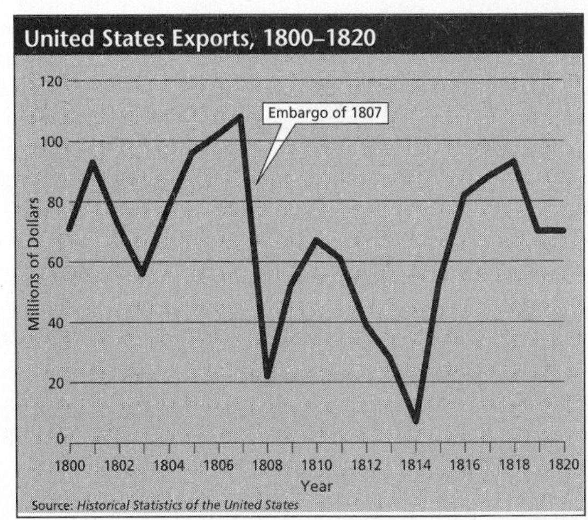

21. In what year during this period were United States exports at their highest level? In what year were they at their lowest?

22. What do you think caused exports to drop between 1812 and 1814?

E. Analyzing a Document

Study the quotations below. Then answer the questions about them on the back of this paper or on a separate sheet of paper. (*12 points*)

Alexander Hamilton

The voice of the people has been said to be the voice of God; and however generally this maxim [statement] has been quoted and believed, it is not true in fact. The people are turbulent and changing; they seldom judge or determine right. (1787)

Thomas Jefferson

Whenever the people are well-informed, they can be trusted with their own government. (1789)

I have great confidence in the common sense of mankind in general. (1800)

23. What was Hamilton's opinion of the American people?

24. Which of these two men do you think would be more likely to support the direct election of leaders? Explain.

NAME ______________________ CLASS ______________ DATE ______________

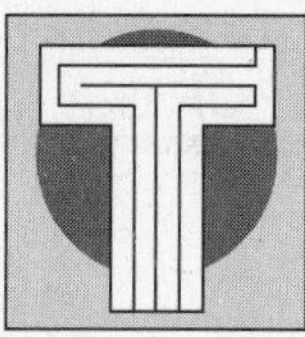

TEST FORM B

The Origins of American Politics (1789-1820)

CHAPTER 6

A. Identifying Key Terms, People, and Places

Match the descriptions in Column I with the terms in Column II. Write the letter of the correct answer in the blank provided. You will not use all the terms. (20 points)

Column I

_____ **1.** not taking sides in a dispute or war

_____ **2.** uprising by Pennsylvania farmers protesting a tax they thought unfair

_____ **3.** legislation that gave the federal government the right to deport citizens and to silence criticism of the government

_____ **4.** principle that said a state could declare a federal law unconstitutional

_____ **5.** practice that allows federal courts to decide if laws are in keeping with the Constitution

_____ **6.** area in which Native Americans were forced to live after losing their homelands

_____ **7.** restriction on trade

_____ **8.** process by which people of one culture merge into and become part of another culture

_____ **9.** William Henry Harrison's fight with Tenskwatawa's warriors

_____ **10.** practice of forcing people into military service

Column II

a. impressment

b. nullification

c. embargo

d. Alien and Sedition Acts

e. neutral

f. Whiskey Rebellion

g. *Marbury* v. *Madison*

h. War of 1812

i. reservation

j. Lewis and Clark expedition

k. judicial review

l. Battle of Tippecanoe

m. Battle of New Orleans

n. assimilation

B. Identifying Main Ideas

Write the letter of the correct answer in the blank provided. (*32 points*)

_____ **11.** Which of the following best describes Jeffersonian Republicans?
- **a.** They favored Federalist policies.
- **b.** They preferred a loose interpretation of the Constitution.
- **c.** They wanted to restore monarchy in the United States.
- **d.** They objected to the national government's interference in local and state government affairs.

_____ **12.** What was the outcome of Gabriel Prosser's rebellion?
a. Slaves in Richmond, Virginia were granted their freedom.
b. The Virginia and Kentucky resolutions were passed.
c. Prosser and other slave rebels were executed.
d. Prosser's master was punished for cruel treatment of his slaves.

_____ **13.** Why was Jefferson not automatically named President after he won the popular vote in 1800?
a. John Adams had more Electoral College votes.
b. Aaron Burr had more Electoral College votes.
c. Congress refused to agree to Jefferson's election.
d. Jefferson did not have a majority of Electoral College votes.

_____ **14.** Which one of the following was a major accomplishment of the Jefferson administration?
a. increasing the size of the army
b. destroying the Bank of the United States
c. making the Louisiana Purchase
d. driving the British out of Canada

_____ **15.** Which was a result of the Treaty of Greenville in 1795?
a. All Native American resistance to American expansion ended.
b. General "Mad Anthony" Wayne resigned his commission.
c. Native Americans had to give up the southern two thirds of Ohio.
d. Handsome Lake declared war on the Legion of the United States.

_____ **16.** Which of the following occurred during the War of 1812?
a. Tecumseh's warriors won the Battle of Tippecanoe.
b. The British navy destroyed Oliver Hazard Perry's force on Lake Erie.
c. British troops set fire to Washington, D.C.
d. United States forces captured Canada.

_____ **17.** Which was an effect of the Panic of 1819?
a. London banks offered to make more investment in the United States.
b. Americans who had borrowed too much money were financially ruined.
c. Americans were not required to immediately repay their loans.
d. The federal government created the Second Bank of the United States.

_____ **18.** Which was a provision of the Missouri Compromise of 1820?
a. Missouri and Maine were denied statehood.
b. Western territories north of Missouri's southern border were closed to slavery.
c. Slavery could not spread to any western lands.
d. Free states could never outnumber slave states.

CHAPTER 6

C. Critical Thinking

Answer the following questions on the back of this paper or on a separate sheet of paper. (*24 points*)

19. Demonstrating Reasoned Judgment Why was the peaceful transfer of power from the Federalists to the Jeffersonian Republicans such an important milestone in American history?

20. Expressing Problems Clearly What problems did the federal government face as a result of westward expansion in the late 1700s and early 1800s?

D. Interpreting a Graph

Use the graph to answer questions 21-22. Write your answers on the back of this paper or on a separate sheet of paper. (*12 points*)

21. What effect did the Embargo of 1807 have on United States exports?

22. What happened to exports after the War of 1812?

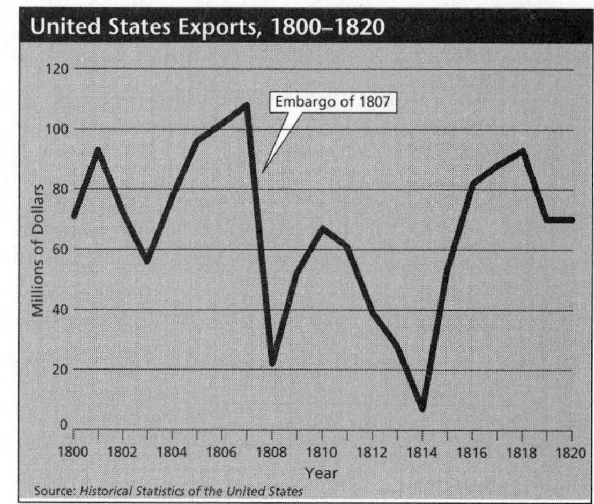

E. Analyzing a Document

Study the quotations below. Then answer the questions about them on the back of this paper or on a separate sheet of paper. (*12 points*)

Alexander Hamilton

The voice of the people has been said to be the voice of God; and however generally this maxim [statement] has been quoted and believed, it is not true in fact. The people are turbulent and changing; they seldom judge or determine right. (1787)

Thomas Jefferson

Whenever the people are well-informed, they can be trusted with their own government. (1789)

I have great confidence in the common sense of mankind in general. (1800)

23. Compare Hamilton's view of common people with Jefferson's.

24. What is Hamilton's view of "the voice of the people"?

NAME ______________________ CLASS ____________ DATE ____________

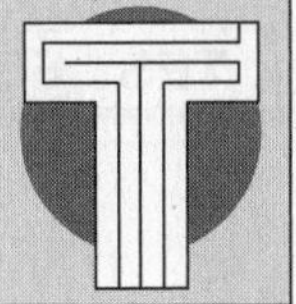

TEST FORM A

Life in the New Nation (1783-1830)

CHAPTER 7

A. Identifying Key Terms, People, and Places

Match the descriptions in Column I with the names in Column II. Write the letter of the correct answer in the blank provided. You will not use all the names. *(14 points)*

Column I

_____ **1.** pioneer who helped cut the Wilderness Road

_____ **2.** inventor who proved steam could be used to power ships

_____ **3.** African American mathematician who surveyed the site of Washington, D.C.

_____ **4.** writer who promoted education and stressed the importance for a standard national language

_____ **5.** New Englander who invented the cotton gin

_____ **6.** British immigrant who constructed the first textile mill in the United States

_____ **7.** minister who helped establish the African Methodist Episcopal Church

Column II

a. Noah Webster
b. Richard Allen
c. William ElleryChanning
d. Eli Whitney
e. John Ross
f. Samuel Slater
g. Benjamin Rush
h. Robert Fulton
i. Daniel Boone
j. Benjamin Banneker

B. Identifying Main Ideas

Write the letter of the correct answer in the blank provided. *(40 points)*

_____ **8.** Which statement best describes population trends in the United States from 1780 to 1830?
a. The population grew older and gradually decreased in size.
b. High birth rates caused rapid population growth.
c. The Native American population grew faster than the white population.
d. Mass immigration from Europe resulted in overpopulation.

_____ **9.** In the Adams-Onís Treaty of 1819,
a. the United States doubled its size.
b. the Cherokees settled their dispute with the American government.
c. Spain ceded Florida to the United States.
d. the United States gained the right to build the Erie Canal.

_____ **10.** How did Native American migration differ from that of white Americans?
a. Most Native Americans migrated after being forced from their land.
b. Most Native Americans migrated south instead of west.
c. Most Native Americans migrated to reclaim their homelands, not to explore.
d. Most Native Americans migrated to cities along the Atlantic coast.

CHAPTER 7

_____ **11.** Americans who believed in republican virtues called on women to
a. take on new political and legal rights.
b. work outside the home.
c. become the recognized heads of families.
d. serve as examples of honesty and discipline.

_____ **12.** How did the invention of interchangeable parts revolutionize the way products like guns could be produced?
a. It demanded that the product maker have a higher level of skill than before.
b. It slowed down the process of making goods, reducing profitability.
c. It speeded up the manufacturing process, increasing profitability.
d. It decreased the money businesspeople wanted to invest in factories.

_____ **13.** What was one important effect of the invention of the cotton gin in 1793?
a. Thousands of southern plantation owners went bankrupt.
b. The demand for slave labor increased.
c. Laws called black codes were passed.
d. Migration from the South to undeveloped lands in the West declined.

_____ **14.** Steam power and canal building were important because they
a. allowed farmers to ship their goods to markets around the country.
b. caused a decline in the demand for slave labor.
c. discouraged the settlement of western regions.
d. increased the cost of transportation and communication.

_____ **15.** Many historians believe that the rise of a mobile society in the United States led to
a. a decline in dueling. **b.** an increase in suicide and alcoholism.
c. a decline in the divorce rate. **d.** an increase in the number of marriages.

_____ **16.** Preachers during the Second Great Awakening taught that
a. churches should be controlled by the wealthy.
b. God can only be understood by highly-educated people.
c. religion is for men only.
d. salvation is available to anyone, rich or poor.

_____ **17.** Which best describes women's role in the Second Great Awakening?
a. They took turns writing and preaching weekly sermons.
b. They assumed leadership roles with their churches.
c. They worked together to help others and to spread Christianity.
d. They did not take much part in it because it did not affect them.

C. Critical Thinking

Answer the following questions on the back of this paper or on a separate sheet of paper. *(22 points)*

18. Recognizing Cause and Effect The United States had a growing and very youthful population during the early 1800s. How do you think this contributed to the settlement of lands west of the Appalachian Mountains?

19. Recognizing Bias In what ways were free African American pioneers discriminated against?

D. Reading a Table

Use the information in the table below to answer questions 20-22. Write your answers on the back of this paper or on a separate sheet of paper. *(12 points)*

20. What was the overall trend for population in all regions from 1800 to 1830?

21. How did the change in New England compare with that of the Middle Atlantic region?

22. Which of these regions contained the states of Ohio and Michigan?

Population for Regions of the United States: 1790 to 1830

Year	New England	Middle Atlantic	North Central[1]	South Atlantic	South Central[2]
1790	1,009,408	958,632	———	1,851,806	109,368
1800	1,233,011	1,402,565	51,006	2,286,494	335,407
1810	1,471,973	2,014,702	272,324	2,674,891	708,590
1820	1,660,071	2,699,845	792,719	3,061,063	1,190,489
1830	1,954,717	3,587,664	1,470,018	3,645,752	1,815,969

1 Ohio, Indiana, Illinois, Michigan
2 Kentucky, Tennessee, Alabama, Missippi

Source: U.S. Bureau of the Census

E. Analyzing a Document

Educator Noah Webster wrote the following paragraphs in support of free public education in 1790. Read them and then answer the questions about them on the back of this paper or on a separate sheet of paper. *(12 points)*

> In several states, we find laws passed establishing provision for colleges and academies where people of property may educate their sons, but no provision is made for instructing the poorer rank of people even in reading and writing…
>
> In our American republics, where government is in the hands of the people, knowledge should be universally diffused [available to all] by means of public schools. Of such consequence [importance] is it to society that the people who make laws should be well informed that I conceive no legislature can be justified in neglecting proper establishments for this purpose.

Noah Webster, On the Education of Youth in America, 1790

23. According to Webster, who was most likely to receive a good education in 1790?

24. Why did Webster feel that public education was important in the United States?

NAME ______________________ CLASS ____________ DATE ____________

TEST FORM B

Life in the New Nation (1783-1830)

CHAPTER 7

A. Identifying Key Terms, People, and Places

Complete each sentence by writing the letter of the correct name in each blank. You will not use all the names. (14 points)

Column I

_____ **1.** _____ was a legendary pioneer who helped cut the Wilderness Road.

_____ **2.** Under the leadership of _____, the Cherokee blended Cherokee and European traditions to create a legal system and government.

_____ **3.** _____ began earning a reputation as a poet following publication of her first poem in 1770.

_____ **4.** _____ established the first successful textile mill in the United States.

_____ **5.** The cotton gin was invented in 1793 by _____.

_____ **6.** _____ built the first steamboat to successfully complete a round trip on an American river.

_____ **7.** In 1794, _____ published a popular moralizing novel entitled *Charlotte Temple.*

Column II

a. Samuel Slater

b. Susanna Haswell Rowson

c. John Ross

d. Noah Webster

e. Eli Whitney

f. Richard Allen

g. Robert Fulton

h. Phillis Wheatley

i. Benjamin Rush

j. Daniel Boone

B. Identifying Main Ideas

Write the letter of the correct ending in the blank provided. *(40 points)*

_____ **8.** The great increase in the United States population during the period before 1830 was mostly a result of

a. immigration from Europe. **b.** an increase in the African slave trade.
c. immigration from Asia. **d.** an increase in the birth rate.

_____ **9.** Through the Adams-Onís Treaty of 1819, the United States

a. gained possession of Florida.
b. made Illinois a free state.
c. made Kentucky a slave state.
d. acquired land west of the Mississippi.

_____ **10.** The Northwest Ordinance of 1787

a. forbade Native Americans to live in Ohio.
b. forbade slavery in territory north of the Ohio River.
c. required Native American groups to develop written languages.
d. required African Americans to post security bonds.

_____ 11. In the early 1800s, American women were expected to
a. be involved in local politics.
b. serve as their husbands' business partners.
c. serve as examples of republican virtues.
d. join the Female Missionary Society.

_____ 12. The ongoing effort to increase production through the use of machines is known as the
a. Great Awakening. b. Second Great Awakening.
c. Industrial Revolution. d. Great Migration.

_____ 13. The construction of canals during the early 1800s was driven by the fact that
a. very few new roads were being built.
b. waterways were the cheapest way to carry goods.
c. they were cheap and easy to build.
d. railroads had proved to be inefficient.

_____ 14. Many historians believe that suicide and drunkenness increased in the early 1800s because
a. so many people were moving from place to place.
b. people had little opportunity to find available land.
c. the number of marriages had decreased.
d. dueling had become a popular pastime.

_____ 15. The evangelical movement that occurred in the early 1800s was
a. highly democratic. b. limited to the poor.
c. limited to the rich. d. aimed at non-white groups.

_____ 16. Outdoor meetings held to bring people back to religious life were known as
a. congregations. b. denominations.
c. spirituals. d. revivals.

_____ 17. Among the Protestant denominations that grew rapidly during the Second Great Awakening were
a. Presbyterians and Congregationalists.
b. Baptists and Methodists.
c. Roman Catholics.
d. Episcopalians.

C. Critical Thinking

Answer the following questions on the back of this paper or on a separate sheet of paper. *(22 points)*

18. Identifying Central Issues Describe the two ways in which society in the United States was "mobile" during the early 1800s.

19. Recognizing Cause and Effect How did the invention of the cotton gin change the economy of the South?

CHAPTER 7

D. Reading a Table

Use the information in the table below to answer questions 20-22. Write your answers on the back of this paper or on a separate sheet of paper. *(12 points)*

20. Which region had the largest population in 1790? In 1830?

21. Which region had the largest population increase between 1790 and 1830?

22. By 1830, how did the size of the population in regions west of the Appalachian Mountains compare with the population of the regions east of the Appalachians?

Population for Regions of the United States: 1790 to 1830

Year	New England	Middle Atlantic	North Central[1]	South Atlantic	South Central[2]
1790	1,009,408	958,632	———	1,851,806	109,368
1800	1,233,011	1,402,565	51,006	2,286,494	335,407
1810	1,471,973	2,014,702	272,324	2,674,891	708,590
1820	1,660,071	2,699,845	792,719	3,061,063	1,190,489
1830	1,954,717	3,587,664	1,470,018	3,645,752	1,815,969

[1] Ohio, Indiana, Illinois, Michigan
[2] Kentucky, Tennessee, Alabama, Missippi

Source: U.S. Bureau of the Census

E. Analyzing a Document

Educator Noah Webster wrote the following paragraphs in support of free public education in 1790. Read them and then answer the questions about them on the back of this paper or on a separate sheet of paper. *(12 points)*

> In several states, we find laws passed establishing provision for colleges and academies where people of property may educate their sons, but no provision is made for instructing the poorer rank of people even in reading and writing...
>
> In our American republics, where government is in the hands of the people, knowledge should be universally diffused [available to all] by means of public schools. Of such consequence [importance] is it to society that the people who make laws should be well informed that I conceive no legislature can be justified in neglecting proper establishments for this purpose.

Noah Webster, On the Education of Youth in America, 1790

23. Did Webster feel that society would benefit from a system of public education? Explain.

24. Who or what did Webster feel should be responsible for creating a system of public schools?

NAME ______________________ CLASS ____________ DATE ____________

TEST FORM A

CHAPTER 8

The Market Revolution (1812-1845)

A. Identifying Key Terms, People, and Places

Complete each sentence in Column I by writing the letter of the correct term from Column II in the blank. You will not use all the terms. *(20 points)*

Column I

_____ **1.** During the _____, Americans began buying rather than making the goods they needed.

_____ **2.** An economic system that is based on privately owned firms competing for profits is called a(n) _____ system.

_____ **3.** The _____ warned European governments not to interfere with nations in the Americas.

_____ **4.** Places made up mostly of one or more cities are called _____ areas.

_____ **5.** Places made up mostly of farms and countryside are called _____ areas.

_____ **6.** A(n) _____ is an organization of workers formed to protect their interests.

_____ **7.** The practice of _____ takes place when elected officials give government jobs to friends and supporters.

_____ **8.** The _____ benefited the manufacturing North but made manufactured goods more expensive for southerners.

_____ **9.** In 1832, South Carolina threatened to _____, or withdraw from the Union.

_____ **10.** The Cherokee referred to their forced westward migration as the _____.

Column II

a. free enterprise
b. rural
c. centralize
d. tenement
e. urban
f. Market Revolution
g. secede
h. labor union
i. Tariff of 1828
j. Monroe Doctrine
k. Trail of Tears
l. Indian Removal Act
m. patronage

B. Identifying Main Ideas

Write the letter of the correct ending in the blank provided. *(32 points)*

_____ **11.** In the early 1800s, banks sparked economic growth by
a. going out of business frequently.
b. printing bank notes with no specie backing.
c. providing capital for investments.
d. being insured by the federal government.

CHAPTER 8

_____ **12.** Increasing farm production in the Old Northwest led to
a. the development of many new businesses.
b. the decline of available farmland in the Northeast.
c. a rise in cotton growing in the South.
d. the Panic of 1837.

_____ **13.** One reason many manufacturing mills were built in New England was
a. the interest in farming.
b. the availability of water power.
c. the New England coal mines.
d. the lack of cities.

_____ **14.** One reason for the growth of cities in the early 1800s was that
a. farmland in the West had become difficult to obtain.
b. centers were needed to process and market farm products.
c. farming was no longer profitable.
d. working conditions had improved in northern cities.

_____ **15.** The South in the early 1800s was
a. crowded and bustling.
b. mainly rural.
c. an area of high population density.
d. predominantly an industrial society.

_____ **16.** After the importation of slaves to the United States was banned,
a. the number of enslaved people shrunk by one half.
b. the slave trade continued within the United States.
c. slavery grew faster in the North than in the South.
d. Virginia outlawed slavery.

_____ **17.** The Monroe Doctrine stated that
a. European countries must give up their colonies in the Western Hemisphere.
b. the United States was free to take sides in European wars.
c. Europe must not try to control any nation in the Western Hemisphere.
d. further European colonization in the Western Hemisphere was welcome.

_____ **18.** Unlike the Jacksonian Democrats, the National Republicans thought
a. the federal government should support internal improvements.
b. the individual states should pay for internal improvements.
c. there should be no national bank.
d. the federal government should remain as inactive as possible.

CHAPTER 8

C. Critical Thinking

Answer the following questions on the back of this paper or on a separate sheet of paper. *(22 points)*

19. Demonstrating Reasoned Judgment Do you think the Market Revolution improved or worsened the lives of most Americans who lived in the Northeast in the early 1800s? Explain your reasoning.

20. Making Comparisons Describe two major differences between the North and the South in the mid-1800s.

D. Interpreting a Political Cartoon

"King Andrew the First"

Study the political cartoon to answer questions 21-23. Write your answers on the back of this paper or on a separate sheet of paper. *(12 points)*

21. What image in the cartoon shows that President Jackson wanted to limit the power of Congress?

22. What images in the cartoon depict Jackson as too powerful a ruler?

23. Which group—the National Republicans or the Jackson Democrats—probably promoted this cartoon? Explain.

E. Analyzing a Document

The excerpt below is from a letter written by Henry Bibb, an escaped slave, to his former master. Read it and answer the questions below. *(14 points)*

> I thank God that I am not property now, but am regarded as a man like yourself, and although I live far north, I am enjoying a comfortable living by my own industry...
>
> You may perhaps think hard of us for running away from slavery, but as for myself, I have but one apology to make for it, which is this: I have only to regret that I did not start at an earlier period. I might have been free long before I was.
>
> *Henry Bibb, 1844*

24. How did Bibb's life change after his escape?

25. What was Bibb's one regret?

NAME ______________________ CLASS ______________ DATE ______________

TEST FORM B

The Market Revolution (1812-1845)

CHAPTER 8

A. Identifying Key Terms, People, and Places

Match the descriptions in Column I with the terms in Column II. Write the letter of the correct answer in the blank provided. You will not use all the terms. *(20 points)*

Column I

_____ **1.** to bring all production tasks together in one place

_____ **2.** economic system in which privately owned companies compete for profit

_____ **3.** wealth that can be used to produce goods and make money

_____ **4.** term that describes places made up mostly of one or more cities

_____ **5.** severe depression marked by high unemployment and increased poverty

_____ **6.** a work stoppage

_____ **7.** policy to prevent European nations from interfering with nations in the Western Hemisphere

_____ **8.** practice of giving government jobs to friends and supporters

_____ **9.** to withdraw

_____ **10.** term used to describe the forced migration of the Cherokee

Column II

a. Monroe Doctrine
b. Panic of 1837
c. spoils system
d. strike
e. Tariff of 1828
f. Trail of Tears
g. urban
h. centralize
i. free enterprise
j. rural
k. secede
l. capital
m. tenement

B. Identifying Main Ideas

Write the letter of the correct answer in the blank provided. *(32 points)*

_____ **11.** Which of the following was an aspect of the Market Revolution?
a. More Americans worked outside the home.
b. The household economy began to dominate American life.
c. Fewer people worked to earn cash.
d. Families became more self-sufficient.

CHAPTER 8

_____ **12.** The most influential new enterprises of the Market Revolution were
a. plantations.
b. banks.
c. canals.
d. universities.

_____ **13.** Increasing farm production in the Old Northwest helped create
a. a decline in factory-building in the Northeast.
b. a rise in specialized businesses to process and transport farm products.
c. a decrease in the desire to settle on lands west of the Appalachians.
d. a ban on the further importation of slaves into the United States.

_____ **14.** Which was a result of industrialization in the United States?
a. a decrease in available jobs
b. a sharp decline in poverty
c. a ban on women in factory jobs
d. the growth of cities

_____ **15.** Which of the following was most important in making cotton "king" in the South?
a. a ban on the further importation of slaves
b. the invention of the cotton gin
c. industrialization in the South
d. rapid urban growth in the South

_____ **16.** How did many southern states react to the uprisings of Vesey and Turner?
a. They passed harsher slave laws.
b. They condemned slave owners who treated their slaves cruelly.
c. They encouraged plantation owners to begin to end slavery.
d. They passed laws to restrict the slave trade.

_____ **17.** How did the Jacksonian Democrats differ from the National Republicans?
a. They opposed government interference with the economy.
b. They thought the federal government should control business.
c. They supported a high tariff on foreign goods.
d. They favored a national bank for the United States.

_____ **18.** How did President Jackson react to Georgia's seizure of Cherokee lands?
a. He supported the Supreme Court rulings that Georgia's action was unconstitutional.
b. He sided with Georgia in defiance of the Supreme Court.
c. He ordered the United States Army to leave the Cherokee alone.
d. He negotiated a compromise that gave one third of the land to Georgia.

C. Critical Thinking

Answer the following questions on the back of this paper or on a separate sheet of paper. *(22 points)*

19. Demonstrating Reasoned Judgment Who was more likely to benefit from the Market Revolution, a middle-class business person or an urban factory worker? Explain.

20. Identifying Central Issues What was the goal of the Monroe Doctrine? Was this policy followed by future Presidents?

D. Interpreting a Political Cartoon

Study the political cartoon. Then write your answers to questions 21-23 on the back of this paper or on a separate sheet of paper. *(12 points)*

21. How does the cartoon tell you that President Jackson probably frustrated Congress?

22. Did the cartoonist view Jackson as a "common man"? Explain.

23. Which political party most likely promoted this cartoon? Explain.

E. Analyzing a Document

The excerpt below is from a letter written by Henry Bibb, an escaped slave, to his former master. Read it and answer the questions below. *(14 points)*

> I thank God that I am not property now, but am regarded as a man like yourself, and although I live far north, I am enjoying a comfortable living by my own industry...
>
> You may perhaps think hard of us for running away from slavery, but as for myself, I have but one apology to make for it, which is this: I have only to regret that I did not start at an earlier period. I might have been free long before I was.
>
> *Henry Bibb, 1844*

24. How did the way Bibb was viewed by other people change once he became free?

25. What was Bibb's one regret?

NAME ______________________ CLASS ____________ DATE ____________

TEST FORM A

CHAPTER 9

Religion and Reform (1800-1850)

A. Identifying Key Terms, People, and Places

Match the descriptions in Column I with the names in Column II. Write the letter of the correct answer in the blank provided. You will not use all the names. *(20 points)*

Column I

_____ **1.** Transcendentalist who wrote about his two years of solitary life at Walden Pond

_____ **2.** Boston teacher who promoted legislation to improve conditions in prisons and poorhouses

_____ **3.** Scottish social reformer who founded the utopian community of New Harmony, Indiana

_____ **4.** African American writer whose 1829 essay *Appeal* promoted the antislavery movement

_____ **5.** Radical abolitionist who published *The Liberator*

_____ **6.** African American abolitionist and publisher of *The North Star*

_____ **7.** former slave and speaker at antislavery and women's rights meetings

_____ **8.** former slave who became a leader of the Underground Railroad

_____ **9.** teacher whose work *A Treatise on Domestic Economy* inspired women to build a strong American society

_____ **10.** Quaker minister who helped organize the Seneca Falls Convention

Column II

a. Robert Owen

b. Dorothea Dix

c. David Walker

d. Sojourner Truth

e. Ralph Waldo Emerson

f. Harriet Tubman

g. Elizabeth Cady Stanton

h. Henry David Thoreau

i. Lucretia Mott

j. Frederick Douglass

k. Catharine Beecher

l. Lyman Beecher

m. William Lloyd Garrison

B. Identifying Main Ideas

Write the letter of the correct answer in the blank provided. *(32 points)*

_____ **11.** Which of the following best describes the ideology of Transcendentalists?

a. Humans are naturally bad.
b. Individuals should rely on outward rituals and group worship.
c. People's lives have been predetermined by God.
d. Humans should be self-reliant and act on their beliefs.

_____ **12.** Temperance societies worked to
a. eliminate the consumption of alcohol.
b. reform education.
c. end slavery.
d. promote women's suffrage.

_____ **13.** What happened to most utopian communities in the early 1800s?
a. They were dissolved by the federal government.
b. They became permanent models of American democracy.
c. They fell prey to crime, poverty, and disease.
d. They fell victim to laziness, selfishness, and infighting.

_____ **14.** Abolitionists all agreed about
a. the importance of women's participation.
b. the need to work within the political system.
c. what tactics to use in their struggle.
d. the need to end slavery.

_____ **15.** What was the purpose of the gag rule?
a. to prevent the reading of antislavery petitions in Congress
b. to stop the activities of temperance supporters
c. to discredit the women's rights movement
d. to expose the Underground Railroad

_____ **16.** By working in reform movements, many women
a. received higher-paying jobs.
b. gained experience in seeking social and political change.
c. became powerful politicians.
d. won the right to vote by the mid-1800s.

_____ **17.** Which group was most active in the reform movements of the 1830s and 1840s?
a. settlers in the West
b. business leaders
c. white southerners
d. northern women

_____ **18.** Which reform movement caused the greatest tension between North and South?
a. the drive for temperance
b. abolitionism
c. women's rights
d. discrimination against immigrants

C. Critical Thinking

Answer the following question on the back of this paper or on a separate sheet of paper. *(24 points)*

19. Testing Conclusions Catharine Beecher argued, "…educate a woman, and the interests of a whole family are secured." Why did she believe it was important for women to be educated?

20. **Recognizing Cause and Effect** Why did many reform movements cause resentment in the South?

D. Interpreting a Graph

Use the graph below to answer questions 21-22. Write your answers on the lines provided. *(12 points)*

21. In what period was Irish immigration at its highest? About how many Irish immigrants arrived during this time?

____

22. Compare German immigration in 1841-1845 with that in 1851-1856.

____

____

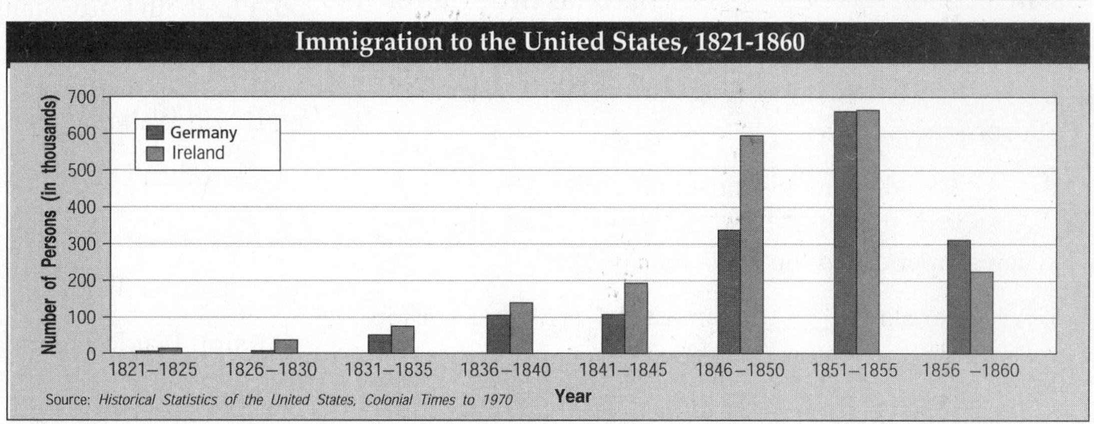

E. Analyzing a Document

The following passage comes from a report on working conditions for women in a Massachusetts textile mill. Read it and answer the questions below. *(12 points)*

> Thirteen hours per day of monotonous labor are exacted from these young women. So fatigued are the girls that they go to bed soon after their evening meal... Upon entering the work room, the noise of the five hundred looms under full operation struck us as frightful. It seemed a great violation to the sense of hearing... Each girl usually attends three looms. Doing so requires constant attention. The atmosphere of the room is full of cotton filaments and dust, which we are told are very harmful to the lungs...
>
> *Report on a visit to the Lowell, Massachusetts, textile mills published in* The Harbinger, *Lowell, 1846*

23. Why was it very loud in the mill work room?

24. Were working conditions dangerous? In what way?

NAME ______________________ CLASS ____________ DATE ____________

TEST FORM B

Religion and Reform (1800-1850)

CHAPTER 9

A. Identifying Key Terms, People, and Places

Complete each sentence by writing the letter of the correct name from Column II in each blank. You will not use all the names. *(20 points)*

Column I

_____ **1.** Charles Grandison Finney and _____ were popular revivalists of the Second Great Awakening.

_____ **2.** Transcendentalist writer _____ launched an "American renaissance" in literature.

_____ **3.** In his book *Walden,* _____ described his two years of solitary life.

_____ **4.** _____ worked to improve conditions in prisons and poorhouses.

_____ **5.** _____ was the nation's most influential African American abolitionist and published an antislavery newspaper called the *North Star*.

_____ **6.** A former slave, _____ became a powerful speaker for abolition and women's rights.

_____ **7.** The antislavery novel *Uncle Tom's Cabin* was written by _____ .

_____ **8.** _____ led hundreds of African Americans to freedom along the Underground Railroad.

_____ **9.** In *A Treatise on Domestic Economy,* _____ stressed the importance of women to the welfare of the United States.

_____ **10.** Lucretia Mott and _____ organized the first convention to discuss the question of women's rights.

Column II

a. Harriet Tubman
b. Horace Mann
c. Lyman Beecher
d. Elizabeth Cady Stanton
e. Catharine Beecher
f. David Walker
g. Dorothea Dix
h. Harriet Beecher Stowe
g. Sojourner Truth
j. Ralph Waldo Emerson
k. Henry David Thoreau
l. Robert Owen
m. Frederick Douglass

B. Identifying Main Ideas

Write the letter of the correct answer in the blank provided. *(32 points)*

_____ **11.** Transcendentalists encouraged people to
a. involve themselves in reforming society.
b. reject all social legislation.
c. become less self-reliant.
d. look to formal religions for profound truths.

_____ **12.** The aim of the temperance movement was to
a. convert Catholic immigrants to Protestantism.
b. help enslaved African Americans to buy their freedom.
c. eliminate all consumption of alcohol.
d. give women the right to vote.

_____ **13.** The American Colonization Society favored returning enslaved African Americans to Africa because of a belief that
a. African Americans desperately wanted to go there.
b. American society would never allow African Americans equal treatment.
c. leaders in Africa wanted enslaved Africans returned there.
d. the United States should begin colonizing throughout the world.

_____ **14.** Supporters of the abolitionist movement were divided over
a. whether slavery should be ended in the United States.
b. which enslaved African Americans should be freed.
c. how great a role women should be allowed to take in the movement.
d. whether they should urge people to take a pledge to practice abstinence.

_____ **15.** Southern members of Congress resisted antislavery efforts by
a. passing the gag rule.
b. establishing the Underground Railroad.
c. abolishing utopian communities.
d. promoting education for enslaved African Americans.

_____ **16.** The Seneca Falls Convention was important because it
a. united various antislavery societies into a single movement.
b. petitioned Congress for a constitutional amendment for emancipation.
c. established a public school system throughout the North.
d. was the first women's rights convention in American history.

_____ **17.** Most immigrants to the United States from 1820 to 1860 came from
a. Asia. **b.** Africa.
c. northern Europe. **d.** the Caribbean.

_____ **18.** In the 1830s and 1840s, most southern whites
a. were beginning to oppose slavery.
b. saw no need to reform their society.
c. promoted prison and public school reforms.
d. encouraged industrial development in the South.

C. Critical Thinking

Answer the following questions on the back of this paper or on a separate sheet of paper. *(24 points)*

19. Demonstrating Reasoned Judgment What problems in the North led to reform movements of the early 1800s?

TEST FORM B *(continued)*

20. Expressing Problems Clearly What are two ways that the rising number of immigrants led to increased tensions in the United States?

D. Interpreting a Graph

Use the graph below to answer questions 21-22. Write your answers on the lines provided. *(12 points)*

21. Compare Irish immigration in 1841-1845 with that in 1846-1850. By how many times did it grow from the first period to the second?

____

22. Compare German immigration in 1846-1850 with that in 1851-1855. By how much did it change in these two periods?

____

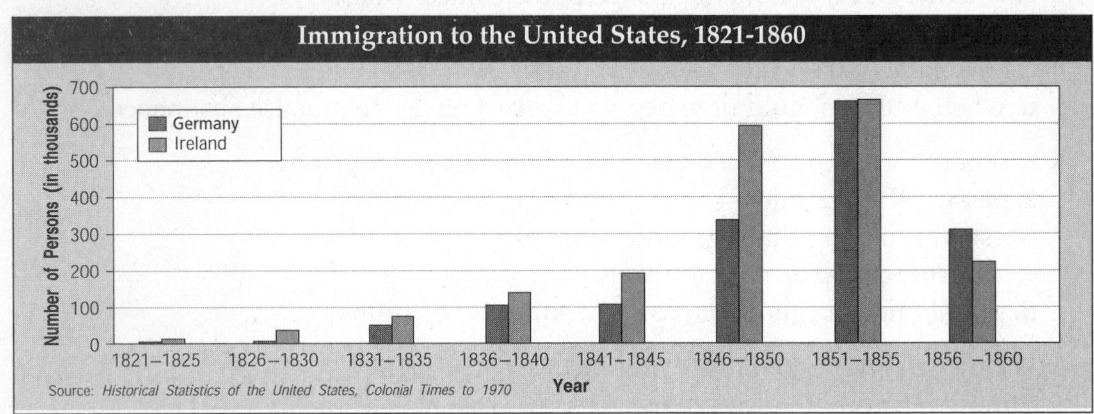

E. Analyzing a Document

The following describes working conditions for women in a Massachusetts textile mill. Read it and answer the questions below. *(12 points)*

> Thirteen hours per day of monotonous labor are exacted from these young women. So fatigued are the girls that they go to bed soon after their evening meal... Upon entering the work room, the noise of the five hundred looms under full operation struck us as frightful. It seemed a great violation to the sense of hearing... Each girl usually attends three looms. Doing so requires constant attention. The atmosphere of the room is full of cotton filaments and dust, which we are told are very harmful to the lungs...
>
> *Report on a visit to the Lowell, Massachusetts, textile mills published in* The Harbinger, *Lowell, 1846*

23. How can you tell that these women worked very hard?

24. Describe the working conditions in this textile mill.

NAME ______________________ CLASS ____________ DATE ____________

TEST FORM A

Beyond the Mississippi (1800-1860)

CHAPTER 10

A. Identifying Key Terms, People, and Places

Complete each sentence in Column I by writing the letter of the correct name from Column II in the blank provided. You will not use all the names. *(20 points)*

Column I

_____ **1.** Member of Congress _____ proposed an amendment to outlaw slavery in the territories acquired from Mexico.

_____ **2.** Under the leadership of _____, the first group of American settlers came to Texas in 1822.

_____ **3.** The dictatorship of General _____ encouraged many American settlers to fight for an independent Texas.

_____ **4.** _____ led Texas rebels at San Jacinto and became the first president of the Republic of Texas.

_____ **5.** Colonel _____ was a leader of the Texans who fought at the Battle of the Alamo.

_____ **6.** _____ was a Presbyterian missionary who worked among the Native Americans in the Oregon Country.

_____ **7.** In 1855, Yakima chief _____ led Native American resistance against being forced onto reservations in Oregon and Washington.

_____ **8.** Captain _____ led an American expedition into California as the Mexican War began.

_____ **9.** In the 1840s, Mormon leader _____ led followers westward to settle in present-day Utah.

_____ **10.** President _____ viewed the Mexican War as a chance for the United States to expand its territories.

Column II

a. Antonio López de Santa Anna
b. John Slidell
c. Narcissa Prentiss Whitman
d. William Travis
e. John C. Frémont
f. James K. Polk
g. Meriweather Lewis
h. Kamiakin
i. Sam Houston
j. David Wilmot
k. Stephen Austin
l. Brigham Young

B. Identifying Main Ideas

Write the letter of the correct ending in the blank provided. *(32 points)*

_____ **11.** The arrival of the horse encouraged many Native Americans to
a. stop trading.
b. become nomads.
c. become farmers.
d. establish permanent villages.

_____ **12.** In nomadic cultures, a main role of Native American women was to
a. serve as influential leaders.
b. produce food and tan buffalo hides.
c. fight as aggressive warriors.
d. learn to be skilled riders and horse thieves.

CHAPTER 10

_____ **13.** In the 1830s, many Americans in Texas opposed the Mexican government's attempt to
a. abolish slavery in Texas. **b.** increase trade with the United States.
c. colonize California. **d.** start a war with the United States.

_____ **14.** In the early 1800s, the United States built strong ties with Texas, New Mexico, and California through
a. religion. **b.** trade.
c. political treaties. **d.** war.

_____ **15.** During the Texas War for Independence, a small Texas army was defeated and slaughtered at
a. the Battle of Buena Vista. **b.** Vera Cruz.
c. Guadalupe Hidalgo. **d.** the Battle of the Alamo.

_____ **16.** The Oregon Country stretched from
a. the Mississippi River to the Pacific Coast.
b. northern California to Alaska's southern border.
c. San Antonio in Texas to Santa Fe in New Mexico.
d. Texas to Utah.

_____ **17.** In the 1840s, the phrase *manifest destiny* referred to the idea that the United States would inevitably
a. abolish slavery.
b. become the most powerful nation in the world.
c. stretch across North America from the Atlantic to the Pacific.
d. spread liberty throughout the world.

_____ **18.** One important result of the Mexican War was that
a. the United States gained control of the entire Oregon Country.
b. the Rio Grande became the accepted American-Mexican border.
c. Mexico and the United States became permanent allies.
d. the Republic of Texas became an independent nation.

C. Critical Thinking

Answer the following questions on the back of this paper or on a separate sheet of paper. (*24 points*)

19. Identifying Central Issues Explain the impact of the successful trade between the United States and Mexico's northern territories of California, New Mexico, and Texas.

20. Demonstrating Reasoned Judgment Some Americans believed that the Mexican War created more problems than it solved. Explain one problem caused by the war.

CHAPTER 10

D. Reading a Table

Use the information in the table below to answer questions 21-22. Write your answers on the back of this paper or on a separate sheet of paper. *(12 points)*

21. What happened to the level of westward migration from 1845 to 1846? What event might have caused this change?

22. In what two-year period did the greatest number of people migrate to the West? What event do you think might have caused this migration boom?

Westward Migration

Year	Estimate	Year	Estimate	Year	Estimate
1841	100	1847	2,000	1853	20,000
1842	200	1848	4,000	1854	10,000
1843	1,000	1849	30,000	1855	5,000
1844	2,000	1850	55,000	1856	5,000
1845	5,000	1851	10,000	1857	5,000
1846	1,000	1852	50,000	1858	10,000

Source: Merrill J. Mattes, Nebraska State Historical Society

E. Analyzing a Document

While under siege at the Alamo during the Texas War for Independence, William Travis wrote the following plea for help. Read it and then answer the questions about it on the back of this paper or on a separate sheet of paper. *(12 points)*

> Fellow citizens & compatriots, I am besieged by thousands or more of the Mexicans under Santa Anna....I call on you in the name of Liberty, of patriotism & everything dear to the American character to come to our aid, with all dispatch....If this call is neglected, I am determined to sustain myself as long as possible & die like a soldier who never forgets what is due to his own honor or that of his country.
>
> *Colonel William B. Travis*

23. Why did Travis need help?

24. How did Travis try to convince people to come to his aid?

NAME ______________________ CLASS __________ DATE __________

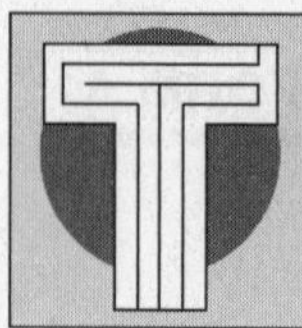

TEST FORM B

Beyond the Mississippi (1800-1860)

CHAPTER 10

A. Identifying Key Terms, People, and Places

Match the descriptions in Column I with the places in Column II. Write the letter of the correct answer in the blank provided. You will not use all the places. *(20 points)*

Column I

_____ **1.** vast grassland that lies between the Mississippi River and the Rocky Mountains

_____ **2.** location of first mission founded by the Spanish in California

_____ **3.** lively market town and capital of New Mexico

_____ **4.** Mexican territory in which settlers' uprising became known as the Bear Flag Revolt

_____ **5.** fortress built on the ruins of a Spanish mission in San Antonio, Texas

_____ **6.** scene of the shooting of 300 Texas prisoners of war

_____ **7.** town in western Missouri that marked the beginning of the 2,000-mile trek to Oregon

_____ **8.** area in Oregon where Presbyterian missionaries settled to convert Native Americans

_____ **9.** official American-Mexican border after the Mexican War

_____ **10.** site of discovery that set off the California Gold Rush

Column II

a. Rio Grande
b. Willamette Valley
c. Great Plains
d. Sutter's Mill
e. Platte River
f. the Alamo
g. Cripple Creek
h. Santa Fe
i. California
j. San Diego
k. Goliad
l. Independence

B. Identifying Main Ideas

Write the letter of the correct answer in the blank provided. *(32 points)*

_____ **11.** What impact did the arrival of the horse have on Native Americans?
a. Farming replaced hunting.
b. Men and women shared more responsibilities.
c. Trading declined.
d. Many Native Americans became nomads.

_____ **12.** Which of the following best describes what happened to Native American women when their cultures became nomadic?
a. They gained influence because they lived in farming villages.
b. They became warriors as warrior cultures developed.
c. They lost influence as farming village life became hunting life.
d. They stayed behind as their husbands and fathers went off to hunt.

_____ **13.** Which of the following contributed to the success of the Spanish missions in California?
a. raids by nomadic Native Americans
b. Native American labor
c. the priests' tolerance and respect for Native American culture
d. good living conditions and excellent medical care

_____ **14.** What contribution did Stephen Austin make to Texas?
a. He blazed the Santa Fe Trail.
b. He led the first organized group of American settlers into Texas.
c. He led the Texans in their fight for independence from Mexico.
d. He fought and died at the Battle of the Alamo.

_____ **15.** What were the hardy fur traders and traders who roamed the Rocky Mountains in search of beaver pelts called?
a. mountain men **b.** forty-niners
c. missionaries **d.** middlemen

_____ **16.** Which statement best describes the relationship between emigrating pioneers and Native Americans in the 1840s?
a. Native Americans usually raided and destroyed the caravans.
b. Native Americans and pioneers usually traded with each other.
c. Native Americans and pioneers rarely interacted at all.
d. Native Americans usually guided and protected the caravans.

_____ **17.** What issue became a major problem for the United States government after the Mexican War?
a. whether slavery should be allowed in the western territories
b. whether Mormons should be allowed to settle in Utah
c. whether the United States should annex Texas
d. whether Americans should migrate to Mexico's northern territories

_____ **18.** What group formed the majority of those who went to California in the 1849 gold rush?
a. Chinese **b.** women and children
c. unmarried men **d.** free African Americans

C. Critical Thinking

Answer the following questions on the back of this paper or on a separate sheet of paper. *(24 points)*

19. Drawing Conclusions Why do you think nomadic Native Americans were more successful than village societies in resisting domination by the United States government?

20. Expressing Problems Clearly After Texas became independent, many Americans disagreed about whether or not to annex Texas. Describe one argument for, and one argument against the annexation of Texas.

CHAPTER 10

D. Reading a Table

Use the information in the table below to answer questions 21-22. Write your answers on the back of this paper or on a separate sheet of paper. *(12 points)*

21. In what year was westward migration at its lowest? In what year did it reach its peak?

22. What impact did the California Gold Rush have on western migration?

Westward Migration

Year	Estimate	Year	Estimate	Year	Estimate
1841	100	1847	2,000	1853	20,000
1842	200	1848	4,000	1854	10,000
1843	1,000	1849	30,000	1855	5,000
1844	2,000	1850	55,000	1856	5,000
1845	5,000	1851	10,000	1857	5,000
1846	1,000	1852	50,000	1858	10,000

Source: Merrill J. Mattes, Nebraska State Historical Society

E. Analyzing a Document

While under siege at the Alamo during the Texas War for Independence, William Travis wrote the following plea for help. Read it and then answer the questions about it on the back of this paper or on a separate sheet of paper. *(12 points)*

> Fellow citizens & compatriots, I am besieged by thousands or more of the Mexicans under Santa Anna....I call on you in the name of Liberty, of patriotism & everything dear to the American character to come to our aid, with all dispatch....If this call is neglected, I am determined to sustain myself as long as possible & die like a soldier who never forgets what is due to his own honor or that of his country.
>
> *Colonel William B. Travis*

23. Describe the situation at the Alamo when Travis wrote this letter.

24. What did Travis expect to happen if he did not receive help?

NAME ______________________ CLASS ____________ DATE ____________

TEST FORM A

The Coming of the Civil War (1848-1861)

CHAPTER 11

A. Identify Key Terms, People, and Places

Complete each sentence in Column I by writing the letter of the correct name from Column II. You will not use all the names. *(20 points)*

Column I

_____ **1.** The book *Uncle Tom's Cabin*, by _____, caused many white Americans to question slavery.

_____ **2.** The Compromise of 1850 was proposed to Congress by Senator _____ of Kentucky.

_____ **3.** Senator _____ of South Carolina declared that the South would not give up its liberty to save the Union.

_____ **4.** Senator _____ of Illinois introduced the Kansas-Nebraska Act of 1854.

_____ **5.** In Congress, Senator _____ of Massachusetts gave a powerful antislavery speech entitled "The Crime Against Kansas."

_____ **6.** In the Dred Scott decision, Chief Justice _____ upheld the right of slaveholders to take their slaves anywhere in the United States and keep them as slaves.

_____ **7.** In 1858, the Republican _____ opposed slavery on moral grounds in debates with Stephen Douglas.

_____ **8.** Abolitionist _____ led the attack on the federal arsenal at Harpers Ferry in Virginia.

_____ **9.** Because his antislavery position seemed too extreme, _____ lost the 1860 Republican presidential nomination.

_____ **10.** _____ of Mississippi was elected president of the Confederate States of America.

Column II

a. John C. Calhoun
b. Robert E. Lee
c. John Brown
d. Jefferson Davis
e. Stephen Douglas
f. Henry Clay
g. Abraham Lincoln
h. Charles Sumner
i. Harriet Beecher Stowe
j. William Henry Seward
k. Roger Taney

B. Identifying Main Ideas

Write the letter of the correct ending in the blank provided. (*32 points*)

_____ **11.** Many northern whites objected to slavery because they believed it
a. made the South better off than the North.
b. made the South politically stronger than the North.
c. violated principles of the Christian religion.
d. made southern whites lazy.

CHAPTER 11

_____ 12. Many southern whites criticized northern business owners for
a. not caring about their workers
b. assuming personal responsibility for workers.
c. trying to control workers' lives.
d. refusing to hire African American workers.

_____ 13. Unlike the South, the North of 1860
a. was committed to the free enterprise system.
b. was not prejudiced against African Americans.
c. was a thriving industrial society.
d. had a democratic form of government.

_____ 14. The purpose of the Fugitive Slave Act was to
a. provide safety for escaped slaves.
b. force all Americans to help catch escaped slaves.
c. offer freed slaves land in the West.
d. ban slavery in Washington, D.C.

_____ 15. Under popular sovereignty, the decision whether or not to allow slavery in a territory was made by
a. Congress.
b. the voters of the territory.
c. the Supreme Court.
d. the President.

_____ 16. Abolitionists objected to the Dred Scott decision because it
a. freed enslaved people who left the South.
b. strengthened the Missouri Compromise.
c. outlawed due process as called for by the Fifth Amendment.
d. meant Congress had no power to ban slavery anywhere.

_____ 17. In 1860 and 1861, seven southern states seceded from the Union in protest of the
a. election of Republican Abraham Lincoln as President.
b. federal government's refusal to punish John Brown.
c. brutal beating of Charles Sumner in the Senate.
d. Dred Scott decision.

_____ 18. The Civil War began with the
a. secession of South Carolina.
b. illegal formation of the Confederate States of America.
c. attack on Lawrence, Kansas, a center of free-soiler activity.
d. the Confederate attack on Fort Sumter.

C. Critical Thinking

Answer the following questions on the back of this paper or on a separate sheet of paper. (*22 points*)

19. Recognizing Ideologies Explain why northern whites who opposed slavery and southern whites who supported slavery both believed they were fighting to defend liberty.

20. Identifying Alternatives In 1861, many northern politicians felt the South should be allowed to secede in peace. For what reasons did Lincoln oppose this argument?

D. Interpreting a Graph

Use the graph to answer questions 21-23. Write your answers on the lines provided. *(12 points)*

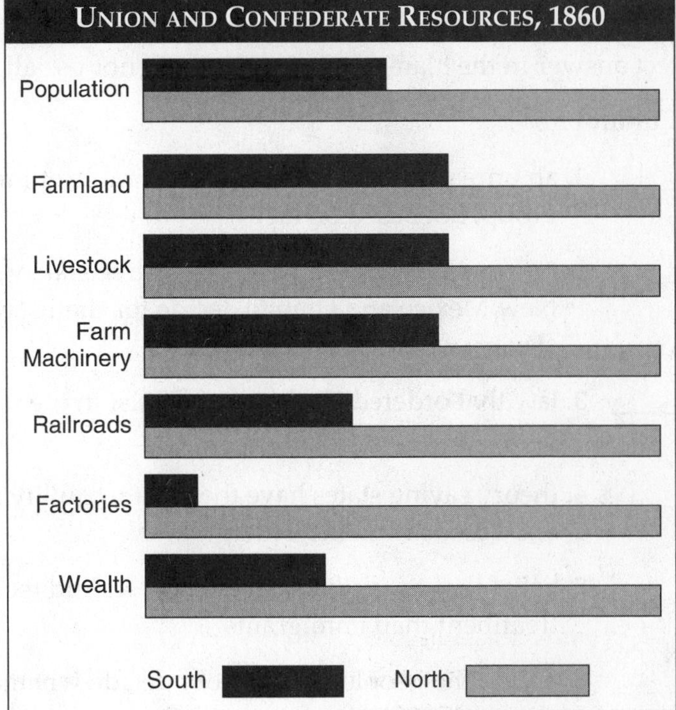

21. Which region had a better transportation system? Which region was more industrial?

____

22. Which region had more farmland in 1860?

____

23. Based on this graph, which region do you think had the advantage in the Civil War? Explain.

____

____

____

E. Analyzing a Document

Shortly before being executed for leading the attack on the federal arsenal at Harpers Ferry, John Brown was interviewed by Senator James Mason of Virginia. Read the following excerpt and answer questions 24-25 on the back of this paper or on a separate sheet of paper. *(14 points)*

> *Senator Mason*: What was your object in coming?
>
> *John Brown*: We came to free the slaves, and only that.
>
> *Senator Mason*: How do you justify your acts?
>
> *John Brown*: I think, my friend, you are guilty of a great wrong against God and humanity… and it would be perfectly right for anyone to interfere with you so far as to free those you willfully and wickedly hold in bondage…

24. What was the goal of John Brown's raid?

25. Was he sorry for the violence he and his men committed? Explain.

NAME ______________________ CLASS ____________ DATE ____________

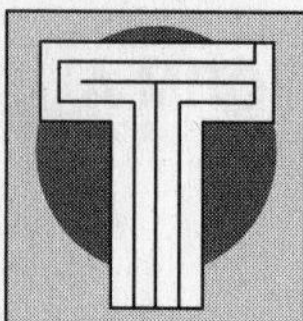

TEST FORM B

The Coming of the Civil War (1848-1861)

CHAPTER 11

A. Identifying Key Terms, People, and Places

Match the descriptions in Column I with the terms in Column II. Write the letter of the correct answer in the blank provided. You will not use all the terms. *(20 points)*

Column I

_____ **1.** an unreasonable and often unfavorable opinion of another group, not based on fact

_____ **2.** proposal to admit California as a free state while allowing New Mexico and Utah to decide for themselves whether slavery would be legal

_____ **3.** law that ordered all citizens to assist in the return of runaway enslaved people

_____ **4.** theory saying states have the right to nullify federal acts and secede from the Union

_____ **5.** belief that native-born Americans should receive better treatment than immigrants

_____ **6.** letting the people of a territory decide whether to allow slavery in their area

_____ **7.** a place where weapons are made or stored

_____ **8.** name given to Delaware, Maryland, Kentucky, and Missouri

_____ **9.** person who wanted the South to leave the Union

_____ **10.** nation created by states of the Lower South when they seceded from the Union

Column II

a. popular sovereignty

b. Fugitive Slave Act

c. Kansas-Nebraska Act

d. Upper South

e. Confederate States of America

f. prejudice

g. nativism

h. secessionist

i. states' rights

j. Border States

k. arsenal

l. Compromise of 1850

B. Identifying Main Ideas

Write the letter of the correct answer in the blank provided. (*32 points*)

_____ **11.** How did the book *Uncle Tom's Cabin* affect American society in the 1850s?
a. It convinced many northerners that enslaved people were property.
b. It resulted in the passage of laws protecting slaves from owners who beat them.
c. It caused some slaveholders to allow slaves to buy their freedom.
d. It convinced many northerners that slavery would ruin the nation.

_____ **12.** Which of the following is true of both the North and the South in the mid-1800s?
a. Both regions cherished their democratic tradition.
b. Both regions had strong communications systems.
c. Cotton was the most important cash crop in both regions.
d. Both regions had about the same amount of industrial production.

_____ **13.** South Carolina Senator John C. Calhoun believed that
a. the South could easily win a war with the North.
b. the South should abandon slavery to save the nation.
c. slavery was morally wrong and a threat to liberty.
d. owning enslaved people was a constitutional right.

_____ **14.** What did Senator Stephen Douglas propose in the Kansas-Nebraska Act?
a. to make Kansas and Nebraska slave states
b. to uphold the Missouri Compromise
c. to rely on popular sovereignty to decide if slavery should be legal in the territories
d. to allow slavery in Nebraska but not in Kansas

_____ **15.** Which of the following did the Supreme Court uphold in the Dred Scott decision?
a. The slave trade should be abolished in Washington, D.C.
b. The federal government should protect the slaveholder, not the slave.
c. Slavery was unconstitutional.
d. Slaveholders could not take slaves into free states or territories.

_____ **16.** During his 1858 senatorial election debates with Stephen Douglas, Abraham Lincoln argued that
a. slavery was a moral issue.
b. whites and African Americans should have social and political equality.
c. slavery should be prohibited in the South.
d. southern states should secede.

_____ **17.** What was the greatest impact of John Brown's raid on Harpers Ferry?
a. Northerners and southerners reached a temporary "cease-fire."
b. The raid deepened the division between North and South.
c. The raid caused the decline of the Whig party.
d. The federal government agreed to let state governments decide all slavery issues.

_____ **18.** Lincoln's call for volunteers to defend Fort Sumter led directly to
a. the succession of the Upper South states.
b. a Union victory in the fighting at Fort Sumter.
c. a split in the Democratic party.
d. the creation of the Confederate States of America.

C. Critical Thinking

Answer the following questions on the back of this paper or on a separate sheet of paper. (*22 points*)

19. Checking Consistency Northern abolitionists and southern slaveholders both believed they were defending the Constitution. Summarize their opposing beliefs on this point.

20. **Recognizing Cause and Effect** How did Lincoln's victory in the 1860 Presidential election help bring about the Civil War?

CHAPTER 11

D. Interpreting a Graph

Use the graph to answer questions 21-23. Write your answers on the lines provided. (*12 points*)

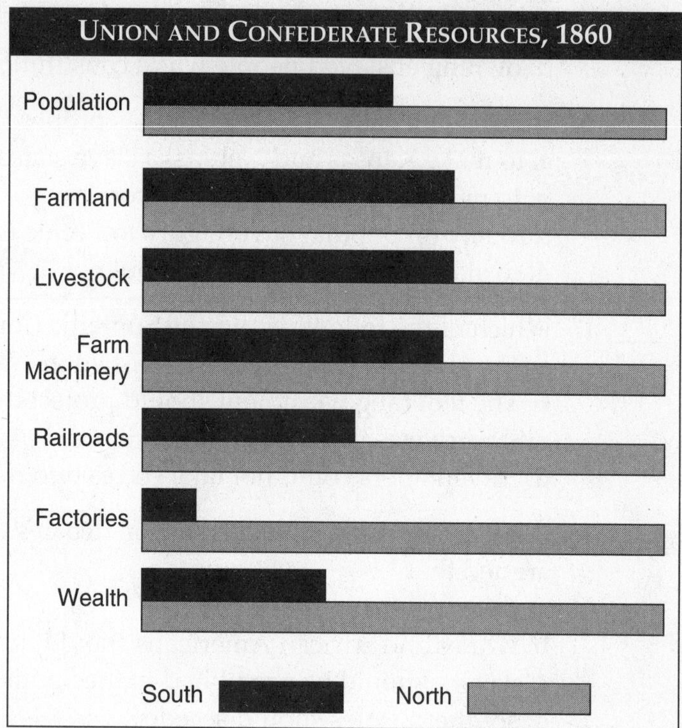

21. In 1860, how did the population of the North compare with the population of the South?

______

22. Which region was more industrial? Which region was wealthier?

______

23. What information in the graph supports this statement from your text: "New technology had a heavier impact on the North than on the South"?

______

______

E. Analyzing a Document

Shortly before being executed for leading the attack on the federal arsenal at Harpers Ferry, John Brown was interviewed by Senator James Mason of Virginia. Read the following excerpt and answer questions 24-25 on the back of this paper or on a separate sheet of paper. (*14 points*)

Senator Mason: What was your object in coming?

John Brown: We came to free the slaves, and only that.

Senator Mason: How do you justify your acts?

John Brown: I think, my friend, you are guilty of a great wrong against God and humanity... and it would be perfectly right for anyone to interfere with you so far as to free those you willfully and wickedly hold in bondage...

24. According to Brown, what "great wrong" is the government guilty of?

25. Why did Brown feel justified in attacking United States property?

NAME ______________________ CLASS ______________ DATE ______________

TEST FORM A

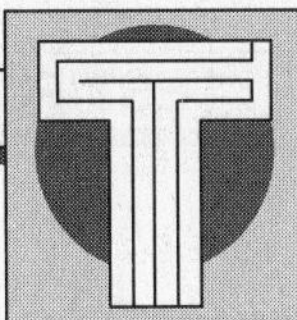

The Civil War (1861-1865)

CHAPTER 12

A. Identifying Key Terms, People, and Places

Match the descriptions in Column I with the terms in Column II. Write the letter of the correct answer in the blank provided. You will not use all the terms. (*16 points*)

Column I

____ **1.** conflict in which one side inflicts continuous losses on its enemy to wear down enemy strength

____ **2.** legal means of forcing people to serve in the armed forces

____ **3.** paper money not backed by gold

____ **4.** emergency rule by military authority

____ **5.** antiwar Northern Democrats

____ **6.** bands of soldiers who use hit-and-run tactics

____ **7.** property seized from one side in a war that becomes the property of the other side

____ **8.** addition to the Constitution that ended slavery

Column II

a. greenbacks
b. contraband
c. recognition
d. war of attrition
e. canister
f. draft
g. Thirteenth Amendment
h. guerrillas
i. Copperheads
j. martial law

B. Identifying Main Ideas

Write the letter of the correct answer in the blank provided. (*40 points*)

____ **9.** What was the first major battle of the Civil War?
a. the Battle of Shiloh
b. the Battle of Chancellorsville
c. the First Battle of Bull Run
d. the Battle of Antietam

____ **10.** Which of the following was an advantage the North had over the South?
a. more experienced generals
b. military support from Britain
c. more money to spend on war
d. full support of all its citizens

____ **11.** What caused President Lincoln to become dissatisfied with General McClellan's command?
a. He thought McClellan took unnecessary risks.
b. He thought McClellan was too slow to take action.
c. He objected to McClellan's political views.
d. He said that McClellan was a coward.

CHAPTER 12

_____ **12.** Which of the following was a strategy of the Confederate government?
a. blockading the North's Atlantic coast
b. attacking the North by way of the Mississippi River
c. seeking support from Britain and France
d. limiting the upper draft age to 35

_____ **13.** During the Civil War, the Republican-controlled Congress
a. removed General Lee as commander of Union forces.
b. dominated the Union military strategy.
c. passed laws repealing the tariffs on manufactured goods.
d. passed a law calling for the construction of a railroad line from Nebraska to the Pacific Coast.

_____ **14.** The Emancipation Proclamation freed
a. all enslaved people living in the United States.
b. enslaved people living in areas controlled by the Confederacy.
c. enslaved people living in the Union states.
d. enslaved people living in the territories.

_____ **15.** After the South's victories at Fredericksburg and Chancellorsville,
a. some Northern leaders began to talk about making peace with the South.
b. the Confederate government declared victory in the war.
c. President Lincoln's popularity increased.
d. Northern industrial production began to fall.

_____ **16.** Grant's victory at Vicksburg
a. ended the South's naval domination.
b. cut the Confederacy in two.
c. caused Lee to surrender.
d. forced Jefferson Davis to resign as president of the Confederacy.

_____ **17.** In the Gettysburg Address, Lincoln
a. condemned the use of total war. **b.** promised the nation a new birth of freedom.
c. declared that slavery was moral. **d.** offered forgiveness to the South.

_____ **18.** What was a major significance of the presidential election of 1864?
a. The Copperheads supported Lincoln.
b. Voters showed their approval of Lincoln's stand against slavery.
c. Voters showed their disapproval of Lincoln's war policy.
d. Voters showed their approval of Lincoln's peace plan.

C. Critical Thinking

Answer the following questions on the back of this paper or on a separate sheet of paper. (*24 points*)

19. Identifying Assumptions Why did the South assume that France and Britain would back the Confederacy? Was this assumption correct?

20. Demonstrating Reasoned Judgement At the start of the Civil War, why do you think many Americans favored the North to win?

D. Interpreting a Map

Use the map to answer questions 21-22. Write your answers on the lines provided. (*10 points*)

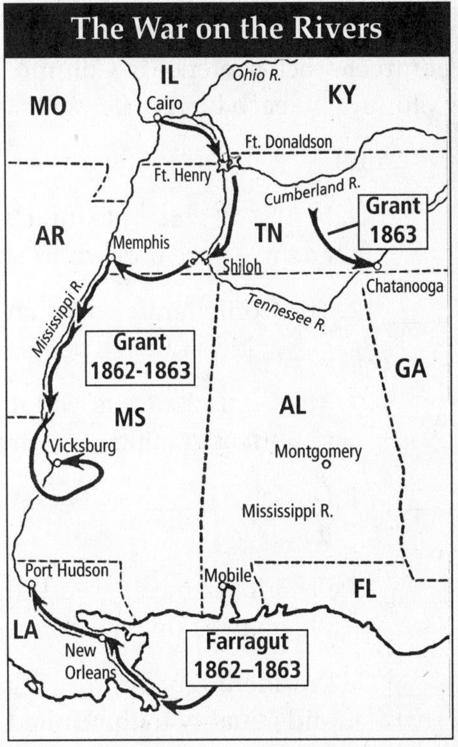

21. Name three rivers that were strategically important for the control of commerce and troops in the Confederacy.

____

____

____

22. What Mississippi city did Grant surround in 1863?

____

____

____

E. Analyzing a Document

Below are the opening lines of the Gettysburg Address. Read them and then answer questions 23-24 on the back of this paper or on a separate sheet of paper. (*10 points*)

> Four score and seven [eighty-seven] years ago our fathers brought forth on this continent a new nation, conceived in Liberty, and dedicated to the proposition that all men are created equal.
>
> Now we are engaged in a great civil war, testing whether that nation, or any nation so conceived and so dedicated, can long endure. We are met on a great battle-field of that war. We have come to dedicate a portion of that field, as a final resting place for those who here gave their lives that that nation might live....
>
> *Abraham Lincoln, 1863*

23. When Lincoln referred to "four score and seven years ago" what year was he talking about?

24. According to Lincoln, what was his purpose in coming to Gettysburg?

NAME ______________________ CLASS ______________ DATE ______________

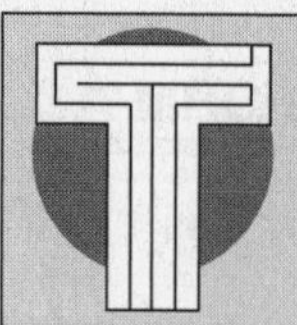

TEST FORM B

The Civil War (1861-1865)

CHAPTER 12

A. Identifying Key Terms, People, and Places

Complete each sentence in Column I by writing the letter of the correct term from Column II in each blank. You will not use all the terms. (*16 points*)

Column I

_____ **1.** In a _____, one side inflicts continuous losses on an enemy to wear down its strength.

_____ **2.** The Confederate government was the first to pass _____ laws to force people to serve in the military.

_____ **3.** The Confederacy hoped to gain status as an independent nation by gaining _____ from Britain and France.

_____ **4.** During a _____, a city is surrounded and starved to make it surrender.

_____ **5.** President Lincoln issued the _____ to free enslaved people in areas under Confederate control.

_____ **6.** President Lincoln's _____ redefined the ideas of freedom and equality in the United States.

_____ **7.** The _____ ended slavery in the United States.

_____ **8.** Northern newspapers called the Union strategy of surrounding the Confederacy the _____.

Column II

a. recognition

b. Internal Revenue Act

c. draft

d. Anaconda Plan

e. contraband

f. Gettysburg Address

g. war of attrition

h. Emancipation Proclamation

i. siege

j. Thirteenth Amendment

B. Identifying Main Ideas

Write the letter of the correct ending in the blank provided. (*40 points*)

_____ **9.** Which of the following was an advantage the South had in the Civil War?
a. larger army **b.** more miles of railroad
c. greater number of factories **d.** more experienced generals

_____ **10.** The First Battle of Bull Run and the Battle of Shiloh proved that the
a. war would be long and difficult.
b. South would soon capture Washington, D.C.
c. Union soldiers were better trained than Confederate soldiers.
d. South could not win the war.

_____ **11.** Lincoln urged General McClellan to attack the Confederate capital of
a. New Orleans, Louisiana. **b.** Memphis, Tennessee.
c. Richmond, Virginia. **d.** Atlanta, Georgia.

_____ 12. The North gained control of important water routes by capturing
- a. Fort Henry and Fort Donelson.
- b. Antietam.
- c. Shiloh.
- d. Fredericksburg and Chancellorsville.

_____ 13. During the Civil War, the South hoped to
- a. capture New York City.
- b. convince Britain and France to intervene on the Confederate side.
- c. form armies of enslaved African Americans.
- d. build a huge, modern navy.

_____ 14. Without Southern opposition in Congress, Republicans were able to
- a. raise tariffs to protect Northern industries.
- b. encourage cotton-growing in the North.
- c. make it impossible to build a railroad from Nebraska to the Pacific coast.
- d. end the threat of Confederate ironclads to Union ships.

_____ 15. The Emancipation Proclamation had the effect of
- a. discouraging white males from joining the Union army.
- b. encouraging African Americans to serve in the Union army.
- c. prohibiting African Americans from service in the Union army.
- d. prohibiting African Americans from service in the Confederate army.

_____ 16. General Lee marched his troops into Pennsylvania because he
- a. had been defeated at Fredericksburg and Chancellorsville.
- b. hoped to win a victory on Union soil.
- c. had been ordered to capture Washington, D.C.
- d. wanted to punish the North for Stonewall Jackson's death.

_____ 17. The single greatest cause of death of Confederate and Union soldiers was
- a. canisters.
- b. shells.
- c. disease.
- d. gunboats.

_____ 18. The reelection of President Lincoln in 1864 showed that most Northern voters
- a. were sick of war.
- b. approved his stand against slavery.
- c. expected the war to last several more years.
- d. approved his plan for peace.

C. Critical Thinking

Answer the following questions on the back of this paper or on a separate sheet of paper. (*24 points*)

19. **Making Comparisons** Identify two advantages that the North had over the South during the Civil War, and two advantages that the South had over the North.

NAME ______ CLASS ______ DATE ______

TEST FORM B *(continued)*

20. **Testing Conclusions** Your text states that for the North "the Fourth of July 1863 was the most joyous independence day since the first one 87 years earlier." Explain this statement.

CHAPTER 12

D. Interpreting a Map

Use the map to answer questions 21-22. Write your answers on the lines provided. (*10 points*)

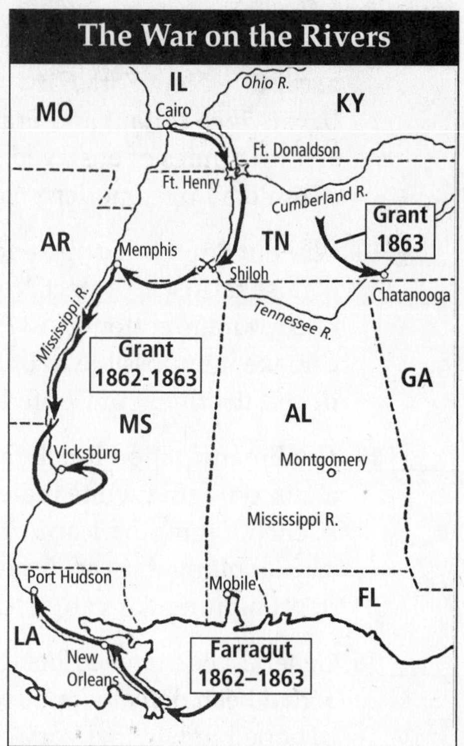

21. What two Confederate strongholds on the Mississippi River did Commodore Farragut and his Union sailors capture?

______

______

______

22. What impact would Union control of the Mississippi River have on the Confederacy?

______

______

______

E. Analyzing a Document

Below are the opening lines of the Gettysburg Address. Read them and then answer questions 23-24 on the back of this paper or on a separate sheet of paper. (*10 points*)

> Four score and seven [eighty-seven] years ago our fathers brought forth on this continent a new nation, conceived in Liberty, and dedicated to the proposition that all men are created equal.
>
> Now we are engaged in a great civil war, testing whether that nation, or any nation so conceived and so dedicated, can long endure. We are met on a great battle-field of that war. We have come to dedicate a portion of that field, as a final resting place for those who here gave their lives that that nation might live....
>
> *Abraham Lincoln, 1863*

23. What did Lincoln say the Civil War was testing?

24. According to Lincoln, how should Union soldiers who died at Gettysburg be remembered?

TEST FORM A

Reconstruction (1865-1877)

A. Identifying Key Terms, People, and Places

Complete each sentence in Column I by writing the letter of the correct term from Column II in each blank. You will not use all the terms. (*16 points*)

Column I

_____ **1.** As part of his Reconstruction policy, Lincoln refused to _____ Confederate military leaders.

_____ **2.** The _____ stated that everyone born or naturalized in the United States was a citizen and was entitled to equal protection of the law.

_____ **3.** After President Johnson tried to fire his Secretary of War, the House of Representatives voted to _____ him.

_____ **4.** With the ratification of the _____, African American males gained the right to vote.

_____ **5.** Southerners called a northern Republican who moved to the South following the Civil War a(n) _____.

_____ **6.** A _____ grows a crop on land owned by someone else and gives the landowner part of the annual yield.

_____ **7.** A _____ rents the land on which he or she grows crops.

_____ **8.** The war-torn South had to rebuild its _____, which included its transportation and communication systems.

Column II

a. pardon
b. impeach
c. Reconstruction
d. carpetbagger
e. scalawag
f. sharecropper
g. infrastructure
h. tenant farmer
i. Fourteenth Amendment
j. Fifteenth Amendment

B. Identifying Main Ideas

Write the letter of the correct ending in the blank provided. (*40 points*)

_____ **9.** The Radical Republicans opposed President Lincoln's Reconstruction plan, saying it was too
a. harsh on the South. **b.** lenient on the South.
c. generous to the freed people. **d.** difficult to carry out.

_____ **10.** In their Reconstruction policies, both President Lincoln and President Johnson insisted upon
a. sworn statements of allegiance from a majority of citizens.
b. immediate elections in all Southern states.
c. Southern approval of the Thirteenth Amendment.
d. a fair redistribution of land.

CHAPTER 13

_____ **11.** The Freedmen's Bureau succeeded in
a. redistributing formerly white-owned land to black southerners.
b. keeping ex-Confederate supporters out of office.
c. providing clothing, medical care, food, and education to many freed people.
d. electing African Americans to southern state governments.

_____ **12.** Southern state governments restricted the rights of former slaves by
a. passing black codes.
b. holding constitutional conventions.
c. refusing to pay war debts.
d. refusing to pass the Thirteenth Amendment.

_____ **13.** Which of these was an important provision of the Radical Republicans' Reconstruction Act of 1867?
a. It ended Reconstruction.
b. It legalized black codes.
c. It offered pardons to Confederate generals.
d. It put the South under military rule.

_____ **14.** During Reconstruction, southern governments tried to improve economic conditions in the South by
a. lowering cotton prices.
b. building railroads and businesses.
c. redistributing land.
d. lowering taxes.

_____ **15.** Which was a major success of Reconstruction in the South?
a. an end to racist government policies
b. the transformation into an industrialized, urban region
c. the creation of a public school system
d. an end to tensions between the South and North

_____ **16.** The main goal of the Ku Klux Klan during Reconstruction was to
a. prevent African Americans from exercising their rights.
b. gain control of state legislatures.
c. restore the Confederacy.
d. improve conditions for poor whites.

_____ **17.** As white southerners regained control of state governments, they began to
a. reverse Reconstruction era reforms.
b. compensate former slaves.
c. join the Republican party.
d. refuse to pay war debts.

_____ **18.** After Rutherford B. Hayes became President in 1877, he
a. ended corruption in government.
b. removed federal troops from the South.
c. promised to regulate the railroads.
d. pledged to promote women's rights.

NAME ______________________ CLASS ____________ DATE ____________

(continued) **TEST FORM A**

C. Critical Thinking

Answer the following questions on the back of this paper or on a separate sheet of paper. (*24 points*)

19. Recognizing Cause and Effect How did the end of slavery change agriculture in the South?

20. Identifying Central Issues Explain one success and one failure of Reconstruction.

CHAPTER 13

D. Interpreting a Cartoon

Use the cartoon to answer questions 21-22. Write your answers on the lines provided. (*10 points*)

21. According to the cartoonist, what was the goal of the Ku Klux Klan?

____

____

22. What is one action the KKK took to make the lives of African Americans "worse than slavery"?

____

____

E. Analyzing a Document

Below is the text of the Thirteenth Amendment to the Constitution. Read it and then answer questions 23-24 on the back of this paper or on a separate sheet of paper. (*10 points*)

> **Section One**
>
> Neither slavery nor involuntary servitude, except as a punishment for crime whereof the party shall have been duly convicted, shall exist within the United States, or any place subject to their jurisdiction.
>
> **Section Two**
>
> Congress shall have power to enforce this article by appropriate legislation.

23. What did the Thirteenth Amendment accomplish?

24. In what case could people still be forced into "involuntary servitude?"

NAME ______________________ CLASS ______________ DATE ______________

TEST FORM B

Reconstruction (1865-1877)

CHAPTER 13

A. Identifying Key Terms, People, and Places

Match the descriptions in Column I with the terms in Column II. Write the letter of the correct answer in the blank provided. You will not use all the terms. *(16 points)*

Column I

_____ **1.** official forgiveness of a crime

_____ **2.** legislation stating that all persons born or naturalized in the United States were citizens and no state could restrict their rights

_____ **3.** personal liberties guaranteed by law

_____ **4.** act of formally charging an official with wrongdoing in office

_____ **5.** legislation stating that no citizen could be denied the vote because of race, color, or previous condition of servitude

_____ **6.** term for a northern Republican who moved to the South after the Civil War

_____ **7.** farmer who grows a crop on someone else's land and gives the landowner part of the annual yield

_____ **8.** unflattering name for a white southern Republican

Column II

a. scalawag

b. carpetbagger

c. impeach

d. sharecropper

e. civil rights

f. Reconstruction

g. Fourteenth Amendment

h. pardon

i. Fifteenth Amendment

j. Freedmen's Bureau

k. tenant farmer

B. Identifying Main Ideas

Write the letter of the correct answer in the blank provided. *(40 points)*

_____ **9.** Which best reflects President Lincoln's hopes for Reconstruction?
a. to severely punish the South for seceding from the Union
b. to replace all white officials in the South with African Americans
c. to strengthen the North's domination of the South
d. to bind the nation together and create a lasting peace

_____ **10.** The Radical Republicans objected to President Lincoln's plan for Reconstruction because they thought it was
a. a threat to Congressional authority.
b. too harsh on the South.
c. unfair to former slave owners.
d. too expensive.

_____ **11.** The goal of the Freedmen's Bureau was to
a. help former slaves adjust to freedom.
b. abolish slavery.
c. prevent African Americans from voting.
d. force African Americans to move north.

_____ **12.** The Radical Republicans passed a series of laws designed to
a. reestablish slavery in a different form.
b. unfairly tax the South.
c. protect the civil rights of African Americans.
d. prohibit free speech in the South.

_____ **13.** What was the verdict in President Johnson's impeachment trial?
a. He was found guilty.
b. He was removed from office.
c. He escaped conviction by one vote.
d. He was forced to confess his guilt.

_____ **14.** Which was a characteristic of agriculture in the South after the Civil War?
a. an abundance of cheap labor **b.** an emphasis on cash crops
c. an even distribution of wealth **d.** a decline in cotton production

_____ **15.** By the mid-1870s, many Americans were tired of Reconstruction partly because
a. no important legislation had been passed.
b. Reconstruction legislatures taxed heavily.
c. all Reconstruction goals had been achieved.
d. the southern economy had fully recovered.

_____ **16.** Rutherford B. Hayes was declared the winner of the 1876 presidential election after he
a. won the popular vote.
b. won the electoral vote by a landslide.
c. made a compromise with the Democrats.
d. won an election in the House of Representatives.

_____ **17.** Reconstruction came to end when
a. the Fifteenth Amendment was ratified.
b. federal troops were removed from the South.
c. President Johnson was impeached.
d. the Freedmen's Bureau was dismantled.

_____ **18.** A major failure of Reconstruction was that
a. the South's cotton production never recovered.
b. war debts remained unpaid.
c. racist attitudes continued in the North and South.
d. no African Americans were voted into Congress.

CHAPTER 13

C. Critical Thinking

Answer the following questions on the back of this paper or on a separate sheet of paper. (*24 points*)

19. Making Comparisons Compare the hardships faced by former slaves, plantation owners, and poor white southerners after the Civil War.

20. Determining Relevance Identify and describe the importance of one major piece of Reconstruction legislation.

D. Interpreting a Cartoon

Use the cartoon to answer questions 21-23. Write your answers on the lines provided. (*10 points*)

21. According to the cartoon, who does the KKK want to run the government?

____

____

22. According to the cartoon, what were conditions like for African Americans after the Civil War?

____

____

E. Analyzing a Document

Below is the text of the Thirteenth Amendment to the Constitution. Read it and then answer questions 23-24 on the back of this paper or on a separate sheet of paper. (*10 points*)

> **Section One**
>
> Neither slavery nor involuntary servitude, except as a punishment for crime whereof the party shall have been duly convicted, shall exist within the United States, or any place subject to their jurisdiction.
>
> **Section Two**
>
> Congress shall have power to enforce this article by appropriate legislation.

23. What was the main goal of the Thirteenth Amendment?

24. What branch of government has the power to enforce this Amendment?

NAME ______________________ CLASS ____________ DATE ____________

TEST FORM A

The Expansion of American Industry (1850-1900)

CHAPTER 14

A. Identifying Key Terms, People, and Places

Match the descriptions in Column I with the names and terms in Column II. Write the letter of the correct answer in each blank. You will not use all the names and terms. (*16 points*)

Column I

_____ **1.** inventor who established the American Telephone and Telegraph Company

_____ **2.** inventor who developed the idea of a central electric power station

_____ **3.** inventor who developed a new way to make steel

_____ **4.** industrialist who preached the "gospel of wealth"

_____ **5.** industrialist who established Standard Oil

_____ **6.** workers called in to replace striking workers

_____ **7.** political radicals who oppose all government

_____ **8.** inventor who patented the telegraph

Column II

a. Thomas A. Edison

b. Alexander Graham Bell

c. anarchists

d. Andrew Carnegie

e. Henry Bessemer

f. scabs

g. Samuel F. B. Morse

h. John D. Rockefeller

i. Homestead

j. Samuel L. Gompers

k. George Pullman

l. social Darwinists

B. Identifying Main Ideas

Write the letter of the correct answer in the blank provided. (*40 points*)

_____ **9.** Which of the following made possible the American industrial growth of the late 1800s?
a. the household economy
b. technological advances
c. government reforms
d. the development of labor unions

_____ **10.** The government contributed to the building of the transcontinental railroad by
a. not allowing immigrants to work for railroad companies.
b. collecting extra taxes from the industries that would use the railroad.
c. awarding loans and land grants to private companies to build the railroad.
d. assigning the Army to lay out a path for the railroad.

TEST FORM A *(continued)*

CHAPTER 14

_____ 11. Which of the following revolutionized American communications in the late 1800s?
a. steam engines and steamships **b.** the telegraph and telephone
c. a workable light filament **d.** refrigeration and sewing machines

_____ 12. Critics of powerful industrialists referred to them as
a. captains of industry. **b.** philanthropists.
c. robber barons. **d.** anarchists.

_____ 13. The goal of the Sherman Antitrust Act was to
a. encourage industries to form cartels.
b. promote fair industrial competition.
c. place higher taxes on business profits.
d. encourage the growth of business monopolies.

_____ 14. According to the theory of social Darwinism, the government should
a. stay out of the affairs of business. **b.** protect the rights of workers.
c. raise taxes on the rich. **d.** outlaw trusts and cartels.

_____ 15. Economists call periods of boom and bust
a. a recovery. **b.** economies of scale.
c. a recession. **d.** the business cycle.

_____ 16. How did industrial growth affect the distribution of wealth in the United States?
a. All Americans enjoyed a higher standard of living.
b. The income gap between farmers and factory workers widened.
c. Wealth was concentrated in the hands of a few industrialists.
d. The income gap between rich and poor grew smaller.

_____ 17. The American Federation of Labor organized
a. farmers, factory workers, and white-collar workers.
b. railway and construction workers.
c. only skilled workers.
d. women and children.

_____ 18. The government responded to the Pullman Strike by
a. taking Pullman officials to court.
b. shutting down all railway operations.
c. using federal troops to control the workers.
d. forcing unions and workers to negotiate.

C. Critical Thinking

Answer the following questions on the back of this paper or on a separate sheet of paper. *(20 points)*

19. Recognizing Cause and Effect What were the main causes of population growth in American cities in the late 1800s?

20. **Making Comparisons** Historians have used the terms "robber barons" and "captains of industry" to describe the powerful industrialists of the late 1800s. Compare the two points of view reflected by these terms.

D. Reading a Cross-Sectional Map

Below is a cross-sectional map of the first transcontinental railroad. The map shows the changes in elevation along the route of the railroad. Use this map to answer questions 21–22. Write your answers on the lines provided. (*12 points*)

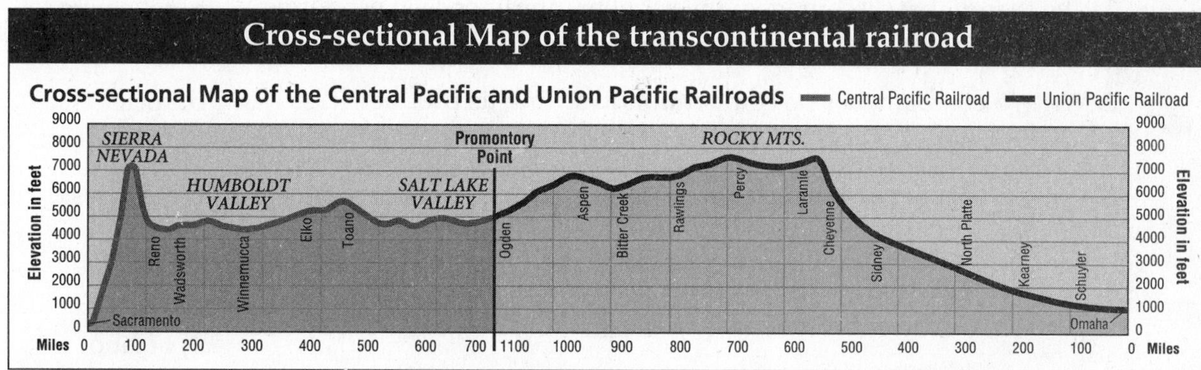

21. What city was the lowest point on the Union Pacific section of the railroad?

______

22. How long was the transcontinental railroad? ______

E. Analyzing a Document

The excerpt below comes from a New York newspaper article that appeared on September 26, 1874. In it the reporter describes the tenement factories in which cigar makers had to live and work. Use it to answer questions 23–24 on the back of this paper or on a separate sheet of paper. (*12 points*)

> ...Entering the narrow hall,...the olfactories [sense of smell] are at once startled by a pungent odor, so strong in some instances as to make a sensitive person sneeze "on sight," or rather "on smell." This is, of course, the tobacco....It was said that in cold weather the odor was so overpowering and pungent, doors and windows being closed, that persons unaccustomed thereto were compelled to shut their eyes in pain. Yet about 4,000 people eat, cook and sleep, as well as work, in these places. Young children fall asleep from the narcotic effects of the pervading odor. Women suffer greatly from it...
>
> *The New York Sun, September 26, 1874*

23. How did working conditions affect the health of workers in cigar factories?

24. During what time of year was the tobacco odor most overpowering? Why?

NAME ______________________ CLASS ____________ DATE ____________

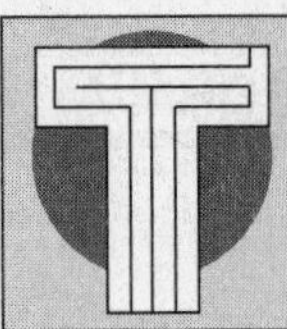

TEST FORM B

The Expansion of American Industry (1850-1900)

CHAPTER 14

A. Identifying Key Terms, People, and Places

Complete each sentence in Column I by writing the letter of the correct term from Column II in each blank. You will not use all the terms. (*16 points*)

Column I

_____ **1.** The theory that discouraged government interference in economic matters was _____.

_____ **2.** When a company has no competition in selling its product, it is said to have a _____.

_____ **3.** A loose arrangement of similar businesses formed to control production and keep prices high is called a _____.

_____ **4.** Breaking a job down into separate tasks and having each worker perform a different task is known as _____.

_____ **5.** _____ is the philosophy that advocates public rather than private control of property.

_____ **6.** When workers negotiate as a group with employers, they are engaging in _____.

_____ **7.** Employers sometimes replace striking workers with other workers called _____.

_____ **8.** Political radicals who violently oppose all government are known as _____.

Column II

a. collective bargaining

b. social Darwinism

c. business cycle

d. patent

e. division of labor

f. scabs

g. anarchists

h. socialism

i. cartel

j. trust

k. monopoly

B. Identifying Main Ideas

Write the letter of the correct ending in the blank provided. (*40 points*)

_____ **9.** The expansion of American industry was sparked mainly by
a. public welfare programs.
b. technological advances and financial investments.
c. a decline in productivity in Europe.
d. government involvement in the economy.

_____ **10.** One of Thomas Edison's major accomplishments was
a. developing a more efficient way to make steel.
b. inventing the telegraph and telephone.
c. helping to make electricity more widely available.
d. preaching the "gospel of wealth."

_____ **11.** John D. Rockefeller gained control over much of the oil industry by
- **a.** managing a trust made up of Standard Oil and allied companies.
- **b.** buying large sections of the transcontinental railroad.
- **c.** going into partnership with Andrew Carnegie.
- **d.** charging higher prices than his competitors.

_____ **12.** Congress passed the Sherman Antitrust Act to
- **a.** encourage the formation of more cartels.
- **b.** tax business profits.
- **c.** keep industries from cutting off competition.
- **d.** end child labor in factories.

_____ **13.** Andrew Carnegie argued that the success of wealthy industrialists
- **a.** helped the entire nation.
- **b.** should be limited by the government.
- **c.** was illegal according to the Sherman Antitrust Act.
- **d.** had no effect on average Americans.

_____ **14.** The business cycle might best be described as
- **a.** unbroken business expansion.
- **b.** a long period of depression.
- **c.** expansion followed by recession.
- **d.** wide unemployment.

_____ **15.** During the late 1800s, children often worked in factories because
- **a.** their parents believed in the process of "natural selection."
- **b.** families needed the income to survive.
- **c.** employers offered high wages to skilled children.
- **d.** there were no public schools for children to attend.

_____ **16.** The nation's first major labor strike was started by
- **a.** anarchists in several city governments.
- **b.** steel workers upset by the use of scabs.
- **c.** railway workers angered by wage cuts.
- **d.** women protesting discrimination.

_____ **17.** Samuel L. Gompers opposed letting women join the American Federation of Labor because he believed that
- **a.** employers would not negotiate with a union having women members.
- **b.** women would get better jobs than men.
- **c.** women in the work force would drive wages down.
- **d.** women were not capable of holding jobs outside the home.

_____ **18.** Some employers forced workers to sign "yellow dog contracts" stating that
- **a.** workers would not join labor unions.
- **b.** workers would work twelve-hour days.
- **c.** no scabs could be hired.
- **d.** women and children would be prohibited from the workplace.

C. Critical Thinking

Answer the following questions on the back of this paper or on a separate sheet of paper. (*20 points*)

19. Recognizing Main Ideas Explain the theory of social Darwinism.

20. **Identifying Alternatives** Which side did the federal government choose to support in the major strikes of the late 1800s? What actions did the government take?

CHAPTER 14

D. Reading a Cross-Sectional Map

Below is a cross-sectional map of the first transcontinental railroad. The map shows the changes in elevation along the route of the railroad. Use this map to answer questions 21–22. Write your answers on the lines provided. (*12 points*)

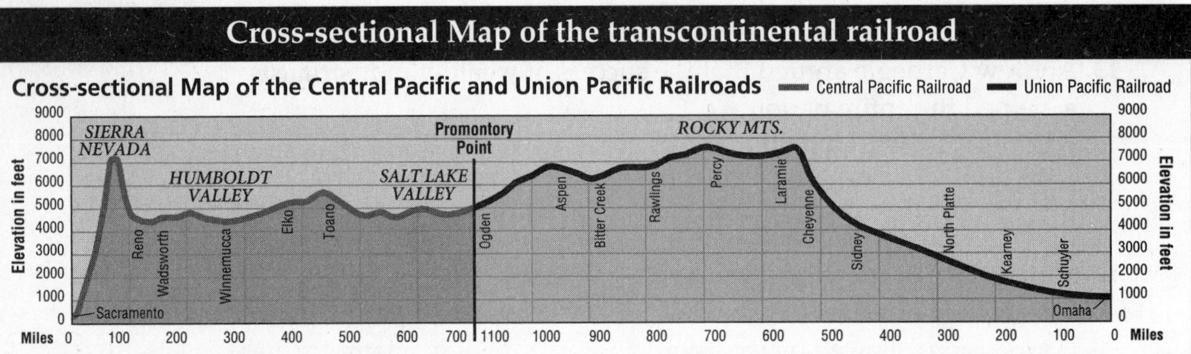

21. What mountain range had the highest point on the Central Pacific section of the railroad?

____

22. Approximately how high was the railroad at Aspen, Colorado? ____________

E. Analyzing a Document

The excerpt below comes from a New York newspaper article that appeared on September 26, 1874. In it the reporter describes the tenement factories in which cigar makers had to live and work. Use it to answer questions 23–24 on the back of this paper or on a separate sheet of paper. (*12 points*)

> ...Entering the narrow hall,...the olfactories [sense of smell] are at once startled by a pungent odor, so strong in some instances as to make a sensitive person sneeze "on sight," or rather "on smell." This is, of course, the tobacco....It was said that in cold weather the odor was so overpowering and pungent, doors and windows being closed, that persons unaccustomed thereto were compelled to shut their eyes in pain. Yet about 4,000 people eat, cook and sleep, as well as work, in these places. Young children fall asleep from the narcotic effects of the pervading odor. Women suffer greatly from it...
>
> *The New York Sun, September 26, 1874*

23. What would you find worst about these conditions if you had to work or live under them? Explain.

24. According to the article, who was most affected by conditions in this cigar factory?

NAME ______________________ CLASS ____________ DATE ____________

TEST FORM A

Looking to the West (1860-1900)

CHAPTER 15

A. Identifying Key Terms, People, and Places

Match the descriptions in Column I with the names and terms in Column II. Write the letter of the correct answer in each blank. You will not use all the names and terms. (*16 points*)

Column I

____ **1.** bought up large areas of land in the hope of selling it later for a profit

____ **2.** migrated to western lands to escape racial violence faced in the South

____ **3.** led the Sioux in war after the federal government allowed miners on Sioux reservation

____ **4.** led the United States cavalry at the Battle of Little Bighorn

____ **5.** led the Nez Percé in their flight from the United States Army

____ **6.** raced across Indian Territory to stake land claims

____ **7.** helped farmers form cooperatives

____ **8.** ran as the Democratic and Populist party nominee in the presidential election of 1896

Column II

a. Chief Joseph

b. Exodusters

c. Populists

d. boomers

e. Chief Sitting Bull

f. land speculators

g. the Grange

h. Frederick Jackson Turner

i. William Jennings Bryan

j. George Armstrong Custer

B. Identifying Main Ideas

Write the letter of the correct answer in the blank provided. (*40 points*)

____ **9.** What did the Morrill Land-Grant Act and the Homestead Act have in common?
- **a.** They provided ways for settlers to acquire western lands.
- **b.** They forced Native Americans onto reservations.
- **c.** They discriminated against African American families.
- **d.** They enabled railroad companies to develop the land near their tracks.

____ **10.** Which statement best describes the lifestyle of homesteaders?
- **a.** Homesteaders lived in isolation and avoided social contact.
- **b.** Most women worked outside their homestead.
- **c.** Homesteaders lived simple and secure lives.
- **d.** Homesteaders often had to struggle even for the necessities.

TEST FORM A *(continued)*

_____ **11.** Many agreements between Native Americans and the federal government fell apart because
a. Native Americans and settlers had differing concepts of land ownership.
b. Native Americans wanted to work as tenant farmers or sharecroppers.
c. Many settlers objected to the reservation system.
d. Most of the treaties were never signed.

_____ **12.** What happened at the Massacre at Wounded Knee?
a. American soldiers killed more than 200 unarmed Sioux.
b. General Custer's cavalry was completely wiped out.
c. The Nez Percé fought for possession of their homeland.
d. The last buffalo of the Great Plains were killed.

_____ **13.** In the West, the combination of big business and new agricultural techniques resulted in
a. placer mines.
b. the long drive.
c. bonanza farms.
d. reservations.

_____ **14.** Which one of the following was a major complaint of farmers in the late 1800s?
a. activities of the Grange
b. runaway inflation
c. rising crop prices
d. high tariffs on manufactured goods

_____ **15.** Western farmers wanted "free silver" because they felt it would
a. stabilize interest rates.
b. increase crop prices.
c. depress crop prices.
d. decrease the amount of money in circulation.

_____ **16.** The Interstate Commerce Act was passed to
a. end the cattle boom.
b. place Native Americans on reservations.
c. regulate railroad rates and practices.
d. tax business profits made in interstate trade.

_____ **17.** Which one of the following did the Populists support?
a. the Turner thesis
b. a progressive income tax
c. staying on the gold standard
d. private ownership of communications and transportation systems

_____ **18.** Which one of the following is a lingering myth about the West?
a. It was settled by a variety of races.
b. Settlers were nearly all white males.
c. Settlers nearly destroyed Native American peoples.
d. Western settlement damaged the environment.

C. Critical Thinking

Answer the following questions on the back of this paper or on a separate sheet of paper. (*24 points*)

19. Formulating Questions Imagine you lived in the late 1800s and were thinking of migrating west. What are four questions you would ask a homesteader in the Dakotas to determine if you would like to migrate there?

20. Making Comparisons Compare the ways in which Native Americans and homesteaders used land on the Great Plains.

D. Interpreting a Graphic

Use the drawing to answer questions 21–22 on the lines provided. (*10 points*)

"GO WEST."

21. What seems to be the white man's attitude toward the Native American?

____

____

22. What important aspect of Native American culture is shown in the graphic? What happened to this part of Native American life?

____

____

E. Analyzing a Document

Below are lines from a song written during the California Gold Rush. Read it and then answer questions 23–24 on the back of this paper or on a separate sheet of paper. (*10 points*)

> Come all ye poor men of the north who are working for your lives
> For to support your families, your children and your wives;
> There is easier ways of gaining wealth than toiling night and day;
> Go and dig the gold that lies in California!
> On every lofty mountain, on every sunny plain,
> The gold dust lies glittering like dewdrops after rain.
> Beneath the shade of every tree, among the flowers so gay,
> It is there we'll dig the gold that lies in California...
>
> *Library of Congress*

23. What was this song encouraging people to do?

24. Does this song present a realistic description of the life of gold miners?

NAME ______________________ CLASS ______________ DATE ______________

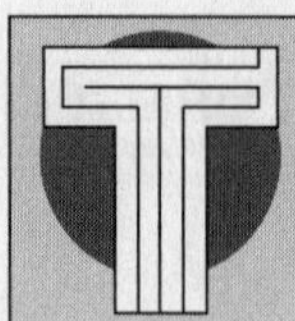

TEST FORM B

Looking to the West (1860-1900)

CHAPTER 15

A. Identifying Key Terms, People, and Places

Complete each sentence in Column I by writing the letter of the correct term from Column II in the blank. You will not use all the terms. (*16 points*)

Column I

_____ **1.** The _____ distributed millions of acres of western lands to state governments.

_____ **2.** _____ bought up large areas of land in the hope of selling it later for a large profit.

_____ **3.** American citizens and immigrants who had applied to become citizens could acquire land directly from the government through the _____.

_____ **4.** Custer's cavalry was wiped out at the _____.

_____ **5.** Homesteaders called _____ staked land claims in Indian Territory before noon on April 22, 1889.

_____ **6.** During the _____, cowboys herded cattle from distant ranges to railroad centers.

_____ **7.** Oliver H. Kelley founded _____ to help farmers form cooperatives.

_____ **8.** Native Americans called African American cavalrymen _____.

Column II

a. the Grange

b. long drive

c. Battle of Little Bighorn

d. Morrill Land-Grant Act

e. Massacre at Wounded Knee

f. Homestead Act

g. sooners

h. buffalo soldiers

i. boomers

j. land speculators

k. Exodusters

B. Identifying Main Ideas

Write the letter of the correct ending in the blank provided. (*40 points*)

_____ **9.** The challenges and hardships of settling the Great Plains led settlers to
- **a.** desire isolation from their neighbors.
- **b.** rely on the government for aid.
- **c.** depend on help from each other.
- **d.** abandon the West.

_____ **10.** Most African American Exodusters migrated west to
- **a.** work as sharecroppers on bonanza farms.
- **b.** escape racial violence in the South.
- **c.** find relatives who had fled during the Civil War.
- **d.** prospect for gold and silver.

_____ **11.** What reason was given by settlers as to why they had a greater right to western lands than the Native Americans?
a. The government already owned all the land of the West.
b. The Native Americans did not want the land.
c. Settlers produced more food and wealth than Native Americans.
d. Native Americans had already agreed to give away their lands.

_____ **12.** The experiences of Chief Joseph and the Nez Percé illustrate how
a. the U.S. government allowed some Native Americans to keep their homelands.
b. Christian missionaries converted Native Americans.
c. violent conflicts arose among settlers, the federal government, and Native Americans.
d. most Native Americans moved peacefully onto reservations.

_____ **13.** One way the government sought to change Native Americans was by
a. teaching them to hunt buffalo.
b. requiring them to farm individual plots.
c. finding them jobs on the railroads.
d. requiring them to move to growing cities.

_____ **14.** Farm mechanization resulted in
a. an increase in farm production.
b. a decline in the number of eastern farms.
c. the end of bonanza farms.
d. stable crop prices.

_____ **15.** One reason that the cattle boom ended in the mid-1880s was that
a. too few Americans ate beef.
b. farmers were using barbed wire to fence in the open range.
c. cattle prices had risen too high for many buyers.
d. the supply of Texas longhorn cattle had run out.

_____ **16.** Most American farmers in the late 1800s protested
a. free silver.
b. high tariffs on manufactured goods.
c. the Interstate Commerce Act.
d. Farmers' Alliances.

_____ **17.** In their platform, the Populists included provisions for
a. free silver, a progressive income tax, and an eight-hour day.
b. changing to the gold standard and ending any government regulation of business.
c. private ownership of communications and transportation systems.
d. excluding African Americans from Populist party membership.

_____ **18.** Frederick Jackson Turner's thesis held that the frontier
a. destroyed the West and the Americans who went there.
b. helped create the strong, individualistic American spirit.
c. would continue to exist for at least another 50 years.
d. had little effect on the American character.

TEST FORM B *(continued)*

C. Critical Thinking

Answer the following questions on the back of this paper or on a separate sheet of paper. (*24 points*)

19. Expressing Problems Clearly Using one sentence for each, express two problems that farming on the Great Plains presented to settlers.

20. Making Comparisons Compare the effects the expanding western railroads had on Native Americans and white settlers.

D. Interpreting a Graphic

Use the drawing to answer questions 21–22 on the lines provided. (*10 points*)

"GO WEST."

21. In this graphic, why does the white settler want the Native American to go west?

____

____

22. In what part of the country is this graphic set? How can you tell?

____

____

E. Analyzing a Document

Below are lines from a song written during the California Gold Rush. Read it and then answer questions 23–24 on the back of this paper or on a separate sheet of paper. (*10 points*)

> Come all ye poor men of the north who are working for your lives
> For to support your families, your children and your wives;
> There is easier ways of gaining wealth than toiling night and day;
> Go and dig the gold that lies in California!
> On every lofty mountain, on every sunny plain,
> The gold dust lies glittering like dewdrops after rain.
> Beneath the shade of every tree, among the flowers so gay,
> It is there we'll dig the gold that lies in California...
>
> *Library of Congress*

23. According to this song, why should men give up their jobs in the North?

24. Does the song suggest that it was difficult to find gold in California? Explain.

NAME ______________________ CLASS ______________ DATE ______________

TEST FORM A

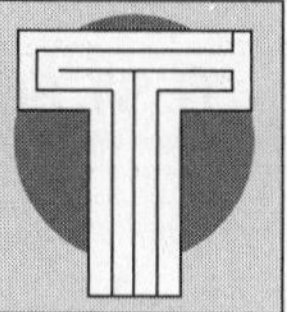

Politics, Immigration, and Urban Life (1870-1915)

CHAPTER 16

A. Identifying Key Terms, People, and Places

Match the descriptions in Column I with the terms in Column II. Write the letter of the correct answer in each blank. You will not use all the terms. (16 points)

Column I

_____ **1.** hands-off approach by government on business matters

_____ **2.** local regulation that prohibits private activities such as drinking alcoholic beverages on Sundays

_____ **3.** legislation to reform the spoils system

_____ **4.** large open area beneath a ship's deck in which most immigrants traveled

_____ **5.** residential community near a city

_____ **6.** section of cities in which certain ethnic and racial groups live

_____ **7.** unofficial organization designed to keep a particular party or group in power

_____ **8.** reform campaign that tried to apply the teachings of Jesus Christ directly to society

Column II

a. steerage

b. ghetto

c. political machine

d. social gospel movement

e. laissez-faire

f. *Munn* v. *Illinois*

g. blue law

h. quarantine

i. Chinese Exclusion Act

j. suburb

k. Pendleton Civil Service Act

B. Identifying Main Ideas

Write the letter of the correct answer in the blank provided. (*40 points*)

_____ **9.** Which of the following best describes key positions held by the Republican party in the Gilded Age?
a. free silver, high immigration, and low tariffs
b. gold standard, high tariffs, and limits on immigration
c. free silver and fewer blue laws
d. no government aid to railroads and no blue laws

_____ **10.** Which of the following best describes key positions held by the Democratic party in the Gilded Age?
a. enforcement of blue laws and higher tariffs
b. gold standard and strict limits on immigration
c. increased money supply, lower tariffs, and higher farm prices
d. pensions for Union soldiers and more government aid to railroads

_____ **11.** Which of the following led to government regulation of businesses during the Gilded Age?
a. declining business profits
b. unfair business practices
c. high tariffs
d. increased factory and farm production

CHAPTER 16

_____ **12.** During the late 1800s, the port of entry for the majority of immigrants was
a. Boston.
b. San Francisco.
c. Philadelphia.
d. New York City.

_____ **13.** What attracted many Asians to the United States in the late 1800s?
a. repeal of the Chinese Exclusion Act
b. the desire for free land
c. jobs with American railroad companies
d. the Gentlemen's Agreement

_____ **14.** President Theodore Roosevelt reached the Gentlemen's Agreement in 1907 with the goal of
a. ending all Japanese immigration to the United States.
b. encouraging Chinese immigration to the United States.
c. slowing the immigration of Japanese laborers.
d. banning Asians from owning farmland.

_____ **15.** Which of the following was a major result of both immigration and the increased productivity of factory jobs in the late 1800s?
a. the rapid expansion of urban areas
b. mechanization of agriculture
c. high wages for factory workers
d. overpopulation of the South

_____ **16.** Why did many immigrants support city political machines?
a. Political machines were free of corruption.
b. Political machines provided them with jobs.
c. Political machines put powerful "bosses" out of business.
d. Political machines fought against crime in the slums.

_____ **17.** Prohibitionists and purity crusaders shared the goal of
a. making charity "scientific."
b. redistributing the nation's wealth.
c. ending immigration from Asia.
d. improving the personal behavior of individuals.

_____ **18.** Which best describes the main goal of the social gospel and settlement movements?
a. to improve living conditions for the poor
b. to strengthen political machines
c. to encourage immigration
d. to create jobs for the unemployed

CHAPTER 16

C. Critical Thinking

Answer the following questions on the back of this paper or on a separate sheet of paper. (*24 points*)

19. Distinguishing False from Accurate Images Many immigrants who came to the United States expected to find streets paved with gold and easy opportunities to make their fortunes. Write a brief description of what they were more likely to find.

20. Testing Conclusions As you read, Mark Twain labeled the years from 1877 to 1900 the "Gilded Age," implying that American society was "a thin layer of glitter over a cheap base." Identify and explain one example that might support Twain's conclusion.

D. Reading a Table

Use the data presented in the table to answer questions 21–22. Write your answers on the lines provided. (*10 points*)

21. How many people in the United States lived in rural areas in 1900? How many in urban areas?

____

22. Describe the population trend that began to develop during the period 1910-1920.

____

____

Rural and Urban Populations in the United States

Year	Rural (in thousands)	Urban (in thousands)
1860	25,227	6,217
1870	28,656	9,902
1880	36,026	14,130
1890	40,841	22,106
1900	45,835	30,160
1910	49,973	41,999
1920	51,553	54,158

Source: Bureau of the Census

E. Analyzing a Document

The excerpt below comes from Jacob Riis's *How the Other Half Lives*, published in 1890. Read it and then answer questions 23–24 on the back of this paper or on a separate sheet of paper. (*10 points*)

> The gang is an institution in New York....The gang is the ripe fruit of the tenement-house growth. It was born there, endowed with [given] a heritage of instinctive hostility to restraint by a generation that sacrificed home to freedom, or left its country for its country's good.... gangs are made up of the American-born sons of English, Irish, and German parents. They reflect exactly the conditions of the tenements from which they sprang....

23. Why did Riis say the gang is "the ripe fruit of tenement-house growth"?

24. According to Riis, who was most likely to be members of a gang?

NAME ______________________ CLASS ____________ DATE ____________

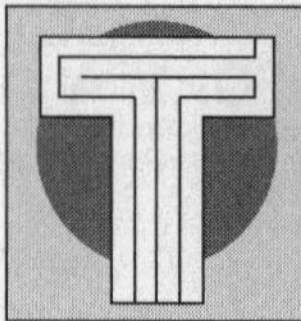

TEST FORM B

Politics, Immigration, and Urban Life (1870-1915)

CHAPTER 16

A. Identifying Key Terms, People, and Places

Complete each sentence in Column I by writing the letter of the correct term from Column II in the blank provided. You will not use all the terms. (*16 points*)

Column I

_____ **1.** A government that practices _____ plays a very limited role in business.

_____ **2.** American railroad companies accepted _____ from the government to help them develop their industries.

_____ **3.** During the Gilded Age, Republicans wanted to enforce _____, which prohibited certain private activities, like drinking alcoholic beverages on Sunday.

_____ **4.** Most immigrants traveled in _____ as they crossed the Atlantic to America.

_____ **5.** Immigrants were placed in _____ if they were thought to carry a contagious disease.

_____ **6.** Some urban areas became _____, home to certain ethnic and racial groups.

_____ **7.** Sometimes homeowners made agreements called _____ promising that they would not sell real estate to certain groups.

_____ **8.** The _____ sought to apply the teachings of Jesus Christ directly to society.

Column II

a. political machines

b. laissez-faire

c. restrictive covenants

d. Gilded Age

e. subsidies

f. social gospel movement

g. blue laws

h. aliens

i. quarantine

j. steerage

k. ghettos

B. Identifying Main Ideas

Write the letter of the correct ending in the blank provided. (40 points)

_____ **9.** During the Gilded Age, Republicans and Democrats held differing views on

a. establishing a state religion.

b. the gold standard and government aid to business.

c. the development of suburbs.

d. repealing the Interstate Commerce Act of 1877.

_____ **10.** The Pendleton Civil Service Act was passed to

a. place additional regulation on the railroads.

b. end Japanese immigration to the United States.

c. end the spoils system.

d. print money backed by silver rather than gold.

_____ **11.** In 1894, Coxey's Army marched on Washington, D.C. with the demand that the government
a. protect union organizers.
b. return the country to the gold standard.
c. maintain its laissez-faire attitude.
d. create jobs for the unemployed.

_____ **12.** During the late 1800s and early 1900s, immigration laws discriminated most against
a. Asians. **b.** Europeans.
c. agricultural workers. **d.** Mexicans.

_____ **13.** In the 1890s, immigration patterns shifted dramatically, with most immigrants now coming from
a. northern European countries.
b. southern and eastern European countries.
c. Mexico and Central America.
d. China and Japan.

_____ **14.** One reason that the United States became more urban during the late 1800s is that
a. farm machines and factory-made goods reduced the need for farm labor.
b. nobody wanted to live on farms anymore.
c. immigrants did not know how to do farm work.
d. union organizing of farm workers had not yet begun.

_____ **15.** One of the reasons that political machines gained power in the late 1800s was that they
a. advocated political reform.
b. refused to accept graft as part of their income.
c. provided jobs and other help for immigrants.
d. provided for the needs of the suburbs.

_____ **16.** The main objective of the nativists was to
a. repeal laws that restricted immigration.
b. help immigrants adjust to American culture.
c. build tenement apartments for immigrants.
d. restrict immigration.

_____ **17.** Prohibitionists and purity crusaders both
a. promoted political machines.
b. opposed government intervention in citizens' daily lives.
c. sought to rid society of behavior they thought immoral.
d. worked to end discrimination against immigrants.

_____ **18.** Most settlement houses of the late 1800s offered poor city dwellers
a. aid in the form of money. **b.** social services.
c. protection from crime. **d.** protection from political machines.

CHAPTER 16

C. Critical Thinking

Answer the following questions on the back of this paper or on a separate sheet of paper. *(24 points)*

19. Demonstrating Reasoned Judgment Imagine that you are a young immigrant living and working in the United States in the 1890s. You hear from a friend from your hometown saying that she and her family are about to emigrate, too. What are two important things you would tell her about life as an immigrant in the United States?

20. Recognizing Ideologies On the issue of immigrants, compare the attitude of a nativist with that of a settlement house worker.

D. Reading a Table

Use the data presented in the table to answer questions 21–22. Write your answers on the lines provided. *(10 points)*

21. How many people in the United States lived in rural areas in 1860? How many in urban areas?

____

22. During what ten-year period did urban population first exceed rural population? Give one reason for this change.

____

____

Rural and Urban Populations in the United States

Year	Rural (in thousands)	Urban (in thousands)
1860	25,227	6,217
1870	28,656	9,902
1880	36,026	14,130
1890	40,841	22,106
1900	45,835	30,160
1910	49,973	41,999
1920	51,553	54,158

Source: Bureau of the Census

E. Analyzing a Document

The excerpt below comes from Jacob Riis's *How the Other Half Lives*, published in 1890. Read it and then answer questions 23–24 on the back of this paper or on a separate sheet of paper. *(10 points)*

> The gang is an institution in New York....The gang is the ripe fruit of the tenement-house growth. It was born there, endowed with [given] a heritage of instinctive hostility to restraint by a generation that sacrificed home to freedom, or left its country for its country's good.... gangs are made up of the American-born sons of English, Irish, and German parents. They reflect exactly the conditions of the tenements from which they sprang....

23. According to Riis, which people made up the gangs of New York?

24. According to Riis, what led to the formation of gangs?

NAME ______________________ CLASS ____________ DATE ____________

TEST FORM A

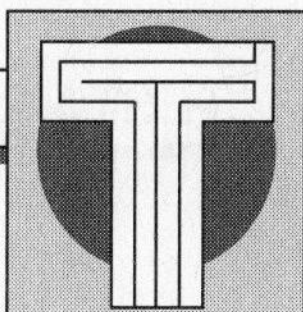

Daily Life in the Gilded Age (1870-1915)

CHAPTER 17

A. Identifying Key Terms, People, and Places

Compete each sentence in Column I by writing the letter of the correct term from Column II in the blank provided. You will not use all the terms. *(16 points)*

Column I

_____ **1.** The ability to read and write is called _____.

_____ **2.** _____ is the process by which people of one culture become part of another culture.

_____ **3.** _____ was a kind of inexpensive variety show that became popular in the 1870s.

_____ **4.** _____ attracted readers by presenting "sensational" news stories.

_____ **5.** To keep African Americans from voting, some southern states charged a(n) _____ to cast a ballot.

_____ **6.** People who gave donations to worthy causes are known as _____.

_____ **7.** A system called _____ legally segregated and degraded African Americans.

_____ **8.** Farm families gained greater access to what cities had to offer through _____.

Column II

a. ragtime
b. vaudeville
c. mail-order catalogues
d. yellow journalism
e. assimilation
f. philanthropists
g. grandfather clause
h. literacy
i. Jim Crow
j. poll tax
k. lynching

B. Identifying Main Ideas

Write the letter of the correct ending in the blank provided. *(40 points)*

_____ **9.** By 1910, nearly 60 percent of American children were in school because
a. families had more money.
b. scholarships were plentiful.
c. immigration was down.
d. many states required school attendance by law.

_____ **10.** Public schools played an important role in
a. teaching religion.
b. helping immigrant children assimilate.
c. training women for the work place.
d. decreasing literacy.

_____ **11.** The Niagara Movement called for
a. legal segregation.
b. an end to immigration.
c. full civil liberties for African Americans.
d. more women's colleges.

CHAPTER 17

_____ **12.** Which became the most popular American sport during the late 1800s?
a. football
b. baseball
c. basketball
d. boxing

_____ **13.** The American dream of rising from "rags to riches" was reflected in
a. Mark Twain's novel *The Gilded Age*
b. novels of social protest.
c. Horatio Alger's *Ragged Dick* stories.
d. minstrel shows.

_____ **14.** During the early 1900s, The National Association for the Advancement of Colored People (NAACP) was an example of how African Americans
a. used the court system to fight discrimination.
b. formed their own political parties.
c. ended all segregation in the South.
d. founded settlement houses in black neighborhoods.

_____ **15.** In the case of *Plessy* v. *Ferguson*, the Supreme Court
a. declared segregation unconstitutional.
b. established the "separate-but-equal" doctrine, upholding segregation.
c. ordered public school districts to upgrade schools for African Americans.
d. ordered universities to enroll more women and African Americans.

_____ **16.** The act of lynching might best be described as
a. seizure and execution of a person by a mob
b. imprisonment of a suspect without a trial
c. illegal search of a home or business
d. illegal seizure of property

_____ **17.** As women began to make their way into professional jobs, they worked mainly in
a. law, engineering, and the ministry.
b. education, health care, and social work.
c. science, music, and manufacturing.
d. architecture, textiles, and the law.

_____ **18.** The "new woman" of the early 1900s promoted the idea that women should
a. adopt more convenient hair and dress styles.
b. reject marriage and motherhood.
c. be chaperoned on dates.
d. have perfect manners.

C. Critical Thinking

Answer the following questions on the back of this paper or on a separate sheet of paper. *(24 points)*

19. Making Comparisons How did W.E.B. Du Bois's attitude toward education of African Americans compare with that of Booker T. Washington?

20. **Recognizing Bias** Identify and explain at least two examples of bias that women faced during the late 1800s and early 1900s.

D. Interpreting a Bar Graph

Use the bar graph to answer questions 21–22. Write your answers on the lines provided. *10 points*)

21. In 1890, about what percentage of women in the labor force were married? What percentage were single?

22. Compare the trend in the percentage of single women in the labor force between 1890 and 1910 with the trend in the percentage of married women in the labor force during the same period.

E. Analyzing a Document

Mary Antin emigrated to the United States from Poland when she was thirteen. The following is an excerpt from a book she wrote about her experiences, entitled *The Promised Land.* Read it and then answer questions 23–24. (*10 points*)

> Education was free. That subject my father had written about repeatedly, as comprising [making up] his chief hope for us children, the essence of American opportunity, the treasure that no thief can touch, not even misfortune or poverty. It was the one thing that he was able to promise when he sent for us; sure, safer than bread or shelter....Father himself conducted us to school. He would not have delegated that mission to the President of the United States. He had awaited the day with impatience equal to mine, and the visions he saw as he hurried us over the sun-flecked pavements transcended [were greater than] all my dreams.

23. What hopes do you think Mary's father had for her?

24. How did Mary's father feel when he took her to school?

NAME ______________________ CLASS ______________ DATE ______________

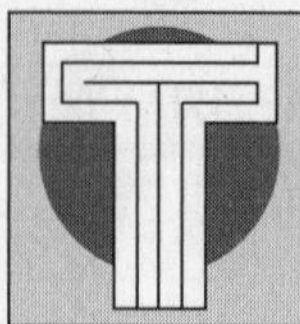

TEST FORM B

Daily Life in the Gilded Age (1870-1915)

CHAPTER 17

A. Identifying Key Terms, People, and Places

Match the descriptions in Column I with the terms in Column II. Write the correct letter in each blank. You will not use all the terms. (*16 points*)

Column I

_____ **1.** the ability to read and write

_____ **2.** process by which people of one culture become part of another culture

_____ **3.** type of variety show for the whole family

_____ **4.** term used to describe "sensational" news coverage

_____ **5.** musical style that originated among African American musicians playing in saloons in the South and Midwest in the 1880s

_____ **6.** fee that some southern states demanded before a person could vote

_____ **7.** mob seizure and execution of a person

_____ **8.** a Post Office service extended to farmers in 1896

Column II

a. philanthropist
b. assimilation
c. lynching
d. literacy
e. mail-order catalogue
f. yellow journalism
g. poll tax
h. grandfather clause
i. rural free delivery
j. department store
k. Jim Crow
l. ragtime
m. vaudeville

B. Identifying Main Ideas

Write the letter of the correct answer in the blank provided. (*40 points*)

_____ **9.** One effect of the public school system was that it
a. created divisions among immigrant children from differing cultures.
b. helped immigrant children become Americanized.
c. denied immigrant children anything more than four years of education.
d. taught immigrant children to retain their native cultures.

_____ **10.** During the late 1800s and early 1900s, what segment of American society was most likely to attend college?
a. wealthy white men **b.** New Englanders
c. gifted students **d.** middle class women

_____ **11.** During the early 1900s, most African Americans who went to college attended
a. fully integrated universities. **b.** African American colleges.
c. religious-based schools. **d.** separate branches of white colleges.

CHAPTER 17

_____ **12.** W.E.B. Du Bois argued that African Americans should educate themselves so they could
a. assimilate into white culture.
b. provide leadership in the fight for civil rights.
c. learn a trade.
d. win acceptance from white politicians.

_____ **13.** Which best describes the popular amusements of the late 1800s?
a. They were available to a small segment of the population.
b. They were heavily censored by the government.
c. They were inexpensive and readily available to large numbers of people.
d. They were mainly imported from Europe and Asia.

_____ **14.** How did the *Plessy* v. *Ferguson* decision affect racial relations in the South?
a. It forced white and African Americans to use the same public facilities.
b. It allowed segregation to continue legally.
c. It improved the quality of African American facilities.
d. It ordered that segregation should be ended in public schools.

_____ **15.** Madam C.J. Walker is remembered for
a. becoming the first African American woman to earn a Ph.D.
b. founding the first African American college.
c. overcoming discrimination to become a self-made millionaire.
d. organizing the Niagara Movement.

_____ **16.** Which of the following factors helped to reduce household chores by 1900?
a. technological advances. **b.** smaller homes.
c. inexpensive domestic help. **d.** division of labor among family members.

_____ **17.** During the late 1800s, women from which of these groups were most likely to work outside the home?
a. older married women **b.** women in the South
c. uneducated women **d.** young single women

_____ **18.** Participation in volunteer organizations helped many women
a. take their first steps toward public life.
b. get higher-paying jobs.
c. gain financial independence.
d. get elected to state governments.

C. Critical Thinking

Answer the following questions on the back of this paper or on a separate sheet of paper. (*24 points*)

19. Recognizing Central Issues What methods did women use to gain a stronger voice in social and political affairs during the Gilded Age?

20. **Recognizing Bias** Compare how bias against African Americans was expressed in the South and the North.

CHAPTER 17

D. Interpreting a Bar Graph

Use the bar graph to answer questions 21–22. Write your answers on the lines provided. (*10 points*)

21. How did the percentage of married women in the labor force change from 1890 to 1910?

____

____

22. Based on this change, what prediction can you make for the percentages of married and single women in the labor force in the decades following 1910?

____

____

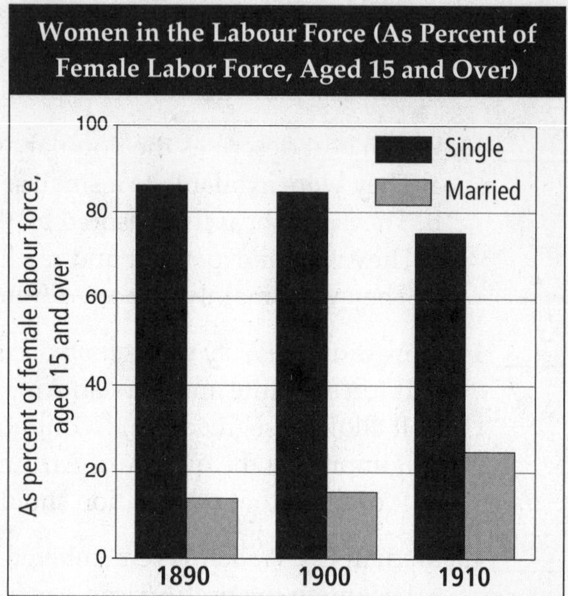

____

E. Analyzing a Document

Mary Antin emigrated to the United States from Poland when she was thirteen. The following is an excerpt from a book she wrote about her experiences, entitled *The Promised Land.* Read it and then answer questions 23–24. (*10 points*)

> Education was free. That subject my father had written about repeatedly, as comprising [making up] his chief hope for us children, the essence of American opportunity, the treasure that no thief can touch, not even misfortune or poverty. It was the one thing that he was able to promise when he sent for us; sure, safer than bread or shelter....Father himself conducted us to school. He would not have delegated that mission to the President of the United States. He had awaited the day with impatience equal to mine, and the visions he saw as he hurried us over the sun-flecked pavements transcended [were greater than] all my dreams.

23. Why was free education so important to Mary's father?

24. How would you explain in your own words why Mary says education is "the treasure that no thief can touch"?

NAME ______________________ CLASS ______________ DATE ______________

TEST FORM A

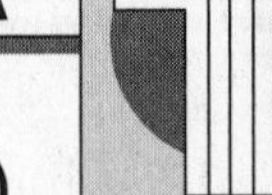

Becoming a World Power (1890-1913)

CHAPTER 18

A. IDENTIFYING KEY TERMS, PEOPLE, AND PLACES

Match the descriptions in Column I with the names in Column II. Write the correct letter in each blank. You will not use all the names. *(10 points)*

Column I

____ **1.** newspaper publisher whose "yellow journalism" influenced public opinion

____ **2.** exiled Cuban journalist who urged the United States to intervene in Cuba

____ **3.** "Rough Rider" who later became President

____ **4.** Admiral who led attack on Spanish ships in the Philippines

____ **5.** President known for his "dollar diplomacy"

Column II

a. Theodore Roosevelt

b. George Dewey

c. William Randolph Hearst

d. Matthew C. Peary

e. Dupuy de Lôme

f. José Martí

g. William Howard Taft

Complete each sentence by writing the letter of the correct place in the blank provided. You will not use all the place names. *(10 points)*

Column I

____ **6.** Guerrillas on the island nation of ____ destroyed American-owned sugar mills to gain support for independence.

____ **7.** The Spanish-American War began in 1898, in ____, when the United States launched a surprise attack on Spanish ships in Manila Bay.

____ **8.** The Rough Riders made ____ the site of a famous incident of the Spanish-American War.

____ **9.** The United States annexed ____ in 1898.

____ **10.** Congress authorized a payment of $25 million to ____ for having used illegal means to acquire the Canal Zone.

Column II

a. San Juan Hill

b. the Philippine Islands

c. Cuba

d. Hawaii

e. Colombia

f. Isthmus of Panama

B. IDENTIFYING MAIN IDEAS

Write the letter of the correct answer in the blank provided. *(32 points)*

____ **11.** Which of the following was a major economic argument for expansion?
  a. The United States needed new markets for its goods.
  b. Many United States industries were short of labor.
  c. Foreign goods were often superior to American products.
  d. Americans needed the respect of foreign countries.

_____ 12. Which of the following demonstrated enforcement of the Monroe Doctrine?
- a. The United States convinced Japan to open trade relations.
- b. The United States allowed Hawaiians to import sugar duty free.
- c. The United States insisted that Great Britain submit a boundary dispute with Venezuela to arbitration.
- d. The United States competed against France and Britain for Asian markets.

_____ 13. Which event led to the Spanish-American War?
- a. Cubans rebelled against Spanish rule.
- b. The United States annexed Cuba.
- c. Spain destroyed American-owned sugar plantations in Cuba.
- d. The Spanish navy sank two American ships in the Pacific.

_____ 14. Which was a result of the Spanish-American War?
- a. Cuba became a Spanish protectorate.
- b. Puerto Rico and Guam were made unincorporated U.S. territories.
- c. Spain admitted it had blown up the *Maine*.
- d. The Philippines won independence from foreign rule.

_____ 15. Why was the Open Door Policy important to the United States?
- a. It gave the United States territory in China.
- b. It gave the United States access to millions of consumers in China.
- c. It increased Chinese investments in the United States.
- d. It kept European goods out of China.

_____ 16. Why did many of Roosevelt's opponents disapprove of his actions in Panama?
- a. They thought Roosevelt paid too much money to lease the Canal Zone.
- b. They thought Roosevelt gave Panama too much control over the canal.
- c. They thought the canal was completely unnecessary.
- d. They opposed Roosevelt's involvement in the Panamanian revolt.

_____ 17. What was the central message of the Roosevelt Corollary?
- a. United States territories could not enter any foreign agreements.
- b. United States territories would remain unincorporated.
- c. The United States would use force to prevent intervention in the affairs of neighboring countries.
- d. The United States would support only those revolutionary movements that promoted democratic principles.

_____ 18. What connection was made between imperialism and the American frontier?
- a. Imperialism would help close the frontier.
- b. Closing the frontier would spur competition.
- c. Imperialism would offer Americans a new frontier.
- d. Imperialism would make the world more like the United States.

C. Critical Thinking

Answer the following questions on the back of this paper or on a separate sheet of paper. *(24 points)*

19. Checking Consistency According to anti-imperialist arguments, how was imperialism inconsistent with basic American principles?

20. Expressing Problems Clearly Identify two problems with "dollar diplomacy" in the early 1900s.

D. Interpreting a Map

Use the map to answer questions 21-22. Write your answers on the back of this paper or on a separate sheet of paper. (*12 points*)

21. Why was the United States concerned with events in Cuba?

22. Why was Panama a logical choice for a Canal Zone?

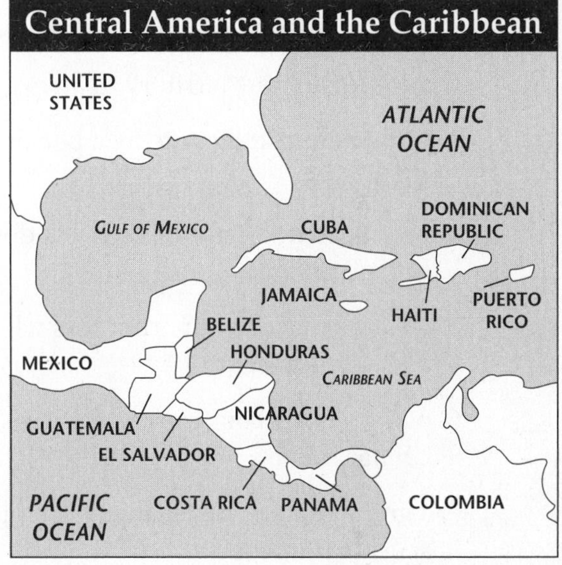

E. Analyzing a Document

Study this 1901 political cartoon, depicting the United States as a large rooster guarding a chicken pen. Then answer questions 23-24 on the back of this paper or on a separate sheet of paper. (*12 points*)

23. According to the cartoon, what purpose did the Monroe Doctrine serve?

24. What does the portrayal of the United States suggest about the country?

NAME ______________________ CLASS ____________ DATE ____________

TEST FORM B

Becoming a World Power (1890-1913)

CHAPTER 18

A. Identifying Key Terms, People, and Places

Match the descriptions in Column I with the terms in Column II. Write the correct letter in each blank. You will not use all the terms. (*16 points*)

Column I

_____ **1.** policy under which stronger nations attempt to create empires by dominating weaker nations

_____ **2.** addition of new territory to an existing country

_____ **3.** settlement of a dispute by a person chosen to listen to both sides

_____ **4.** national pride combined with a desire for an aggressive foreign policy

_____ **5.** area outside a nation's borders where it exercises economic and political control

_____ **6.** policy giving countries equal access to trading rights in China

_____ **7.** a grant of land in exchange for a promise to use it for a specific purpose

_____ **8.** policy that established the United States as "an international police power"

Column II

a. Roosevelt Corollary
b. imperialism
c. dollar diplomacy
d. jingoism
e. sphere of influence
f. Open Door Policy
g. arbitration
h. concession
i. annexation
j. compulsory service
k. Rough Riders

B. Identifying Main Ideas

Write the letter of the correct ending in the blank provided. (*40 points*)

_____ **9.** The United States followed a policy of expansionism in the late 1800s because
a. European nations were eager to sell rights to their colonies.
b. many Americans were demanding high-quality foreign goods.
c. U.S. factories needed foreign laborers.
d. the nation sought more markets for its goods.

_____ **10.** Alfred T. Mahan argued that to protect its trade, the United States must build up its
a. army. **b.** navy.
c. labor unions. **d.** pioneer spirit.

_____ **11.** The United States reaffirmed the Monroe Doctrine in the late 1800s by
a. passing the Platt Amendment.
b. warning Great Britain to back out of a territorial dispute with Venezuela.
c. allowing Hawaiians to import sugar duty free.
d. refusing to support the Cuban guerrillas.

CHAPTER 18

_____ **12.** In the 1890s, William R. Hearst and Joseph Pulitzer used their newspapers to
a. help start the Boxer Rebellion.
b. increase public sympathy for Cuban rebels.
c. repeal the Monroe Doctrine.
d. elect Theodore Roosevelt President.

_____ **13.** A main goal of the United States during the Spanish-American War was to
a. annex Florida.
b. gain spheres of influence in South America.
c. protect business investments in Spain.
d. free Cuba from Spanish rule.

_____ **14.** As a result of the Spanish-American War,
a. Puerto Rico became an unincorporated territory of the United States.
b. Cuba was divided into spheres of influence.
c. the Philippines became a Spanish colony.
d. the United States gained rights to the Panama Canal.

_____ **15.** The building of the Panama Canal was important because it
a. helped stabilize the economies of Latin American countries.
b. improved relations between Colombia and the United States.
c. facilitated movement between Atlantic and Pacific ports.
d. promoted European investment in the United States.

_____ **16.** President Theodore Roosevelt is often remembered for
a. promoting "dollar diplomacy."
b. promoting self-government in former colonies.
c. expanding presidential power.
d. opposing the annexation of new territories.

_____ **17.** To support their view, anti-imperialists argued that
a. imperialism would reduce U.S. military forces.
b. the United States should get more involved in foreign affairs.
c. imperialism rejected the American ideal of "liberty for all."
d. imperialism would make the United States more admired in the world.

_____ **18.** The United States acquired control of the Canal Zone by
a. paying Panama $25 million. **b.** passing the Roosevelt Corollary.
c. signing a treaty with Spain. **d.** organizing a revolt in Panama.

C. Critical Thinking

Complete the following activities on the back of this paper or on a separate sheet of paper. *(24 points)*

19. Making Comparisons Compare President Theodore Roosevelt's approach to foreign policy with that of President William Howard Taft. How were they alike and different?

CHAPTER 18

20. **Recognizing Bias** Explain how racism was displayed in both imperialist and anti-imperialist viewpoints.

D. Interpreting a Map

Use the map to answer questions 21–22 on the back of this paper or on a separate sheet of paper. (*10 points*)

21. Geographically, why was Panama a better site for a canal than Nicaragua?

22. Why was the United States wary of a European presence in Central America and the Caribbean in the 1800s?

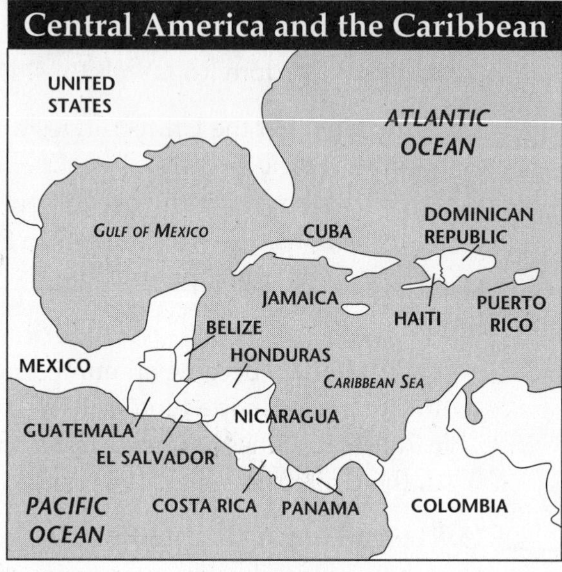

E. Analyzing a Document

Study this 1901 political cartoon, depicting the United States as a large rooster guarding a chicken pen. Then answer questions 23–24 on the back of this paper or on a separate sheet of paper. (*10 points*)

23. What does the chicken coop represent in the cartoon? Explain how the symbol works.

24. How is the figure representing the United States different from other figures in the cartoon? What do these differences suggest?

NAME ______________________ CLASS __________ DATE __________

TEST FORM A

CHAPTER 19

The Era of Progressive Reform (1890-1920)

A. Identify Key Terms, People, and Places

Complete the sentences in Column I with the terms in Column II. Write the letter of the correct answer in each blank. You will not use all the terms. (*16 points*)

Column I

_____ **1.** In the 1890s, business leaders often asked the courts for _____, prohibiting workers from striking.

_____ **2.** Under _____, cities exercised a limited degree of self-government.

_____ **3.** Progressives wanted government to create various _____ to ensure a basic standard of living for all Americans.

_____ **4.** In a(n) _____, voters cast ballots to select nominees for upcoming elections.

_____ **5.** Citizens can propose new laws through the _____ process.

_____ **6.** Voters can remove public officials from office before the next election through the _____ procedure.

_____ **7.** The _____ legalized strikes and peaceful picketing.

_____ **8.** Calling his policy the _____, Woodrow Wilson promised to enforce antitrust laws without threatening free economic competition.

Column II

a. direct primary

b. Clayton Antitrust Act

c. New Freedom

d. muckrakers

e. initiative

f. home rule

g. New Nationalism

h. injunctions

i. recall

j. social welfare programs

B. Identifying Main Ideas

Write the letter of the correct ending in the blank provided. (*40 points*)

_____ **9.** In the late 1800s, journalists Henry George and Edward Bellamy both
- **a.** discouraged single-tax speculation.
- **b.** wrote about ideas for reforming society.
- **c.** promoted plans to increase free enterprise profits.
- **d.** warned Americans about the pace of industrialization.

_____ **10.** Most Progressives agreed that the government should
- **a.** nationalize industries.
- **b.** abolish home rule in cities and states.
- **c.** protect workers and help the poor.
- **d.** outlaw unions.

TEST FORM A *(continued)*

_____ **11.** The efforts of Florence Kelley convinced many states to abolish
a. child labor.
b. direct primaries.
c. minimum wage legislation.
d. single-tax colonies.

_____ **12.** Municipal reformers aimed to
a. solve rural problems.
b. end government corruption.
c. increase immigrant rights.
d. curb union power.

_____ **13.** President Roosevelt's progressive record included all the following *except*
a. conservation of forest land.
b. break-up of several trusts deemed harmful to the public.
c. regulation of food and drugs.
d. establishment of the Federal Reserve System.

_____ **14.** President Taft continued Roosevelt's progressive program by
a. actively promoting women's right to vote.
b. pursuing antitrust cases.
c. selling several million acres of Alaska's public lands.
d. abolishing Jim Crow practices in federal offices.

_____ **15.** Woodrow Wilson won the Presidential election of 1912, partly due to
a. Taft's decision not to run for a second term.
b. the fact that he was the only candidate with a reform platform.
c. a split in the Republican vote.
d. the lack of competition.

_____ **16.** President Wilson established the Federal Reserve system to
a. reorganize the federal banking system.
b. enforce the Clayton Antitrust Act.
c. make federal loans available to farmers.
d. end child labor in all states.

_____ **17.** A basic anti-suffrage argument was that women would
a. prevent prohibition.
b. fail to exercise their voting rights.
c. become too masculine.
d. refuse to pay taxes.

_____ **18.** Progressivism was halted by
a. the efforts of the NAACP.
b. World War I.
c. the repeal of the prohibition amendment.
d. the victory of the Bull Moose party.

C. Critical Thinking

Answer the following questions on the back of this paper or on a separate sheet of paper. (*24 points*)

19. Recognizing Cause and Effect How did progressivism affect the role of the federal government in the early 1900s?

20. Making Comparisons How was President Wilson's approach to economic reform similar to that of Theodore Roosevelt? How was it different?

Write answers to sections D and E on the other side of this page, or on a separate sheet of paper.

D. Interpreting a Map

Use the map below to answer questions 21–22. (*10 points*)

21. By 1900, which states had granted women equal suffrage?

22. In which region of the United States was the women's suffrage movement most successful? Why?

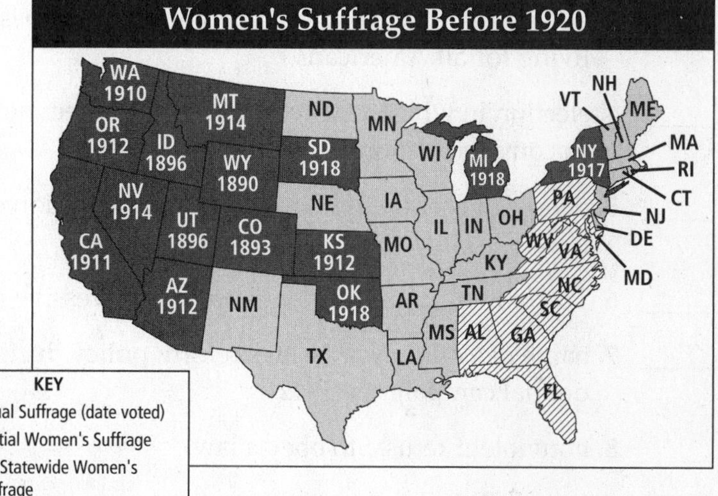

E. Analyzing a Document

The excerpt below, about men seeking work in the meatpacking industry, is from Upton Sinclair's novel *The Jungle*. Read the excerpt, and then answer questions 23–24. (*10 points*)

> All day long the gates of the packing houses were besieged by starving and penniless men; they came, literally, by the thousands every single morning, fighting with each other for a chance for life. Blizzards and cold made no difference to them, they were always on hand... Sometimes their faces froze, sometimes their feet and hands; sometimes they froze all together—but still they came, for they had no other place to go....

23. What problems of concern to Progressives does this passage address?

24. Which parts of this account do you think might have been based on fact, and which might have been exaggerations to influence public opinion?

NAME ______________________ CLASS ____________ DATE ____________

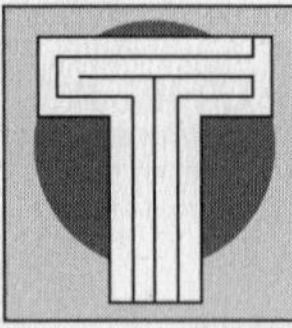

TEST FORM B

The Era of Progressive Reform (1890-1920)

CHAPTER 19

A. Identifying Key Terms, People, and Places

Match the descriptions in Column I with the terms in Column II. Write the letter of the correct answer in each blank. You will not use all the terms. (*16 points*)

Column I

_____ **1.** having to do with city government

_____ **2.** a limited degree of self-government for cities

_____ **3.** efforts made by the government to ensure a basic standard of living for all Americans

_____ **4.** election in which voters cast ballots to select nominees for upcoming elections

_____ **5.** people concerned with the care and protection of the environment

_____ **6.** Theodore Roosevelt's name for his progressive reform program

_____ **7.** name of Woodrow Wilson's reform policy during the presidential campaign of 1912

_____ **8.** nonviolent refusal to obey a law

Column II

a. New Freedom
b. direct primary
c. muckrakers
d. municipal
e. home rule
f. New Nationalism
g. civil disobedience
h. conservationists
i. holding company
j. social welfare programs

B. Identifying Main Ideas

Write the letter of the correct answer in the blank provided. (*40 points*)

_____ **9.** According to journalist Henry George, how could Americans eliminate poverty?
a. by nationalizing industries
b. by allowing home rule in cities and states
c. by ending capitalism
d. by discouraging land speculation

_____ **10.** Which belief was held by most Progressives?
a. The government should own American industries.
b. Housing and health care should remain private.
c. The government should protect agricultural interests.
d. The government should intervene in unfair business practices.

_____ **11.** Which of the following was Florence Kelley a major force in reforming?
a. labor laws
b. referendum procedures
c. antitrust legislation
d. the Federal Reserve system

_____ **12.** Which did municipal reformers favor in the early 1900s?
a. strong, independent political machines
b. city control of utilities
c. abolishment of home rule
d. federal regulation of city services

_____ **13.** What action did President Roosevelt take in the United Mine Workers' strike in 1902?
a. He dissolved the union.
b. He sent the army to seize and operate the mines.
c. He sent in arbitrators to resolve the dispute.
d. He refused to interfere with labor and management relations.

_____ **14.** Over what were Republican insurgents angry at President Taft?
a. his support of the Seventeenth Amendment
b. his support of women's suffrage
c. his handling of the Ballinger-Pinchot affair
d. his refusal to enforce antitrust cases

_____ **15.** How did Woodrow Wilson's reform platform during the 1912 campaign differ from that of Theodore Roosevelt?
a. Wilson supported federal regulation of business.
b. Wilson promised to preserve free economic competition.
c. Wilson supported tariff reduction.
d. Wilson promised to enforce antitrust laws.

_____ **16.** Which was a major contributor to Woodrow Wilson's winning the presidency in 1912?
a. a split between northern and southern Democrats
b. Taft's decision not to run for a second term
c. Roosevelt's splitting the Republican vote
d. the candidacy of Eugene V. Debs

_____ **17.** Which of the following caused a split in the women's suffrage campaign?
a. Alice Paul's aggressive strategy
b. Carrie Chapman Catt's "Winning Plan"
c. the decision to press for a constitutional amendment
d. World War I

_____ **18.** How did World War I affect the cause of women's suffrage?
a. It ended major support for it.
b. It set aside arguments about separate spheres for men and women.
c. It reinforced the idea that the vote would make women more masculine.
d. It strengthened the liquor interests that opposed woman suffrage.

TEST FORM B *(continued)*

CHAPTER 19

C. Critical Thinking

Answer the following questions on the back of this paper or on a separate sheet of paper. (*24 points*)

19. Formulating Questions What are two questions that Progressives would likely ask candidates in the 1912 presidential campaign? What answers to these questions might win Progressives votes?

20. Identifying Alternatives What two main strategies did woman suffrage activists use in the late 1800s and early 1900s? How did each strategy contribute to the passage of the Nineteenth Amendment?

D. Interpreting a Map

Use the map below to answer questions 21–22. Write your answers on the back of this paper or on a separate sheet of paper. (*10 points*)

21. Which state was the first to grant women the vote, and in what year did it do so?

22. In 1920, where were most of the equal suffrage states located? Why was the suffrage movement more successful in this region?

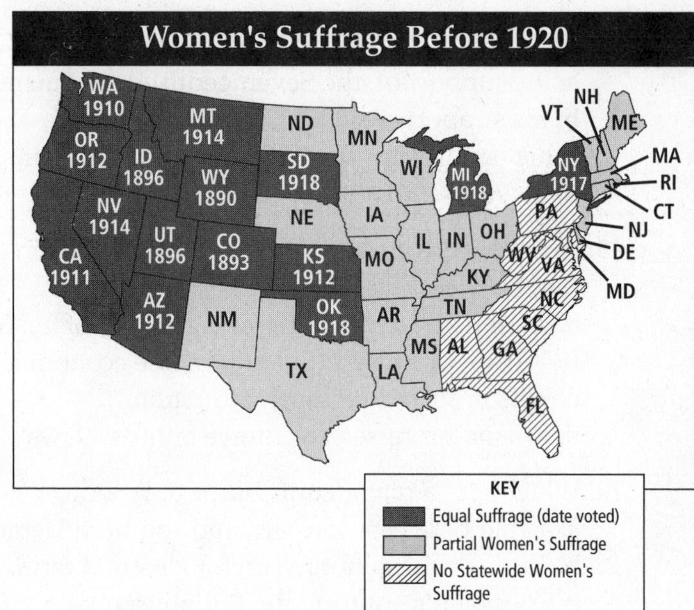

E. Analyzing a Document

The excerpt below, about men seeking work in the meatpacking industry, is from Upton Sinclair's novel *The Jungle*. Read the excerpt, and then answer questions 23–24. (*10 points*)

> All day long the gates of the packing houses were besieged by starving and penniless men; they came, literally, by the thousands every single morning, fighting with each other for a chance for life. Blizzards and cold made no difference to them, they were always on hand... Sometimes their faces froze, sometimes their feet and hands; sometimes they froze all together—but still they came, for they had no other place to go....

23. What were Sinclair's probable goals in writing this passage?

24. In what ways is the excerpt an example of "muckraking"?

NAME ______________________________ CLASS ______________ DATE ______________

TEST FORM A

The World War I Era (1914-1920)

CHAPTER 20

A. Identifying Key Terms, People, and Places

Match the descriptions in Column I with the terms in Column II. Write the letter of the correct answer in each blank. You will not use all the terms. (*16 points*)

Column I

_____ **1.** countries that fought against Germany and Austria-Hungary during World War I

_____ **2.** Germany's promise that its U-boats would warn ships before attacking

_____ **3.** speech or actions that encourage rebellion

_____ **4.** cease-fire between opponents in a war

_____ **5.** organized killing of an entire people

_____ **6.** President Wilson's program for peace

_____ **7.** worldwide organization aimed at ensuring security and peace

_____ **8.** payment from one nation to another for economic injury suffered during a war

Column II

a. Sussex pledge
b. Versailles Treaty
c. Allies
d. Fourteen Points
e. reparations
f. League of Nations
g. mobilization
h. genocide
i. sedition
j. armistice
k. Central Powers

B. Identifying Main Ideas

Write the letter of the correct answer in the blank provided. (*40 points*)

_____ **9.** Which event sparked World War I?
a. the sinking of the *Lusitania*
b. the German-French dispute over Alsace-Lorraine
c. Russia's quest for a warm-water port
d. the assassination of the heir to the Austro-Hungarian throne

_____ **10.** Which of the following best describes the first few years of World War I?
a. Both sides were locked in a stalemate.
b. The Central Powers had conquered most of Europe.
c. Victory for the Allies seemed to be coming soon.
d. There was little actual fighting.

_____ **11.** Which country actively encouraged anti-German feeling in the United States?
a. Mexico **b.** Great Britain
c. Russia **d.** Austria-Hungary

TEST FORM A *(continued)*

_____ **12.** Which of the following was a major factor in the United States' decision to enter World War I?
a. Britain's naval blockade of Germany
b. Germany's unrestricted submarine warfare
c. Vladimir Lenin's rise to power in Russia
d. France's fall to the Central Powers

_____ **13.** What was the purpose of the convoy system?
a. to hire workers for war factories
b. to place women in the work force
c. to get troops safely across the Atlantic
d. to drop bombs on the enemy

_____ **14.** Which was true of African Americans during World War I?
a. Almost as many African Americans served in the war as did white Americans.
b. African Americans were not allowed to serve in the war.
c. African American troops were usually reserved for battle.
d. African American troops were segregated and rarely allowed to fight.

_____ **15.** What role did the federal government play in the economy during the war?
a. The government gave industries more economic freedom.
b. The government lowered taxes to promote economic growth.
c. The government stripped the corporate world of its power.
d. The government regulated the production of war goods.

_____ **16.** Which best describes the Great Migration?
a. the increase in European immigration during World War I
b. the movement of African Americans to northern cities
c. the movement of women into jobs formerly held by men
d. the progress of Allied troops across France

_____ **17.** Why did the "irreconcilable" senators oppose the Versailles Treaty?
a. They did not want the United States to join the League of Nations.
b. They wanted harsher terms for Germany.
c. They believed the treaty violated the Fourteen Points.
d. They opposed reparations for the Allies.

_____ **18.** Which of the following made postwar adjustment difficult in the United States?
a. The United States became the world's largest debtor nation.
b. There were more jobs available than workers to fill them.
c. There was no plan for merging returning troops back into society.
d. The government continued to control the economy.

C. Critical Thinking

Answer the following questions on the back of this paper or on a separate sheet of paper. (*24 points*)

19. Determining Relevance What role did public opinion play in the United States' decision to enter World War I?

20. Testing Conclusions Your text states, "Waging war required many sacrifices at home." What evidence can you cite to support this conclusion?

D. Interpreting a Table

Use the table below to answer questions 21–22. Write your answers on the back of this paper or on a separate sheet of paper. (*10 points*)

United States Foreign Trade During World War I

	1914	1915	1916
To Allied Countries	$824,860,237	$1,991,747,493	$3,214,480,547
To Central Powers	$169,289,775	$11,878,153	$1,159,653
To Northern Neutrals	$187,667,040	$330,110,646	$279,786,219

21. With which group of countries did the United States have the strongest commercial ties in 1914?

22. Based on the table, what conclusions can you draw about relations between the United States and the Central Powers during the early years of World War I?

E. Analyzing a Document

Study this 1915 American newspaper clipping. Then answer questions 23–24 on the back of this paper or on a separate sheet of paper. (*10 points*)

23. Who placed this notice, and why?

24. Did the warning in the notice apply to the ship advertised at right? Why or why not? What happened to the *Lusitania*?

NOTICE!

TRAVELLERS intending to embark on the Atlantic voyage are reminded that a state of war exists between Germany and her allies and GreatBritian and her allies; that the zone of war includes the waters adjacent to the British Isles; that, in accordance with formal notice given by the Imperial German Government, vessels flying the flag of Great Britian, or of any of her allies, are liable to destruction in those waters and that travellers sailing in the war zone on ships of Great Britian or her allies do so at their own risk.

IMPERIAL GERMAN EMBASSY,
WASHINGTON, D. C., APRIL 22, 1915.

CUNARD

EUROPE VIA LIVERPOOL

LUSITANIA

Fastest and Largest Steamer
now in Atlantic Service Sails
SATURDAY, MAY 1, 10 A. M.
Transylvania - Fri., May 7, 5 P.M.
Orduna, - - - Tues., May 18, 10 A.M.
Tuscania, - - - Fri., May 21, 5 P.M.
LUSITANIA, - Sat., May 29, 10 A.M.
Transylvania, 5 P.M.

NAME ______________________ CLASS ______________ DATE ______________

TEST FORM B

The World War I Era (1914-1920)

CHAPTER 20

A. Identifying Key Terms, People, and Places

Complete the sentences in Column I with the terms in Column II. Write the letter of the correct answer in each blank. You will not use all the terms. *(16 points)*

Column I

_____ **1.** German use of the _____ changed the rules of naval warfare.

_____ **2.** In the _____, Germany proposed an alliance with Mexico.

_____ **3.** The United States sold _____ to help it finance the war.

_____ **4.** President Wilson's program for peace came to be known as the _____.

_____ **5.** Austria-Hungary's ethnic groups sought _____, the power to make decisions about their own future.

_____ **6.** President Wilson hoped that membership in the _____ would ensure security and peace for all members.

_____ **7.** Britain wanted _____, payment for economic injuries suffered during the war.

_____ **8.** The _____ was signed by European powers, ending World War I.

Column II

a. Fourteen Points
b. self-determination
c. Liberty Bonds
d. Zimmermann note
e. U-boat
f. Versailles Treaty
g. reparations
h. Sussex Pledge
i. League of Nations
j. American Expeditionary Force
k. price controls

B. Identifying Main Ideas

Write the letter of the correct ending in the blank provided. *(40 points)*

_____ **9.** The incident that triggered World War I was the
a. sinking of the *Lusitania*.
b. Serbian invasion of Hungary.
c. assassination of the heir to the Austro-Hungarian throne.
d. German seizure of Alsace-Lorraine, claimed by France.

_____ **10.** An underlying cause of World War I was
a. the ongoing dispute over the convoy system.
b. the web of alliances European nations created for their defense.
c. an alliance between the autocratic rulers of Germany and Russia.
d. American insistence on neutrality.

CHAPTER 20

_____ **11.** Under the terms of the Sussex pledge, the German government promised that
a. the German navy would not attack any American ships.
b. German ships would not blockade Britain and France.
c. German U-boats would warn ships before attacking.
d. the German army would never invade Russia.

_____ **12.** The United States decided to enter the war in response to
a. Germany's return to unrestricted submarine warfare.
b. France's fall to the Central Powers.
c. the Czar's growing support in Russia.
d. a filibuster by United States senators.

_____ **13.** The Selective Service Act was a means of
a. getting money to support the war effort.
b. getting women to take over jobs formerly done by men.
c. drafting young men for the military forces.
d. finding jobs for men after they left military service.

_____ **14.** After Vladimir Lenin seized control of Russia in 1917,
a. Germany surrendered.
b. the Allies declared war on Russia.
c. the United States entered the war.
d. Russia withdrew from the war.

_____ **15.** The government increased control of the economy during World War I by
a. filing a record number of antitrust suits.
b. enacting price controls and rationing.
c. overseeing war-related production.
d. forbidding any unions to strike.

_____ **16.** Fears of spies and sabotage in the United States during the war led to
a. restrictions on immigration.
b. discrimination and violence toward Germans.
c. repression of free speech.
d. all of the above.

_____ **17.** President Wilson convinced the Allies to
a. divide the spoils of war among the victors.
b. accept his plan for the League of Nations.
c. make Germany pay heavy war reparations.
d. allow Germany to keep its overseas colonies.

_____ **18.** Many senators opposed American entry into the League of Nations because
a. they feared it would weaken the country's independence.
b. they disapproved of its other member countries.
c. they wanted stronger promises of support from other countries.
d. they had already approved the Versailles Treaty.

CHAPTER 20

C. Critical Thinking

Answer the following questions on the back of this paper or on a separate sheet of paper. (*24 points*)

19. Recognizing Bias What role did bias play in Americans' response to the war?

20. Recognizing Cause and Effect How were civil liberties restricted during the war? What were some responses to these restrictions?

D. Interpreting a Table

Use the table below to answer questions 21–22. Write your answers on the back of this paper or on a separate sheet of paper. (*10 points*)

United States Foreign Trade During World War I

	1914	1915	1916
To Allied Countries	$824,860,237	$1,991,747,493	$3,214,480,547
To Central Powers	$169,289,775	$11,878,153	$1,159,653
To Northern Neutrals	$187,667,040	$330,110,646	$279,786,219

21. If the United States had entered World War I in 1914 to protect its commercial interests, with which side would it likely have sided? Why?

22. Use the table to support or refute the following conclusion: *Commercial relations between the United States and Germany deteriorated rapidly during the early years of World War I.*

E. Analyzing a Document

Study this 1915 American newspaper clipping. Then answer questions 23–24 on the back of this paper or on a separate sheet of paper. (*10 points*)

23. Whom is the notice addressing, and what is its main message?

24. What is the connection between the ship advertised on the right and the notice on the left?

NOTICE!

TRAVELLERS intending to embark on the Atlantic voyage are reminded that a state of war exists between Germany and her allies and GreatBritian and her allies; that the zone of war includes the waters adjacent to the British Isles; that, in accordance with formal notice given by the Imperial German Government, vessels flying the flag of Great Britian, or of any of her allies, are liable to destruction in those waters and that travellers sailing in the war zone on ships of Great Britian or her allies do so at their own risk.

IMPERIAL GERMAN EMBASSY,
WASHINGTON, D. C., APRIL 22, 1915.

CUNARD

EUROPE VIA LIVERPOOL

LUSITANIA

Fastest and Largest Steamer now in Atlantic Service Sails
SATURDAY, MAY 1, 10 A. M.

Transylvania - Fri., May 7, 5P.M.
Orduna, - - - Tues., May 18, 10A.M.
Tuscania, - - - Fri., May 21, 5 P.M.
LUSITANIA, - Sat., May 29, 10A.M.
Transylvania, - 5P.M.

NAME ______________________ CLASS ____________ DATE ____________

TEST FORM A

The Twenties (1920-1929)

CHAPTER 21

A. Identifying Key Terms, People, and Places

Match the descriptions in Column I with the terms in Column II. Write the letter of the correct answer in the blank provided. You will not use all the terms. (*10 points*)

Column I

_____ **1.** policy of avoiding alliances with foreign countries

_____ **2.** statistics that describe a population

_____ **3.** African American literary movement of the 1920s

_____ **4.** numerical limit

_____ **5.** set of religious beliefs based on a literal interpretation of the Bible

Column II

a. demographics

b. quota

c. Cotton Club

d. fundamentalism

e. isolationism

f. communism

g. Harlem Renaissance

Complete each sentence in Column I by writing the letter of the correct name from Column II in the blank. You will not use all the names. (*10 points*)

Column I

_____ **6.** Elected in 1920, Republican President _____ promised a "return to normalcy."

_____ **7.** "The business of the American people is business," observed _____, President from 1923 to 1927.

_____ **8.** _____ became a national hero after flying nonstop from New York to Paris.

_____ **9.** One of the most celebrated jazz musicians of the 1920s was pianist, composer, and bandleader _____.

_____ **10.** Harlem writer _____ gained fame with the novel, *Their Eyes Were Watching God.*

Column II

a. Calvin Coolidge

b. Charles Lindbergh

c. Edna St. Vincent Millay

d. Zora Neale Hurston

e. Warren G. Harding

f. Duke Ellington

g. Herbert Hoover

B. Identifying Main Ideas

Write the letter of the correct ending in the blank provided. (*32 points*)

_____ **11.** Key features of Republican administrations of the 1920s included
- **a.** expansionism and business regulation.
- **b.** isolationism and laissez-faire business policy.
- **c.** a buildup of armaments and armed forces.
- **d.** reduction of quotas and increased immigration.

TEST FORM A *(continued)*

_____ **12.** The Red Scare was a response to
- **a.** Prohibition.
- **b.** the Teapot Dome scandal.
- **c.** the Russian Revolution.
- **d.** the Kellogg-Briand Pact.

_____ **13.** The economy grew in the 1920s as consumers
- **a.** carefully conserved electricity.
- **b.** invested most of their money in government bonds.
- **c.** learned to ignore advertisements.
- **d.** began to buy goods on credit.

_____ **14.** Though relatively few in number, flappers represented
- **a.** a sign of social stability.
- **b.** women's desire to break with the past.
- **c.** women's desire to return to the past.
- **b.** the significant impact of women on national elections.

_____ **15.** One major demographic shift of the 1920s was the movement of
- **a.** large numbers of Americans to the suburbs.
- **b.** large numbers of Americans from the North to the South.
- **c.** French-speaking Canadians into barrios.
- **d.** Mexican workers to New England.

_____ **16.** The rapid development of the mass media during the 1920s
- **a.** promoted a mass migration to rural areas.
- **b.** encouraged Americans to work longer hours.
- **c.** promoted the creation of a national culture.
- **d.** simplified life for most Americans.

_____ **17.** One result of Prohibition during the 1920s was
- **a.** an increase in alcoholism.
- **b.** a decline in dancing and socializing.
- **c.** the rise of organized crime.
- **d.** the creation of urban artistic colonies.

_____ **18.** Marcus Garvey led a movement to
- **a.** segregate African Americans in northern cities.
- **b.** build up African American self-respect and economic power.
- **c.** unionize African American workers.
- **d.** create new African American homelands in the Caribbean Islands.

C. Critical Thinking

Answer the following questions on the back of this paper or on a separate sheet of paper. (*26 points*)

19. Recognizing Ideologies Why did so many Americans fear the spread of communist ideology?

20. Recognizing Cause and Effect Explain how the mass production of automobiles in the 1920s affected the economy of the United States.

D. Interpreting a Bar Graph

Examine the graph below. Then write your answers to questions 21–23 on the back of this paper or on a separate sheet of paper. (*12 points*)

21. (a) From which part of the world did the largest number of immigrants come in 1921? (b) About how many immigrants came from this region in 1921?

22. From which region did the United States accept the most immigrants in 1926?

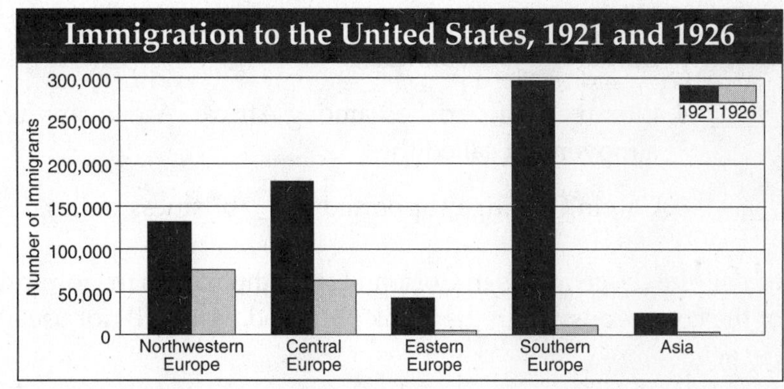

23. Describe the overall trend of immigration from 1921 to 1926. How did United States policy affect this trend?

E. Analyzing a Document

The excerpt below comes from a statement that Representative Fiorello La Guardia of New York made to a Congressional committee in 1926. Read it and answer questions 24–25 on the back of this paper or on a separate sheet of paper. (*10 points*)

> It is impossible to tell whether Prohibition is a good thing or a bad thing. It has never been enforced in this country....
>
> I will concede that the saloon was odious, but we now have delicatessen stores, pool rooms, drug stores, millinery shops, private parlors, and 57 other varieties of speakeasies selling liquor and flourishing.

24. Why did La Guardia claim it was impossible to judge prohibition?

25. What evidence did La Guardia cite to show that Prohibition was not working?

NAME ______________________ CLASS ______________ DATE ______________

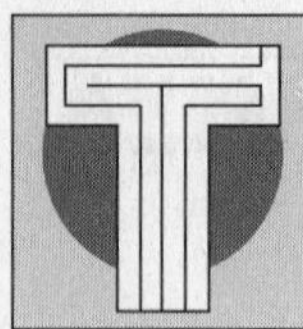

TEST FORM B

The Twenties (1920-1929)

CHAPTER 21

A. Identifying Key Terms, People, and Places

Complete each sentence in Column I by writing the letter of the correct term from Column II in the blank provided. You will not use all the terms. (*10 points*)

Column I

_____ **1.** The _____ scandal tarnished the reputation of the Harding administration.

_____ **2.** The _____ made it possible for Henry Ford to produce cars quickly and cheaply.

_____ **3.** The 1920s became known as the _____, after a popular, influential form of music.

_____ **4.** Literary life flourished among African Americans as part of a movement called the _____.

_____ **5.** Calvin Coolidge supported _____ business policy.

Column II

a. Harlem Renaissance
b. assembly line
c. laissez-faire
d. Teapot Dome
e. Jazz Age
f. red scare
g. flapper

Match the descriptions in Column I with the names in Column II. Write the letter of the correct answer in the blank provided. You will not use all the names. (*10 points*)

Column I

_____ **6.** immigrant whose murder conviction provoked controversy

_____ **7.** "silent" Republican President who opposed government interference in American business

_____ **8.** flyer whose feats included a solo flight across the Atlantic

_____ **9.** popular jazz trumpeter and singer

_____ **10.** Jamaican-born leader of movement promoting African American pride

Column II

a. Calvin Coolidge
b. Nicola Sacco
c. Georgia O'Keefe
d. Marcus Garvey
e. Louis Armstrong
f. Amelia Earhart
g. Warren G. Harding

B. Identifying Main Ideas

Write the letter of the correct answer in the blank provided. (*32 points*)

_____ **11.** Why did many Americans fear Vladimir I. Lenin and his followers, the Bolsheviks?
a. They promoted a system that was hostile to American values.
b. They refused to pay back Russia's war debts.
c. They had abolished the Russian monarchy.
d. They encouraged other nations to reject socialism.

_____ **12.** Which caused labor unrest in the United States after World War I?
a. International trade collapsed.
b. The cost of living rose significantly.
c. Returning veterans refused to work in low-paying factory jobs.
d. Consumer demand outstripped factory production.

_____ **13.** How did installment plans affect the American economy in the 1920s?
a. They led to a sharp decline in average wages.
b. They inspired Americans to cut back on luxury items.
c. They fueled the growth of the consumer economy.
d. They reinforced the demand for lower tariffs.

_____ **14.** Which was a result of the boom in the automobile industry?
a. The tourist industry declined.
b. New roads were built.
c. Gasoline had to be rationed.
d. Workers in Ford plants received low wages.

_____ **15.** How did life change for American women in the 1920s?
a. Many women felt freer to experiment with bolder styles and manners.
b. Married women found it much easier to balance careers and family life.
c. Most women grew long hair and stopped using makeup.
d. Women began to dominate the workforce, often taking leadership positions.

_____ **16.** Why did many Americans become fascinated with heroes in the 1920s?
a. They longed to return to the days of World War I.
b. They longed for symbols of old-fashioned virtues.
c. They had little leisure time to pursue their own interests.
d. They objected to being reminded of basic American ideals.

_____ **17.** Which of the following was a long-term effect of Prohibition?
a. the consumer economy
b. the growth of organized crime
c. an end to alcoholism in the United States
d. the rise of fundamentalism

_____ **18.** Why did some states ban the teaching of evolution in the schools?
a. The theory challenged scientific beliefs.
b. The theory appeared to violate the Constitution.
c. The theory seemed to contradict the Bible's account of creation.
d. The theory was unknown to most teachers.

CHAPTER 21

C. Critical Thinking

Answer the following questions on the back of this paper or on a separate sheet of paper. (*26 points*)

19. Making Comparisons Compare the governments of the United States and the Soviet Union in the 1920s.

20. Identifying Assumptions What did supporters of Prohibition assume outlawing alcohol would accomplish? How accurate were their assumptions?

D. Interpreting a Bar Graph

Examine the graph below. Then write your answers to questions 21–23 on the back of this paper or on a separate sheet of paper. (*12 points*)

21. Which group experienced the sharpest decline in immigration from 1921 to 1926?

22. (a) From which region did the most immigrants come in 1926? (b) About how many immigrants came from this region in 1926?

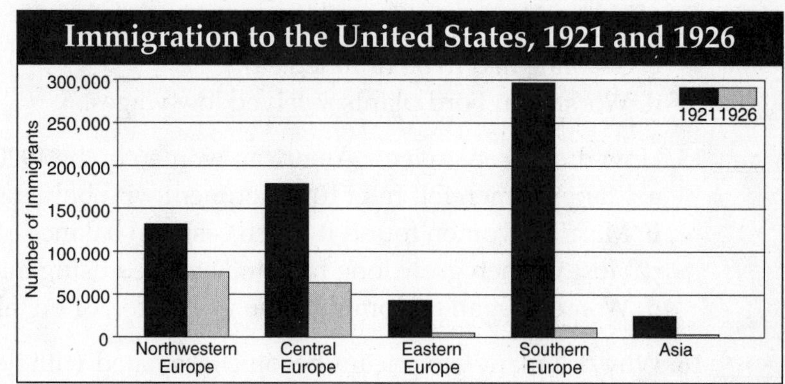

23. Explain the graph's data based on what you know about American attitudes toward immigrants in the 1920s.

E. Analyzing a Document

The excerpt below comes from a statement that Representative Fiorello La Guardia of New York made to a Congressional committee in 1926. Read it and answer questions 24–25 on the back of this paper or on a separate sheet of paper. (*10 points*)

> It is impossible to tell whether Prohibition is a good thing or a bad thing. It has never been enforced in this country....
>
> I will concede that the saloon was odious, but we now have delicatessen stores, pool rooms, drug stores, millinery shops, private parlors, and 57 other varieties of speakeasies selling liquor and flourishing.

24. What argument did La Guardia make about Prohibition?

25. How did the existence of speakeasies support his point?

NAME ______________________ CLASS ____________ DATE ____________

TEST FORM A

Crash and Depression (1929-1933)

CHAPTER 22

A. Identifying Key Terms, People, and Places

Match the descriptions in Column I with the terms in Column II. Write the letter of the correct answer in the blank provided. You will not use all the terms. *(10 points)*

Column I

_____ **1.** employers' practice of meeting some of workers' needs without demands from unions

_____ **2.** practice of making high-risk investments in hopes of high gain

_____ **3.** purchasing stock by borrowing part of the price from stockbrokers

_____ **4.** total annual value of goods and services a country produces

_____ **5.** 1930 import tax, the highest in history

Column II

a. Hawley-Smoot tariff

b. speculation

c. welfare capitalism

d. Dow Jones Industrial Average

e. buying on margin

f. Gross National Product

g. Twenty-first Amendment

Complete each sentence in Column I by writing the letter of the correct name from Column II in the blank. You will not use all the names. *(10 points)*

Column I

_____ **6.** The photographer ____ showed the nation the realities of the Depression.

_____ **7.** During the Depression, the followers of Harlem evangelist ____ ran soup kitchens that fed thousands daily.

_____ **8.** By the time her husband ran for President, ____ was an experienced political worker and social reformer.

_____ **9.** President ____ argued that the key to recovery was confidence.

_____ **10.** British economist ____ said that massive government spending could help a collapsing economy.

Column II

a. Dorothea Lange

b. Herbert Hoover

c. Eleanor Roosevelt

d. Father Divine

e. John Maynard Keynes

f. Franklin Delano Roosevelt

g. Douglas MacArthur

CHAPTER 22

B. Identifying Main Ideas

Write the letter of the correct ending in the blank provided. (32 points)

_____ **11.** Throughout most of the 1920s, Americans were generally
a. worried that the Stock Market would crash.
b. confident that business would bring continued prosperity.
c. delighted that wealth was evenly distributed.
d. concerned with economic danger signs.

_____ **12.** One sign that the economy might be weakening in the 1920s was
a. the failure of many rural banks.
b. underproduction of consumer goods.
c. an increase in personal savings.
d. the collapse of large corporations.

_____ **13.** When the Dow Jones Industrial Average began to drop sharply in late October 1929,
a. investors bought record shares of stock.
b. bankers pardoned personal loans and mortgages.
c. President Hoover warned Americans to stop investing.
d. investors raced to get their money out of the stock market.

_____ **14.** European economies were hurt during the Depression when
a. President Hoover pardoned war debts.
b. Congress lowered tariffs.
c. United States companies stopped investing in Germany.
d. the United States increased its exports.

_____ **15.** A major environmental crisis of the 1930s was known as
a. the Dust Bowl. **b.** the Grapes of Wrath.
c. Black Tuesday. **d.** the Great Crash.

_____ **16.** During the Depression, African Americans, Hispanics, and Asian Americans
a. made great strides in equal rights legislation.
b. often lost jobs to white laborers.
c. were less affected than other groups.
d. were encouraged to start their own businesses.

_____ **17.** In 1933 the Twenty-first Amendment brought an end to
a. Prohibition. **b.** stock speculation.
c. the Depression. **d.** the United States Communist party.

_____ **18.** The 1932 presidential election served as a turning point in the way Americans viewed
a. presidential elections.
b. the Bill of Rights.
c. the responsibilities of the federal government.
d. local relief programs and private charities.

C. Critical Thinking

Answer the following questions on the back of this paper or on a separate sheet of paper. *(24 points)*

19. Distinguishing False from Accurate Images Did President Hoover present a false or an accurate image of the Depression to the American public? Cite examples to support your answer.

20. Drawing Conclusions What kind of advice do you think a survivor of the Great Depression might give younger adults today?

D. Interpreting a Line Graph

Use the graph to answer questions 21-23. Write your answers on the back of this paper or on a separate sheet of paper. *(12 points)*

21. By how much did the Gross National Product (GNP) decrease from 1929 to 1932?

22. What appears to be the relationship between personal income and a country's GNP?

23. Why is 1939 considered the last year of the Great Depression?

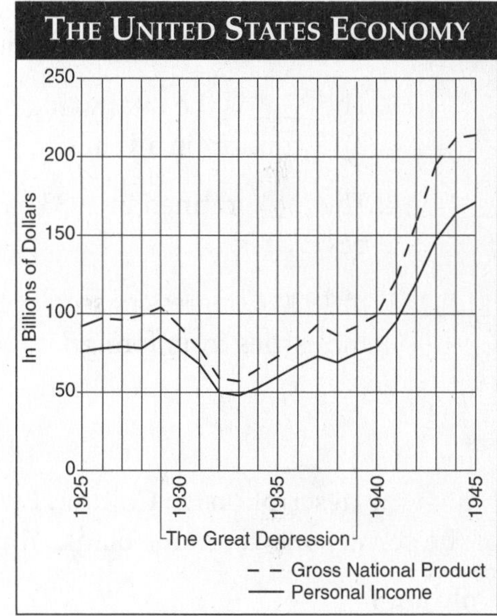

E. Analyzing a Document

The excerpt below comes from a campaign speech that President Hoover gave in 1932. Read it and then answer questions 24-25 on the back of this paper or on a separate sheet of paper. *(12 points)*

> Our system is...founded on the conception that only through ordered liberty, through freedom to the individual, and equal opportunity to the individual will his initiative and enterprise be summoned to spur the march of progress....
>
> It is in the further development of this cooperation and a sense of its responsibility that we should find solution for many of our complex problems, and not by the extension of government into our economic and social life. ...

24. How did Hoover believe the country's economic problems would be solved?

25. How did Franklin Delano Roosevelt's view of government differ from the view expressed here?

NAME ______________________ CLASS ____________ DATE ____________

TEST FORM B

Crash and Depression (1929-1933)

CHAPTER 22

A. Identifying Key Terms, People, and Places

Complete each sentence in Column I by writing the letter of the correct term from Column II in the blank. You will not use all the terms. (10 points)

Column I

_____ **1.** To keep unions weak, many companies turned to ____ to meet some of their workers' needs.

_____ **2.** Information about stock prices is reflected in the ____.

_____ **3.** The ____ is the total value of goods and services produced by a country in a year.

_____ **4.** The ____, ratified in 1933, repealed the ban on alcoholic beverages.

_____ **5.** In 1930 Congress passed the ____ to protect domestic industries from foreign imports.

Column II

a. speculation

b. Twenty-first Amendment

c. welfare capitalism

d. Gross National Product

e. Bonus Army

f. Dow Jones Industrial Average

g. Hawley-Smoot tariff

Match the descriptions in Column I with the names in Column II. Write the letter of the correct answer in the blank. You will not use all the names. (10 points)

Column I

_____ **6.** photographer who showed the realities of the Depression to the nation

_____ **7.** "Everybody Ought to Be Rich" author and corporate leader who financed the Empire State Building

_____ **8.** baseball legend who joked that he "had a better year" than the President

_____ **9.** economist who believed that massive government spending programs could revive a failing economy

_____ **10.** President who promised the nation a "new deal"

Column II

a. Herbert Hoover

b. Babe Ruth

c. Douglas MacArthur

d. John J. Raskob

e. John Maynard Keynes

f. Franklin Delano Roosevelt

g. Dorothea Lange

B. Identifying Main Ideas

Write the letter of the correct answer in the blank provided. (32 points)

_____ **11.** Which statement best describes the American economy in the 1920s?
a. Wages decreased and the economy appeared weak.
b. Unemployment was at an all-time high.
c. Stock prices rose and the economy appeared healthy.
d. Small businesses dominated American industry.

_____ **12.** Which group faced hard times during much of the 1920s?
a. urban bankers
b. farmers
c. small investors
d. owners of large corporations

_____ **13.** Which of the following was a sign of an unsound economy during the 1920s?
a. Personal debt was decreasing.
b. Wages were keeping pace with production.
c. More goods were being produced than consumers could buy.
d. The Dow Jones Industrial Average was steady.

_____ **14.** How did most investors react to a sudden fall in stock prices in 1929?
a. They called in their loans.
b. They pooled money to buy stock.
c. They raced to sell their stocks.
d. They pledged their stocks as collateral.

_____ **15.** Which was one effect of the wage cuts and unemployment of the 1930s?
a. The divorce rate nearly tripled.
b. Banks pardoned thousands of farm mortgages.
c. Hoovervilles sprang up in the nation's cities.
d. Most industries gave top jobs to married women.

_____ **16.** During the Depression, many African Americans
a. took low-paying jobs previously held by white workers.
b. experienced worsening conditions and discrimination in job and relief programs.
c. returned from northern cities to the South.
d. won new civil rights, such as access to education and health care.

_____ **17.** President Hoover believed that the best strategy for ending the Depression was
a. encouraging massive government spending.
b. lowering import duties.
c. setting up federal relief programs.
d. encouraging voluntary controls in the business sector.

_____ **18.** A fundamental disagreement between the candidates in the 1932 presidential election concerned whether or not
a. the Depression existed.
b. the federal government should try to fix people's problems.
c. Americans should offer aid to European economies.
d. any relief efforts were necessary to ease the economic crisis.

CHAPTER 22

C. Critical Thinking

Answer the following question on the back of this paper or on a separate sheet of paper. *(24 points)*

19. Checking Consistency Explain whether the maxim "Work hard, be thrifty, don't borrow" from Benjamin Franklin's *Poor Richard's Almanac* is consistent or inconsistent with attitudes displayed in the United States in the 1920s.

20. Recognizing Cause and Effect In your opinion, what was the greatest single effect of the Depression on the United States? Support your answer.

D. Interpreting a Line Graph

Use the graph to answer questions 21-23. Write your answers on the back of this paper or on a separate sheet of paper. (12 points)

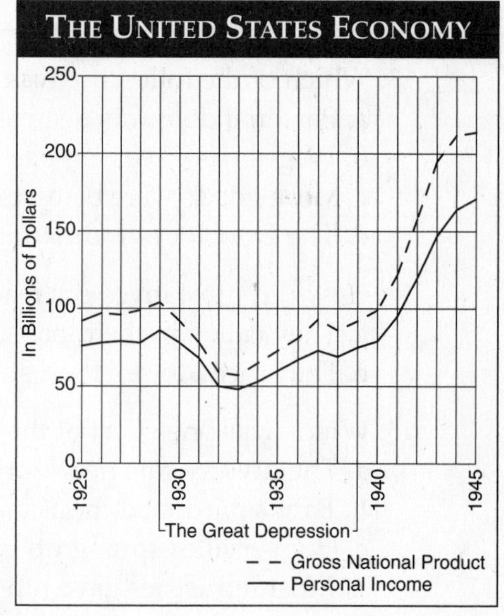

21. Which year of the Great Depression do you think was most difficult for Americans? Support your answer.

22. Explain how Roosevelt might have used the data in the graphs during the 1932 presidential campaign.

23. If the total Gross National Product increased, what would most likely happen to personal income?

E. Analyzing a Document

The excerpt below comes from a campaign speech that Herbert Hoover gave in 1932. Read it and then answer questions 24-25 on the back of this paper or on a separate sheet of paper. (12 points)

> Our system is…founded on the conception that only through ordered liberty, through freedom to the individual, and equal opportunity to the individual will his initiative and enterprise be summoned to spur the march of progress….
>
> It is in the further development of this cooperation and a sense of its responsibility that we should find solution for many of our complex problems, and not by the extension of government into our economic and social life. …

24. On what did Hoover believe the American system was based?

25. Given the context of the speech, what was Hoover arguing *against?*

NAME ______________________ CLASS ______________ DATE ______________

TEST FORM A

The New Deal (1933-1938)

CHAPTER 23

A. Identifying Key Terms, People, and Places

Match the descriptions in Column I with the terms in Column II. Write the letter of the correct answer in the blank provided. You will not use all the terms. (*16 points*)

Column I

_____ **1.** Roosevelt's program of relief, recovery, and reform

_____ **2.** government-funded projects to build public facilities

_____ **3.** project that helped farmers and created jobs by reactivating a hydroelectric power facility

_____ **4.** legislation that allowed collective bargaining and set up a National Labor Relations Board

_____ **5.** program that provided old-age pensions for workers, unemployment insurance, and other benefits

_____ **6.** group that spearheaded much of the opposition to the New Deal

_____ **7.** the total amount of borrowed money the federal government has yet to pay back

_____ **8.** an alliance of groups with similar goals

Column II

a. coalition

b. revenue

c. Tennessee Valley Authority

d. New Deal

e. national debt

f. public works programs

g. Wagner Act

h. demagogues

i. Social Security system

j. American Liberty League

B. Identifying Main Ideas

Write the letter of the correct answer in the blank provided. (*40 points*)

_____ **9.** Why did FDR declare a "bank holiday" early in his administration?
a. to cut off the use of cash
b. to weaken the banking industry
c. to inspect the financial health of the banks
d. to give people in the banking industry a well-earned vacation

_____ **10.** Which New Deal agency was created to help businesses?
a. Federal Reserve Board
b. National Recovery Administration
c. Civilian Conservation Corps
d. Home Owners' Loan Corporation

_____ **11.** Which best describes FDR's "brain trust"?
a. the members of FDR's Cabinet
b. an informal group of intellectuals who helped devise New Deal policies
c. the heads of the new government agencies
d. the presidents of the country's leading universities

CHAPTER 23

_____ **12.** What was the Second New Deal?
a. a series of tax laws that primarily benefited the rich
b. a program designed to balance the national budget
c. a repeal of most New Deal policies
d. a wave of legislation including more social welfare benefits

_____ **13.** Which of the following did New Deal programs fail to address?
a. protection of domestic workers
b. low prices for agriculture products
c. the decline of industrial prices
d. Native Americans' need for schools, hospitals, and irrigation systems

_____ **14.** What criticism did many Progressives make of the New Deal?
a. It unfairly taxed successful, hardworking people.
b. It promoted a regimented, militaristic society.
c. It did not do enough to redistribute wealth.
d. Many of its programs smacked of "Bolshevism."

_____ **15.** Why are Huey Long and Father Charles E. Coughlin referred to as demagogues?
a. They manipulated people with half-truths and scare tactics.
b. They called for state ownership of factories and farms.
c. They planned, but did not receive credit for, most New Deal programs.
d. They resorted to bribery in order to pass FDR's programs.

_____ **16.** Which of the following aroused the greatest opposition?
a. the Wagner Act
b. the Social Security system
c. FDR's attempt to "pack" the Supreme Court
d. government funding of the arts

_____ **17.** Why did FDR cut back on expensive relief programs in 1937?
a. He had lost faith in government programs.
b. He was worried about the rising national debt.
c. He wanted to put the money into weapons programs instead.
d. He wanted to lower the Social Security tax.

_____ **18.** Which of the following was part of the New Deal legacy?
a. guaranteed health insurance for all citizens
b. an end to recessions in the economy
c. a restored sense of hope among the people
d. an end to discrimination against African Americans and women

C. Critical Thinking

Answer the following questions on the back of this paper or on a separate sheet of paper. (*24 points*)

19. Determining Relevance The text quotes Harry Hopkins as saying: "Give a man a dole [handout] and you save his body and destroy his spirit. Give him a job and pay him an assured wage and you save both the body and the spirit." Explain the relevance of this way of thinking to the New Deal.

20. **Drawing Conclusions** Why do you think some critics of the New Deal feared that its programs might lead to socialism or communism?

D. Interpreting A Line Graph

Study this line graph showing the number of unemployed people in each year from 1933 to 1940. Then answer questions 21-22 on the back of this page or on a separate piece of paper. *(10 points)*

21. (a) In which year shown was unemployment lowest? (b) About how many people were unemployed that year?
22. How might Roosevelt have used the information in this graph to defend his New Deal programs?

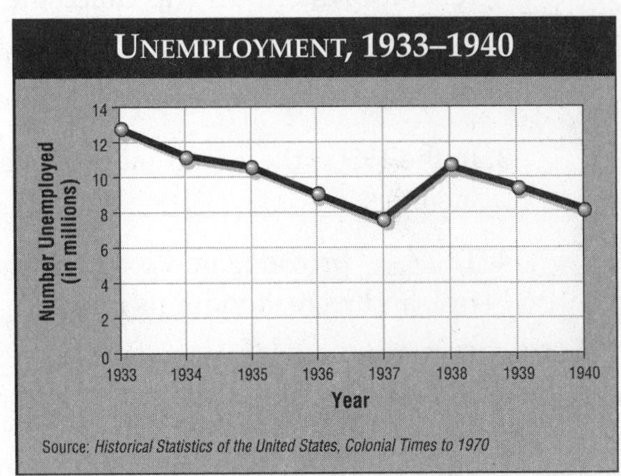

Source: *Historical Statistics of the United States, Colonial Times to 1970*

E. Analyzing A Document

Study this cartoon about President Franklin D. Roosevelt and answer questions 23-24 on the back of this paper or on a separate sheet of paper. (*10 points*)

23. What was the significance of the Supreme Court building outside FDR's door?
24. How does the cartoonist show that many Supreme Court justices were angry at FDR's court-packing attempt?

NAME _______________ CLASS _______________ DATE _______________

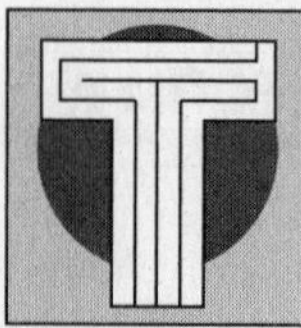

TEST FORM B

The New Deal (1933-1938)

CHAPTER 23

A. Identifying Key Terms, People, and Places

Complete each sentence in Column I by writing the letter of the correct term from Column II in each blank. You will not use all the terms. (*16 points*)

Column I

_____ **1.** FDR's broad program to spur economic recovery and provide relief for Americans was called the ____.

_____ **2.** Early in his administration, FDR pushed many programs through Congress in the period known as the ____.

_____ **3.** In the 1930s, the government sponsored ____ to build public facilities.

_____ **4.** The ____ provided new jobs, cheap electric power, flood control, and recreation for its region.

_____ **5.** The ____ provided federal protection for the activities of labor unions.

_____ **6.** Funded through contributions from employers and workers, the ____ established several types of social insurance.

_____ **7.** A group called the ___ spearheaded much of the opposition to the New Deal.

_____ **8.** The ____ is the total amount of borrowed money that the federal government has yet to repay.

Column II

a. Wagner Act

b. hundred days

c. New Deal

d. nationalization

e. Tennessee Valley Authority

f. national debt

g. revenue

h. public works programs

i. Social Security system

j. American Liberty League

B. Identifying Main Ideas

Write the letter of the correct ending in the blank provided. (*40 points*)

_____ **9.** In his first few months in office, President Roosevelt
- **a.** abolished the banking system and government building projects.
- **b.** avoided direct action and sent problems to committees for study.
- **c.** pushed Congress to pass legislation to improve the economy.
- **d.** concentrated on programs that strengthened big business.

_____ **10.** The National Industrial Recovery Act aimed to help business by
- **a.** removing regulations.
- **b.** bolstering industrial prices.
- **c.** helping industries to get rid of excess workers.
- **d.** giving consumers money to spend.

_____ 11. The "black cabinet" was
- a. an unofficial group of African American office-holders.
- b. a loose coalition of opponents to the New Deal.
- c. the nickname given to Roosevelt advisers Harry Hopkins and Harold Ickes.
- d. African American Cabinet members who opposed the New Deal.

_____ 12. First Lady Eleanor Roosevelt defied tradition by
- a. serving as one of her husband's Cabinet members.
- b. refusing most public appearances.
- c. actively and aggressively promoting the New Deal.
- d. rallying opposition to many of her husband's programs.

_____ 13. The Second New Deal aimed to
- a. relax controls over business.
- b. slow down legislative activity.
- c. lower taxes on the rich.
- d. do more for ordinary Americans.

_____ 14. Many Republicans criticized the New Deal for
- a. going too far in its attempts to reform the economy.
- b. not doing enough to address the nation's ills.
- c. failing to address unemployment.
- d. trying to put an end to the unequal distribution of wealth.

_____ 15. FDR aroused the most opposition when he
- a. failed to balance the budget.
- b. refused to use the militia against the General Motors strike.
- c. attempted to "pack" the Supreme Court.
- d. earmarked WPA funds for the arts.

_____ 16. The recession of 1937 was caused in part by
- a. the sudden collapse of world markets.
- b. crop failures in the Midwest.
- c. increased federal borrowing.
- d. increased consumer spending.

_____ 17. In the short run, the Wagner Act led to
- a. a rise in union membership and a wave of strikes.
- b. a decline in union membership.
- c. rapid unionization of agricultural workers.
- d. an end to the National Labor Relations Board.

_____ 18. In the late 1930s' movies
- a. declined in importance as other art forms received more attention.
- b. almost always focused on the harsh realities of the Depression.
- c. often provided a temporary escape for struggling Americans.
- d. suffered tremendous losses, as very few people could afford to see them.

CHAPTER 23

C. Critical Thinking

Answer the following questions on the back of this paper or on a separate sheet of paper. (24 points)

19. Recognizing Ideologies What beliefs do you think lay beneath New Deal legislation that put women at a disadvantage in the workforce?

20. Checking Consistency Many New Deal programs were biased against African Americans, yet FDR had the support of a large share of African American voters. How can you explain this apparent inconsistency?

D. Interpreting A Line Graph

Study this line graph showing the number of unemployed people in each year from 1933 to 1940. Then answer questions 21-22 on the back of this page or on a separate piece of paper. *(10 points)*

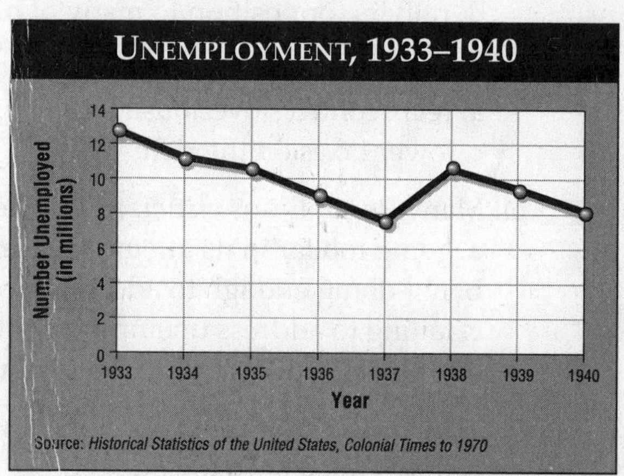

21. (a) In which year shown was unemployment highest? (b) About how many people were unemployed that year?

22. Does the information in this graph suggest that New Deal programs addressing unemployment were successful or unsuccessful? Explain.

E. Analyzing a Document

Study this cartoon about President Franklin D. Roosevelt and answer questions 23-24 on the back of this paper or on a separate sheet of paper. *(10 points)*

23. How can you tell that the valentines in the cartoon were sent to FDR by the Supreme Court?

24. Select one valentine and explain how it relates to FDR's court-packing attempt.

NAME ______________________ CLASS ______________ DATE ______________

TEST FORM A

World War II (1939-1945)

CHAPTER 24

A. Identifying Key Terms, People, and Places

Match the descriptions in Column I with the names in Column II. Write the letter of the correct answer in each blank. You will not use all the names. (*16 points*)

Column I

_____ **1.** Fascist party leader who became dictator of Italy

_____ **2.** leader of the Nazi party in Germany

_____ **3.** leader of the Soviet Union during World War II

_____ **4.** British prime minister during World War II

_____ **5.** American general who commanded Allied forces in the D-Day invasion

_____ **6.** top American general and Army Chief of Staff during World War II

_____ **7.** general who became prime minister of Japan

_____ **8.** President who authorized the dropping of the atomic bomb during World War II

Column II

a. Hideki Tojo
b. Adolph Hitler
c. Joseph Stalin
d. Chester Nimitz
e. George Marshall
f. Harry S. Truman
g. Winston Churchill
h. Benito Mussolini
i. Dwight D. Eisenhower
j. Jiang Jieshi

B. Identifying Main Ideas

Write the letter of the correct answer in the blank provided. (*40 points*)

_____ **9.** What did Italy, Germany, and Japan have in common in the 1930s?
a. They overturned traditional governments and established democracies.
b. They were economic giants and together controlled world trade.
c. They sought to solve their nations' problems through conquest.
d. They angered other nations by their persecution of the Jews.

_____ **10.** Which was part of American policy during the early years of World War II?
a. denouncing Britain and France for declaring war on Germany
b. following a foreign policy of appeasement
c. remaining neutral while making war supplies available to Britain
d. terminating all trade agreements with warring nations

_____ **11.** What prompted the United States to enter the war in 1941?
a. the imprisonment of Jews in German concentration camps
b. the Japanese attack on Pearl Harbor
c. the pact that the Soviet Union signed with Germany
d. Germany's invasion of the Rhineland

_____ **12.** Which of the following best describes "code talkers"?
a. aides to Roosevelt and Churchill who relayed messages between the leaders
b. German Americans who served as translators for the Allies
c. women who worked as airfield control tower operators
d. Navajo radio operators who helped secure communications in the Pacific

_____ **13.** Which of the following took place on D-Day?
a. the last fight to get American supplies across the Atlantic to Britain
b. the first British and American landings in North Africa
c. the start of the Allied invasion of Italy
d. the landing of Allied forces on France's Normandy coast

_____ **14.** In what part of the world were the battles of the Coral Sea, Midway, and Guadalcanal fought?
a. the Atlantic
b. the Pacific
c. the Asian mainland
d. the Italian peninsula

_____ **15.** Which of the following best describes Japanese *kamikazes*?
a. one-man submarines that attacked American ships at Pearl Harbor
b. guerrilla fighters who hid in caves on the Pacific islands
c. bomb-loaded planes whose pilots deliberately crashed into targets
d. guards at the prisoner-of-war camps operated by the Japanese

_____ **16.** What finally brought an end to World War II?
a. a massive Soviet invasion of the Japanese islands
b. the appeasement of Germany
c. a U.S. naval blockade of Japan
d. the dropping of atomic bombs on Hiroshima and Nagasaki

_____ **17.**What is the term used to describe Nazi Germany's systematic annihilation of European Jews?
a. *blitzkrieg*
b. the Holocaust
c. *Kristallnacht*
d. the Manhattan Project

_____ **18.** Who was tried at the Nuremberg Trials?
a. Japanese generals accused of war crimes
b. Soviet soldiers who had helped capture Berlin
c. members of the War Refugee Board
d. Nazi leaders accused of crimes against humanity

C. Critical Thinking

Answer the following questions on the back of this paper or on a separate sheet of paper. (*22 points*)

19. Recognizing Cause and Effect What factors motivated Italian, German, and Japanese leaders to pursue aggressive foreign policies in the 1930s?

20. Demonstrating Reasoned Judgment Do you think the Allies would have won World War II without the aid of the United States? Explain.

D. Interpreting a Map

Use the map to answer questions 21-23. Write your answers on the back of this page or on a separate piece of paper. (*12 points*)

21. Which countries remained neutral during World War II?

22. How did Britain's location help that nation to avoid a German invasion?

23. Why might it have been a mistake for Germany to have broken its pact and invaded the Soviet Union?

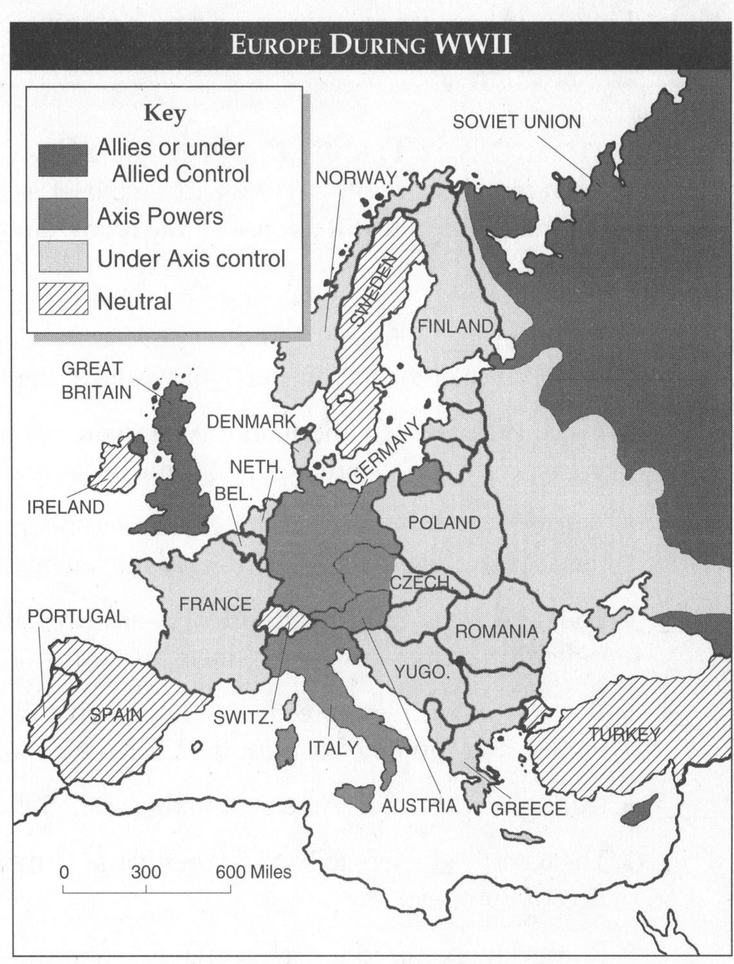

E. Analyzing a Document

The following excerpt comes from a letter that the Chief of Naval Personnel sent to U.S. Navy commandants in June 1945. It deals with a new order to send black and white recruits to the same training camps. Study the excerpt and then answer questions 24-25 on the back of this page or on a separate piece of paper. (*10 points*)

> …[The] Recruiting and Induction Service has been instructed to assign Negroes to Recruit Training Centers on the same basis as whites. The purpose of this change of policy is to obtain more complete utilization of all personnel and facilities.
>
> It is recognized that this policy is at variance with some individual ideas and attitudes. However, at activities where similar experiences have been encountered and met with intelligent and forceful planning and leadership, the results have been satisfactory….

24. Why was the policy changed?

25. To what "individual ideas and attitudes" do you think the writer was referring?

NAME ______________________ CLASS ____________ DATE ____________

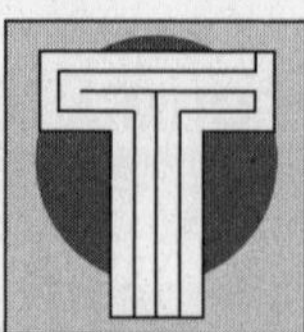

TEST FORM B

World War II (1939-1945)

CHAPTER 24

A. Identifying Key Terms, People, and Places

Complete each sentence in Column I by writing the letter of the correct term from Column II in the blank. You will not use all the terms. (*16 points*)

Column I

_____ **1.** The term ____ refers to a political philosophy that places the importance of the nation above the value of the individual.

_____ **2.** In the 1930s, Britain and France tried to prevent war by following a policy of ____, giving in to some of Germany's demands.

_____ **3.** The term ____ means "lightning war" and refers to Germany's tactic of striking quickly and deeply into enemy territory.

_____ **4.** The ____ authorized the President to aid any nation whose defense was seen as vital to American security.

_____ **5.** The ____, principles agreed to by Roosevelt and Churchill, would later form the basis for the United Nations.

_____ **6.** During World War II, American soldiers called themselves ____.

_____ **7.** The term ____ refers to Nazi Germany's systematic annihilation of European Jews.

_____ **8.** Roosevelt organized the top secret ____ to develop the atomic bomb.

Column II

a. Manhattan Project
b. GIs
c. appeasement
d. Holocaust
e. Atlantic Charter
f. fascism
g. Lend-Lease Act
h. *blitzkrieg*
i. *Kristallnacht*
j. anti-Semitism

B. Identifying Main Ideas

Write the letter of the correct ending in the blank provided. (*40 points*)

_____ **9.** During the 1930s, Hitler, Mussolini, and the military leaders of Japan
a. had a monopoly on world trade.
b. began invading neighboring lands.
c. organized the League of Nations.
d. bolstered national pride by calling for free elections.

_____ **10.** During the early years of World War II, the United States
a. organized several peace talks between the Allies and the Axis powers.
b. stopped trading with all nations at war.
c. tried to remain neutral while supplying weapons to Britain and France.
d. sent military and economic aid to all nations at war.

_____ **11.** Americans fought to keep German submarines from isolating Great Britain in
a. the Battle of Midway. **b.** the Battle of the Atlantic.
c. the Battle of the Coral Sea. **d.** the Battle of Stalingrad.

_____ **12.** The Japanese attack on Pearl Harbor
a. prompted the United States to enter the war.
b. marked the final Japanese victory of the war.
c. did not cause significant damage to American warships or planes.
d. led directly to the liberation of the Philippines.

_____ **13.** V-E Day, May 8, 1945, marked
a. the start of the largest landing by sea in history.
b. the Allied attack on North Africa.
c. the end of the war in Europe.
d. the end of the war in the Pacific.

_____ **14.** With the words "I shall return," General Douglas MacArthur promised to come back to
a. the Philippines. **b.** France.
c. Pearl Harbor. **d.** the Soviet Union.

_____ **15.** An important strategy used by American forces in the Pacific was
a. *blitzkrieg*. **b.** island-hopping.
c. *kamikaze* attacks. **d.** the Bataan Death March.

_____ **16.** After the United States dropped atomic bombs on Hiroshima and Nagasaki,
a. the Soviet Union allied itself with Japan.
b. the League of Nations was created to end global war.
c. the Allied powers divided Japan into peace-keeping zones.
d. Japan accepted American terms for surrender.

_____ **17.** In 1935, the Nazis passed the Nuremberg Laws to
a. send political prisoners to labor camps.
b. strip Jews of their German citizenship.
c. end the requirement that Jews carry identity cards.
d. outlaw the activities of Communists in Poland.

_____ **18.** People considered by the Nazis to be "undesirable" were
a. imprisoned in concentration camps.
b. forced to join *Einsatzgruppen*.
c. offered automatic refuge in the United States.
d. placed in war refugee camps.

C. Critical Thinking

Answer the following questions on the back of this paper or on a separate sheet of paper. (*22 points*)

19. Making Comparisons What similar strategies did leaders in Germany, Italy, and Japan use to transform their nations into strong world powers?

20. Identifying Alternatives What were some alternatives to using the atomic bomb against Japan? Do you think any of these alternatives would have been better than the action taken? Explain why or why not.

TEST FORM B *(continued)*

CHAPTER 24

D. Interpreting a Map

Use the map to answer questions 21-23. Write your answers on the back of this page or on a separate sheet of paper. (*12 points*)

21. Which parts of Europe were under Axis control?

22. How did geography help Great Britain remain free of Axis control?

23. What status did Spain, Sweden, and Turkey have during World War II?

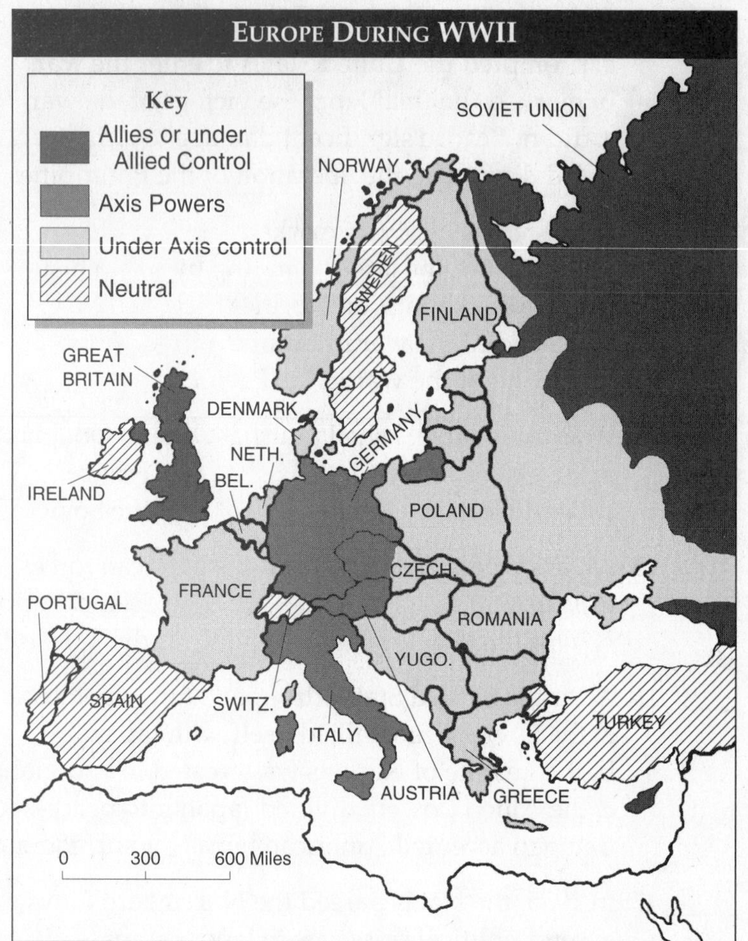

E. Analyzing a Document

The following excerpt comes from a letter that the Chief of Naval Personnel sent to U.S. Navy commandants in June 1945. It deals with a new order to send black and white recruits to the same training camps. Study the excerpt and then answer questions 24-25 on the back of this page or on a separate piece of paper. (*10 points*)

> …[The] Recruiting and Induction Service has been instructed to assign Negroes to Recruit Training Centers on the same basis as whites. The purpose of this change of policy is to obtain more complete utilization of all personnel and facilities.
>
> It is recognized that this policy is at variance with some individual ideas and attitudes. However, at activities where similar experiences have been encountered and met with intelligent and forceful planning and leadership, the results have been satisfactory….

24. How do you know that the writer of the letter expected the new policy to cause problems?

25. What did the writer suggest would solve these problems?

NAME ____________________ CLASS ____________ DATE ____________

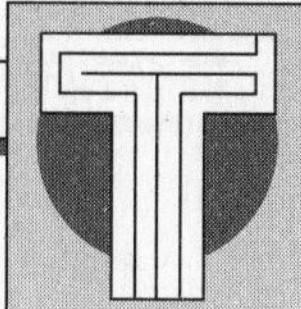

TEST FORM A

CHAPTER 25

World War II at Home (1941-1945)

A. Identifying Key Terms, People, and Places

Match the descriptions in Column I with the terms in Column II. Write the letter of the correct answer in each blank. You will not use all the terms. (*16 points*)

Column I

_____ **1.** vessels built in the United States that usually carried troops or war supplies

_____ **2.** work stoppages organized by workers and not endorsed by unions

_____ **3.** government savings notes bought by Americans to help finance World War II

_____ **4.** home projects that raised vegetables during World War II

_____ **5.** image used to attract women to the wartime work force

_____ **6.** status derived from length of service in a job

_____ **7.** effort launched to win both the war overseas against the Axis powers and the war at home for racial equality

_____ **8.** centers in remote inland areas where Japanese Americans were confined during World War II

Column II

a. internment camps

b. war bonds

c. rations

d. "Double V" campaign

e. wildcat strikes

f. victory gardens

g. U-boats

h. Rosie the Riveter

i. seniority

j. Liberty ships

B. Identifying Main Ideas

Write the letter of the correct answer in the blank provided. (*40 points*)

_____ **9.** Why did President Franklin Roosevelt create the Office of War Mobilization?
a. to replace the Office of Price Administration
b. to centralize agencies dealing with war production
c. to build up wartime morale
d. to reduce the government's role in war production

_____ **10.** How did the government seek to guarantee profits for businesses engaged in war production?
a. by rationing scarce resources
b. by freezing prices of all consumer goods
c. by establishing the "cost-plus" system for military contracts
d. by reducing deficit spending

_____ **11.** Which of the following was an example of deficit spending during the war?
a. raising taxes to finance government programs
b. using a "pay-as-you-go" method of collecting income taxes
c. freezing prices to head off inflation
d. using borrowed money to finance war production

CHAPTER 25

_____ 12. What prevented Americans from spending the high wages they earned in wartime jobs?
a. shortages of consumer items
b. fear of going into debt
c. desire to build up savings after the hardships of the Depression
d. inflated prices for consumer goods

_____ 13. What was the overriding goal of the Office of War Information?
a. to introduce mass production techniques into shipbuilding
b. to develop codes that the enemy could not decipher
c. to boost morale and patriotism on the home front
d. to set up a system of rationing

_____ 14. Which of the following best describes women who went to work during wartime?
a. young and unmarried
b. primarily African American
c. white and middle class
d. of all ages and ethnic and economic backgrounds

_____ 15. In general, how did women's status compare with that of men in the war production work force?
a. Women were paid less for the same work.
b. Women were paid more for the same work.
c. Women were granted more seniority.
d. Women received equal work for equal pay.

_____ 16. Which statement best describes the effect the war had on racial conditions in the United States?
a. It highlighted the injustice of racism in the country.
b. It brought about an end to the Jim Crow system.
c. It improved race relations in the northern and western cities.
d. It improved conditions only for Mexicans and Native Americans.

_____ 17. Which was true of the North during the war years?
a. The Jim Crow system was as strong as it was in the South.
b. There was no legal or actual segregation.
c. African Americans faced discrimination in employment, housing, and education.
d. African Americans received preferential treatment from government agencies.

_____ 18. What led the government to evacuate Japanese Americans from the West Coast?
a. long-held prejudice, and fears inflamed by the Japanese attack on Pearl Harbor
b. terrorist attacks by immigrants living on the West Coast
c. fear for the safety of Japanese Americans on the West Coast
d. refusal of the Nisei to accept United States citizenship

C. Critical Thinking

Answer the following questions on the back of this paper or on a separate sheet of paper. (*22 points*)

19. Identifying Assumptions The Supreme Court ruled in *Korematsu* v. *United States* that the wartime internment of Japanese Americans was justified because of "the military urgency of the situation." What assumptions might have influenced the Court's decision?

20. **Distinguishing False from Accurate Images** Was the image of Rosie the Riveter a false or accurate representation of women doing war production work? Explain your answer.

D. Interpreting Graphs

Use the graphs below to answer questions 21-23. Write your answers on the back of this page or on a separate sheet of paper. *(12 points)*

21. Between which two consecutive years did production of passenger cars undergo the steepest drop?

22. About how many military aircraft were produced in 1944?

23. What was the general relationship between auto production and military aircraft production in the war years?

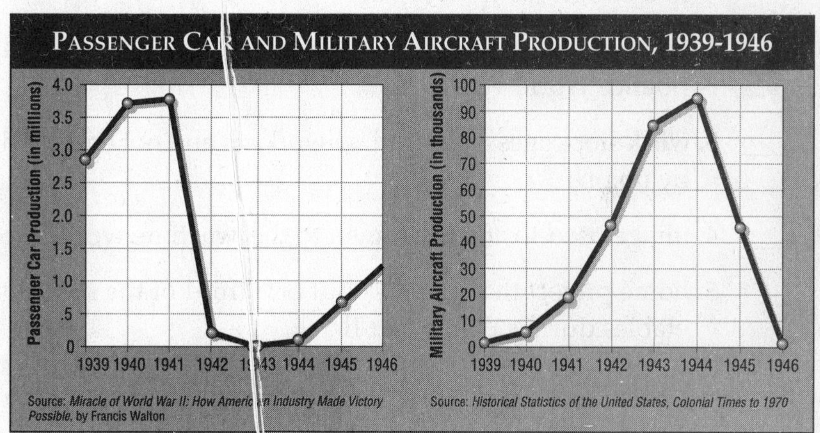

E. Analyzing a Document

Use this poster showing a man in the military and a farmer during World War II to answer questions 24-25. Write your answers on the back of this paper or on a separate sheet of paper. (*10 points*)

24. What was the main idea expressed by the poster?

25. According to the poster, in what way were overalls like a military uniform?

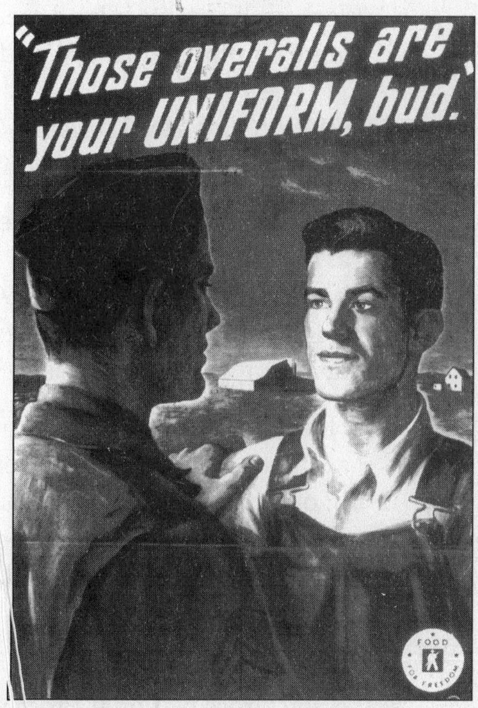

NAME ______________________ CLASS ______________ DATE ______________

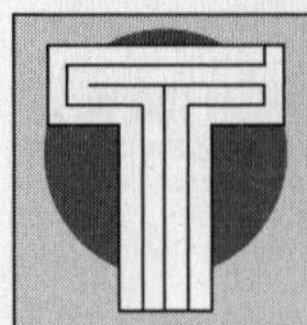

TEST FORM B

World War II at Home (1941-1945)

CHAPTER 25

A. Identifying Key Terms, People, and Places

Match the descriptions in Column I with the terms in Column II. Write the letter of the correct answer in each blank. You will not use all the terms. (*16 points*)

Column I

_____ **1.** Japanese Americans born in the United States of parents who had emigrated from Japan

_____ **2.** government savings notes bought by Americans to help finance World War II

_____ **3.** work stoppages organized by workers and not endorsed by unions

_____ **4.** image used to attract women to the wartime work force

_____ **5.** home project that raised about one third of the nation's vegetables during World War II

_____ **6.** superagency established to centralize agencies dealing with war production

_____ **7.** agency set up to boost Americans' patriotism and sense of participation in the war effort

_____ **8.** centers in remote inland areas where Japanese Americans were confined during World War II

Column II

a. Office of War Mobilization

b. internment camps

c. Nisei

d. "Double V" campaign

e. wildcat strikes

f. victory gardens

g. Office of War Information

h. Rosie the Riveter

i. war bonds

j. Liberty ships

B. Identifying Main Ideas

Write the letter of the correct ending in the blank provided. (*40 points*)

_____ **9.** The United States began to emerge from the depression as a result of
a. freezing rents and prices.
b. producing goods for the Allied forces.
c. increasing production of consumer goods.
d. allocating raw materials.

_____ **10.** Henry Kaiser contributed to wartime production by
a. creating new markets over seas.
b. organizing the War Production Board.
c. using mass production techniques to build Liberty ships.
d. converting automobile plants to aircraft production.

_____ **11.** Financing the war with borrowed money was an example of
a. the cost-plus system. **b.** deficit spending.
c. the Gross National Product. **d.** wartime conversion.

_____ **12.** On the home front, popular culture was characterized by
a. weariness and low spirits. **b.** pessimism and fear.
c. resentment and hostility. **d.** patriotism and high morale.

_____ **13.** The goal of wartime rationing was
a. to speed up war production. **b.** to distribute scarce items fairly.
c. to ensure business profits. **d.** to end racial discrimination.

_____ **14.** Campaigns to collect scrap metal, kitchen fats, and other materials were promoted mainly to
a. keep the people on the home front actively involved in the war effort.
b. create paying jobs for children and older adults.
c. distribute such materials without rationing.
d. lend these supplies to Great Britain and France.

_____ **15.** During wartime, women in the work force were generally paid
a. the same wages as men doing the same job.
b. higher wages than men, to cover child care costs.
c. lower wages than men doing the same jobs.
d. less than they had earned during the Depression.

_____ **16.** The government assumed that after the war most working women would
a. go back to school to learn job skills.
b. become full-time homemakers again.
c. switch to part-time work.
d. continue in their jobs.

_____ **17.** The "Double V" campaign
a. encouraged workers to join labor unions.
b. promoted victory in war and racial equality at home.
c. tried to help keep their jobs after the war ended.
d. motivated Americans to plant gardens to grow their own vegetables.

_____ **18.** On the home front during the war years,
a. racial discrimination in employment practices ended.
b. the Jim Crow system was banned by executive order.
c. segregation ended in northern cities.
d. African Americans took direct action to promote racial equality.

C. Critical Thinking

Answer the following questions on the back of this paper or on a separate sheet of paper. (*20 points*)

19. Demonstrating Reasoned Judgment How do you think World War II might have changed American women's attitudes toward their roles in the work-place?

TEST FORM B *(continued)*

20. Checking Consistency Were the United States goals overseas consistent or inconsistent with its goals on the home front? Explain.

D. Interpreting Graphs

Use the graphs below to answer questions 21-23. Write your answers on the back of this page or on a separate sheet of paper. *(12 points)*

21. In which year shown were the fewest passenger cars produced?

22. About how many military aircraft were produced in 1943?

23. How were the trends shown in the two graphs related?

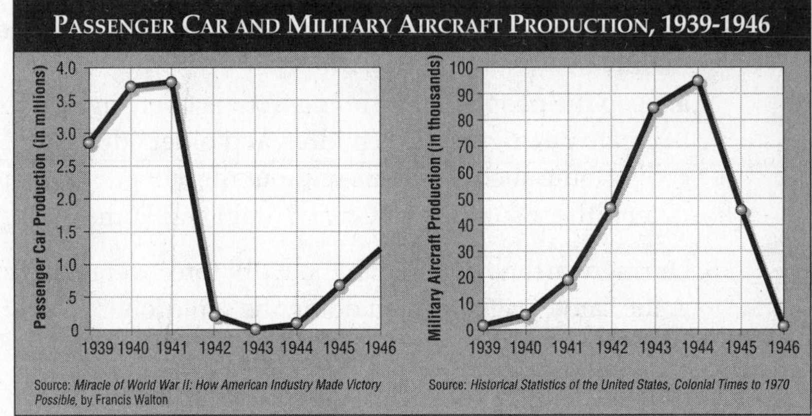

E. Analyzing a Document

Use this poster showing a man in the military and a farmer during World War II to answer questions 24-25. Write your answers on the back of this paper or on a separate sheet of paper. (*12 points*)

24. How does the slogan "FOOD FOR FREEDOM," found in the circle in the bottom right corner of the poster, relate to the poster's main message?

25. What assumption do you think the artist made about farmers in creating this poster?

NAME ________________ CLASS ________ DATE ________

TEST FORM A

The Cold War (1945–1960)

A. Identifying Key Terms, People, and Places

Complete each sentence by circling the correct name in parentheses. (*16 points*)

1. In 1946, (*Winston Churchill, Harry Truman*) proclaimed that an iron curtain separated communist Eastern Europe from capitalist Western Europe.

2. (*Vyacheslav Molotov, Josip Broz [Tito]*) defied Stalin and ruled Yugoslavia relatively free of Soviet interference.

3. Secretary of State (*George C. Marshall, Joseph McCarthy*) drafted a plan to help European nations rebuild after World War II.

4. American General (*Douglas MacArthur, George Patton*) led United Nations forces during the Korean War.

5. (*Mao Zedong, Jiang Jieshi*) led the Communist forces that took control of China in 1949.

6. The trial and execution of (*Pat McCarran, Ethel and Julius Rosenberg*) in 1953 intensified the fear of communism as an internal threat to the United States.

7. In 1959, revolutionary leader (*Fulgencio Batista, Fidel Castro*) overthrew the Cuban dictatorship.

8. Secretary of State (*John Foster Dulles, Whittaker Chambers*) made it clear that the United States would risk war to protect its national interests, a policy known as brinkmanship.

B. Identifying Main Ideas

Write the letter of the correct answer in the blank provided. (*40 points*)

_____ **9.** Disagreement over which issue worsened post-war relations between the United States and the Soviet Union?
- **a.** the United Nations charter
- **b.** Soviet sympathy for Nazi Germany
- **c.** the future of Poland
- **d.** the discovery of Russian spies in California

_____ **10.** Which of the following best describes satellite nations?
- **a.** nations in debt to the World Bank
- **b.** nations that belonged to NATO
- **c.** nations west of the iron curtain
- **d.** nations dominated by the Soviet Union

_____ **11.** What did President Truman promise in the Truman Doctrine?
- **a.** to support nations trying to resist Soviet control.
- **b.** to fight hunger anywhere in the world.
- **c.** to enforce the American foreign policy of brinkmanship.
- **d.** to reject the former policy of containment.

TEST FORM A *(continued)*

_____ **12.** How did the Soviet Union react to the Marshall Plan?
a. The Soviet Union offered to share the plan's cost with the United States.
b. The Soviet Union refused to participate in the plan.
c. The Soviet Union condemned the plan as unrealistic.
d. The Soviet Union offered Western Europe a competing plan.

_____ **13.** The Berlin airlift was President Truman's response to the
a. reunification of East and West Germany.
b. German development of the atomic bomb.
c. Soviet blockade of West Berlin.
d. construction of the Berlin wall.

_____ **14.** In response to the formation of NATO, the Soviet Union
a. created the Warsaw Pact. **b.** left the United Nations.
c. ended the Berlin airlift. **d.** joined the Marshall Plan.

_____ **15.** Members of the House Un-American Activities Committee (HUAC) charged numerous Hollywood figures with
a. promoting anti-Semitism. **b.** avoiding the issue of racism.
c. spying for the Soviet Union. **d.** being sympathetic to communist ideas.

_____ **16.** What was the outcome of the Korean War?
a. Korea was unified under a communist government.
b. North Korea surrendered after the threat of atomic warfare.
c. Korea remained divided at almost exactly the same place as before the war.
d. China controlled North Korea while South Korea remained independent.

_____ **17.** What impact did Joseph McCarthy have on American society?
a. He encouraged a widespread fear of communism.
b. He strengthened the United States Army.
c. He encouraged Americans to stand up for their civil rights.
d. He created opposition to United States involvement in Latin American affairs.

_____ **18.** Which of the following is a reason the United States became involved in affairs in the Middle East following World War II?
a. to limit Jewish immigration into the region
b. to prevent oil-rich Arab nations from falling under Soviet influence
c. to discourage the founding of a Jewish homeland in the region
d. to overthrow dictatorships in Arab nations

C. Critical Thinking

Answer the following questions on the back of this paper or on a separate sheet of paper. (*24 points*)

19. Demonstrating Reasoned Judgment How do you think the leaders of the Soviet Union viewed the formation of the Marshall Plan and NATO? Support your answer.

20. Checking Consistency Explain how United States foreign policy during the Cold War was consistent in Asia, the Middle East, and Latin America. Give one example from each region.

D. Using Map Skills

Use the map to answer questions 21–22. Write your answers on the lines provided. (*10 points*)

21. Name three European nations that were not members of NATO or the Warsaw Pact in 1955.

______

______

______

22. Other than the Soviet Union, name four Warsaw Pact nations.

______

______

______

______

E. Analyzing a Document

This excerpt is from President Truman's "Truman Doctrine" speech, made to Congress in March 1947. Read it and then answer questions 23–24 on the back of this paper or on a separate sheet of paper. (*10 points*)

> "Nearly every nation must choose between alternative ways of life. The choice is too often not a free one. One way of life is based on the will of the majority....The second way of life is based upon the will of a minority forcibly imposed [forced] upon the majority....I believe that it must be the policy of the United States to support free peoples who are resisting attempted subjugation [conquest] by armed minorities or by outside pressures. I believe that we must assist free peoples to work out their own destinies in their own way."

23. When Truman used the phrase "alternate ways of life," what two ways of life was he talking about?

24. What did Truman mean when he said, "The choice is too often not a free one"?

NAME ______________________ CLASS ______________ DATE ______________

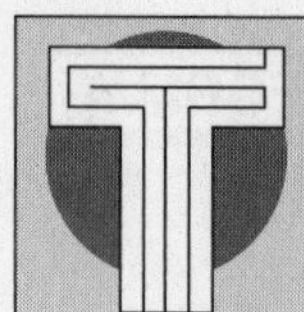

TEST FORM B

The Cold War (1945–1960)

CHAPTER 26

A. Identifying Key Terms, People, and Places

Complete each sentence in Column I by writing the letter of the correct term from Column II in the blank provided. You will not use all the terms. (*20 points*)

Column I

_____ **1.** A(n) ____ in Eastern Europe was controlled politically and economically by the Soviet Union.

_____ **2.** The ____ was the imaginary line that divided Europe between capitalist West and communist East.

_____ **3.** The term ____ refers to the competition that developed between the United States and the Soviet Union for power and influence in the world.

_____ **4.** After World War II, American leaders developed a policy of ____ to resist and stop the spread of communism.

_____ **5.** The ____ pledged American financial aid to all European nations following World War II.

_____ **6.** The ____ provided vital supplies to a region blockaded by the Soviet Union.

_____ **7.** In the late 1940s, the ____ investigated the motion picture industry for communist influences.

_____ **8.** A(n) ____ shows the names of people whom employers agree not to hire.

_____ **9.** According to the ____, if one country falls to communism, its neighbors will soon follow.

_____ **10.** The struggle between the United States and the Soviet Union to gain weapons superiority was the ____.

Column II

a. NATO

b. Marshall Plan

c. arms race

d. iron curtain

e. domino theory

f. blacklist

g. Berlin airlift

h. containment

i. Truman Doctrine

j. HUAC

k. Cold War

l. brinkmanship

m. satellite nation

B. Identifying Main Ideas

Write the letter of the correct ending in the blank provided. (*32 points*)

_____ **11.** At the Yalta conference, Roosevelt, Churchill, and Stalin decided to
- **a.** keep the Soviet Union out of the war with Japan.
- **b.** divide the defeated Germany into four sectors—American, British, French, and Soviet.
- **c.** rearm Germany as soon possible.
- **d.** set up a world organization that would share knowledge of atomic weapons.

_____ **12.** As World War II ended, a major disagreement between the United States and the Soviet Union involved

a. Soviet domination of Poland.
b. the division of Latin America.
c. the role of Britain in postwar Europe.
d. the wording of the United Nations charter.

_____ **13.** Which was an immediate result of the Truman Doctrine?

a. Congress approved $400 million to help Turkey and Greece resist Soviet influence.
b. The state of Israel was founded.
c. The Soviet Union took control over Yugoslavia.
d. Congress established the House Un-American Activities Committee (HUAC).

_____ **14.** The Berlin airlift began when

a. West Berliners began fleeing into East Berlin.
b. the British and French had a dispute over German zone boundaries.
c. the Soviets blocked Allied access to West Berlin.
d. the Marshall Plan ended.

_____ **15.** The North Atlantic Treaty Organization (NATO) was based on the principle of

a. free trade.
b. collective security.
c. appeasement.
d. isolationism.

_____ **16.** As a result of the Korean War, the United States succeeded in

a. keeping South Korea free of communism.
b. unifying Korea under a democratic government.
c. ending communism in Southeast Asia.
d. pushing Chinese troops out of North Korea.

_____ **17.** Both President Truman's Federal Employee Loyalty Program and Senator Joseph McCarthy's hearings aimed to

a. fight discrimination in government jobs.
b. defend Americans' civil liberties.
c. reinvigorate the American economy.
d. expose Communists in the United States.

_____ **18.** During the Cold War, a major goal of United States policy in Latin America was to

a. build nuclear weapons bases in Central America.
b. encourage the countries of Latin America to join the United Nations.
c. protect American financial investments in Latin America.
d. prevent Fidel Castro from taking over Cuba.

C. Critical Thinking

Answer the following questions on the back of this paper or on a separate sheet of paper. (*24 points*)

19. Determining Relevance How were the Truman Doctrine and the Marshall Plan relevant to the American foreign policy goal of containment?

CHAPTER 26

20. Recognizing Cause and Effect Explain how the contrasting post-World War II goals of the Soviet Union and the United States led to the Cold War.

D. Using Map Skills

Use the map to answer questions 21-22. Write your answers on the lines provided. (*12 points*)

21. By 1955, into what two military camps was Europe divided?

____

____

22. What was the post-war military status of Germany?

____

____

____

____

____

____

E. Analyzing a Document

This excerpt is from President Truman's "Truman Doctrine" speech, made to Congress in March 1947. Read it and then answer questions 23-24 on the back of this paper or on a separate sheet of paper. (*12 points*)

> "Nearly every nation must choose between alternative ways of life. The choice is too often not a free one. One way of life is based on the will of the majority.... The second way of life is based upon the will of a minority forcibly imposed [forced] upon the majority ....I believe that it must be the policy of the United States to support free peoples who are resisting attempted subjugation [conquest] by armed minorities or by outside pressures. I believe that we must assist free peoples to work out their own destinies in their own way."

23. Of the two ways of life Truman discussed, which one did the United States support?

24. How did Truman propose to show this support?

TEST FORM A

CHAPTER 27

The Postwar Years at Home (1945-1960)

A. Identifying Key Terms, People, and Places

Complete each sentence in Column I by writing the letter of the correct term in Column II in the blank provided. You will not use all the terms. (*16 points*)

Column I

_____ **1.** From 1945 to 1960, the average income per person, or _____, nearly doubled.

_____ **2.** A giant corporation becomes a _____ by investing in a wide range of businesses that produce different kinds of goods and services.

_____ **3.** A(n) _____ gives a group or individual the right to market a company's goods or services.

_____ **4.** A tiny circuit that improved the transmission of electronic signals is called a(n) _____.

_____ **5.** The high birth rate that followed World War II continued the _____ that had begun during the war.

_____ **6.** In 1944, Congress passed the _____ to give World War II veterans benefits like college tuition and low-interest mortgage loans.

_____ **7.** President Eisenhower's conservative approach to government was known as _____.

_____ **8.** The process of bringing together different races is known as _____.

Column II

a. transistor
b. franchise
c. beatnik
d. per capita income
e. modern republicanism
f. baby boom
g. GI Bill
h. conglomerate
i. National Defense Education Act
j. integration
k. gross national product

B. Identifying Main Ideas

Write the letter of the correct ending in the blank provided. (*40 points*)

_____ **9.** During the postwar years, the gross national product of the United States
a. more than doubled. **b.** returned to Depression levels.
c. shrank by half. **d.** stayed about the same.

_____ **10.** One effect of business expansion after World War II was
a. lower wages for most workers.
b. the weakening of labor unions.
c. a shift in the work force from blue-collar to white-collar jobs.
d. a major decline in working conditions for most Americans.

_____ **11.** One long-lasting effect of the major highway-building projects of the 1950s was
a. a reduction in the number of cars built.
b. less reliance on the public transportation system.
c. a shrinkage of the trucking industry.
d. the disappearance of suburban housing.

_____ 12. Unlike Betty Friedan, pediatrician Benjamin Spock believed that women should
a. stay home with their children.
b. contribute to the family income.
c. remain mainly in teaching and nursing.
d. explore creative new roles for themselves.

_____ 13. The beatniks of the 1950s promoted
a. traditional social patterns.
b. family values.
c. segregation of African Americans.
d. spontaneity over conformity.

_____ 14. One of President Truman's greatest challenges in reconverting to a peacetime economy was
a. keeping inflation in check.
b. appeasing women who lost their jobs to returning soldiers.
c. securing passage of the Taft-Hartley Act.
d. encouraging mass production of consumer goods.

_____ 15. The 1957 launching of *Sputnik*
a. proved the superiority of American technology.
b. greatly increased Eisenhower's popularity.
c. plunged the United States into a series of three recessions.
d. caused Congress to increase spending on teaching science and mathematics.

_____ 16. Jackie Robinson, Thurgood Marshall, Rosa Parks, and Martin Luther King, Jr,. were alike in that they
a. helped ignite a religious revival in the 1950s.
b. were the first African Americans to play professional sports.
c. fought the government's reconversion policies.
d. took actions to end segregation.

_____ 17. In 1954, the Supreme Court ruled in *Brown* v. *Board of Education* that
a. bus segregation was unconstitutional.
b. the federal government must increase financial aid to education.
c. segregation was no longer permissible in public schools.
d. the government must provide loans to low-income college students.

_____ 18. President Eisenhower placed the Arkansas National Guard under federal command to
a. integrate Central High School.
b. end the bus boycott.
c. protect Mexican American rights.
d. end segregation in the armed forces.

C. Critical Thinking

Answer the following questions on the back of this paper or on a separate sheet of paper. (*22 points*)

19. Demonstrating Reasoned Judgment How did the development of franchises encourage nationwide businesses while sometimes discouraging local businesses?

20. Recognizing Ideologies In what way was President Eisenhower's approach to government similar to the ideologies of the Republican Presidents of the 1920s? How did his approach differ?

D. Reading a Table

Examine the table below. Then write your answers to questions 21-22 on the back of this paper or on a separate sheet of paper. (*12 points*)

21. Based on the data in this table, why did Congress pass the Taft-Hartley Act in 1947?

22. Explain whether you think the Taft-Hartley Act was successful or unsuccessful in curbing labor strikes.

	Work Stoppages	Workers Involved (in thousands)	Percent of Total Workers Employed
1945	4,750	3,470	8.2
1946	4,985	4,600	10.5
1947	3,693	2,170	4.7
1948	3,419	1,960	4.2
1949	3,606	3,030	6.7
1950	4,843	2,410	5.1
1951	4,737	2,220	4.5
1952	5,117	3,540	7.3
1953	5,091	2,400	4.7
1954	3,468	1,530	3.1
1955	4,320	2,650	5.2
1956	3,825	1,900	3.6

Source: Bureau of the Census

E. Analyzing a Document

The excerpt below comes from the Supreme Court's 1954 decision in *Brown* v. *Board of Education*. Read it and then answer questions 23-24 on the back of this paper or on a separate sheet of paper. (*10 points*)

> Today, education . . . is the very foundation of good citizenship. . . a principal instrument in awakening the child to cultural values, in preparing him for later professional training . . . . It is doubtful that any child may reasonably be expected to succeed in life if he is denied the opportunity of an education. Such an opportunity must be made available to all on equal terms.
>
> . . . Does segregation of children in public schools solely on the basis of race deprive the children of minority groups of equal educational opportunities? We believe that it does . . .
>
> To separate them from others of similar age and qualifications solely because of their race generates a feeling of inferiority . . . that may affect their hearts and minds in a way unlikely ever to be undone.

23. The Court cited several reasons why education is so important to a democratic society. Identify the one you think most important and explain why.

24. Why did the Court think that education is "a right which must be available to all on equal terms"?

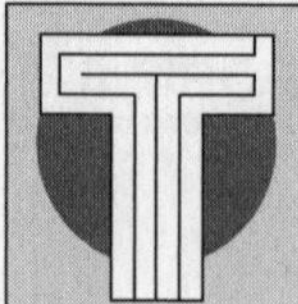

TEST FORM B

The Postwar Years at Home (1945-1960)

CHAPTER 27

A. Identifying Key Terms, People, and Places

Match the descriptions in Column I with the names in Column II. Write the letter of the correct answer in each blank. You will not use all the names. (*16 points*)

Column I

_____ **1.** doctor who developed a vaccine against polio

_____ **2.** developer who mass-produced new communities in suburbs

_____ **3.** pediatrician who wrote a highly influential book on child care

_____ **4.** author of *The Feminine Mystique*

_____ **5.** Democratic candidate for President in 1952 and 1956

_____ **6.** Eisenhower's vice-presidential running mate

_____ **7.** first African American to play major league baseball

_____ **8.** spokesperson for the Montgomery bus boycott

Column II

a. Richard M. Nixon

b. Adlai Stevenson

c. William J. Levitt

d. Jackie Robinson

e. Betty Friedan

f. Benjamin Spock

g. Jonas Salk

h. J. D. Salinger

i. Martin Luther King, Jr.

j. Rosa Parks

B. Identifying Main Ideas

Write the letter of the correct answer in the blank provided. (*40 points*)

_____ **9.** How did the gross national product and per capita income change in the 1950s?
- **a.** The gross national product increased while per capita income decreased.
- **b.** Both gross national product and per capita income fell sharply.
- **c.** Both gross national product and per capita income increased dramatically.
- **d.** The gross national product decreased while per capita income increased.

_____ **10.** What effect did conglomerates and the franchise system have on the American economy in the 1950s?
- **a.** They inadvertently slowed industrial growth.
- **b.** They promoted diversity and individualism within the business world.
- **c.** They contributed to major business expansion.
- **d.** They eliminated thousands of service-oriented, white-collar jobs.

_____ **11.** What major effect did the transistor have on technology?
- **a.** It made nuclear power possible.
- **b.** It ended the popularity of radio.
- **c.** It reduced the size of electronic appliances.
- **d.** It temporarily slowed the development of new technology.

_____ 12. What roles were most American women expected to fulfill in the 1950s?
a. active politicians **b.** full-time homemakers
c. leaders in social causes **d.** second income earners

_____ 13. Which of the following best describes the beatniks of the 1950s?
a. They rebelled against conformity and traditional social patterns.
b. They worked to revive organized religion.
c. They organized campaigns against racial injustice.
d. They valued American middle-class culture above diverse cultural heritages.

_____ 14. Why did Congress pass the Taft-Hartley Act in 1947?
a. to protect union officials against undue invasion of privacy
b. to raise wages
c. to increase unemployment benefits
d. to restrict labor strikes that threatened the national interest

_____ 15. Which of the following factors made it seem that Harry Truman had little chance of winning reelection in 1948?
a. He had lost some support in his own party.
b. He had opposed the Taft-Hartley Act.
c. He had received illegal gifts.
d. His campaign style was dull.

_____ 16. How did President Eisenhower's domestic policy reflect that of his Republican predecessors Coolidge and Hoover?
a. He encouraged the growth of unions. **b.** He favored big business.
c. He favored a national health plan. **d.** He discouraged highway building.

_____ 17. Why did Branch Rickey, the general manager of the Brooklyn Dodgers, choose Jackie Robinson to break the color line in baseball?
a. Robinson had proven his ability to tolerate racial injustice.
b. Robinson had a record of standing up against racial injustice.
c. Robinson promised he would act violently against those who insulted him.
d. Robinson was the first African American to join the armed forces.

_____ 18. What role did Rosa Parks play in the struggle for equal rights?
a. She helped the Montgomery bus boycott.
b. She argued the case of *Brown* v. *Board of Education*.
c. She took part in desegregating Central High School in Little Rock, Arkansas.
d. She was a leader in the Native American movement for equal rights.

C. Critical Thinking

Answer the following questions on the back of this paper or on a separate sheet of paper. (*22 points*)

19. Identifying Assumptions What assumption did President Truman make about what the American people wanted when he introduced his Fair Deal in late 1945 and early 1946?

CHAPTER 27

20. Recognizing Cause and Effect What effect did developments in technology have on the American way of life in the 1950s?

D. Reading a Table

Examine the table below. Then write your answers to questions 21-22 on the back of this paper or on a separate sheet of paper. (*12 points*)

21. What data from the table might have been used to convince members of Congress to support the Taft-Hartley Act in 1947?

22. Use the information in the table to agree or disagree with the following statement: Workers were more content during Eisenhower's first term (1953-1956) than during the Truman years (1945-1952).

	Work Stoppages	Workers Involved (in thousands)	Percent of Total Workers Employed
1945	4,750	3,470	8.2
1946	4,985	4,600	10.5
1947	3,693	2,170	4.7
1948	3,419	1,960	4.2
1949	3,606	3,030	6.7
1950	4,843	2,410	5.1
1951	4,737	2,220	4.5
1952	5,117	3,540	7.3
1953	5,091	2,400	4.7
1954	3,468	1,530	3.1
1955	4,320	2,650	5.2
1956	3,825	1,900	3.6

Source: Bureau of the Census

E. Analyzing a Document

The excerpt below comes from the Supreme Court's decision in *Brown* v. *Board of Education*. Read it and then answer questions 23-24 on the back of this paper or on a separate sheet of paper. (*10 points*)

> Today, education . . . is the very foundation of good citizenship. . . a principal instrument in awakening the child to cultural values, in preparing him for later professional training . . . . It is doubtful that any child may reasonably be expected to succeed in life if he is denied the opportunity of an education. Such an opportunity must be made available to all on equal terms.
>
> . . . Does segregation of children in public schools solely on the basis of race deprive the children of minority groups of equal educational opportunities? We believe that it does . . .
>
> To separate them from others of similar age and qualifications solely because of their race generates a feeling of inferiority . . . that may affect their hearts and minds in a way unlikely ever to be undone.

23. What reasons did the Court give to justify its statement that "it is doubtful that any child may reasonably be expected to succeed in life if he is denied the opportunity of an education"?

24. Why did the Court conclude that segregated education deprives minority children of equal educational opportunities?

NAME ______________________ CLASS ______________ DATE ______________

TEST FORM A

The Kennedy and Johnson Years (1960-1968)

CHAPTER 28

A. Identifying Key Terms, People, and Places

Use each key term in a sentence that shows the meaning of the term. (*21 points*)

1. mandate ______________________

2. Great Society ______________________

3. Volunteers in Service to America (VISTA) ______________________

4. Immigration Act of 1965 ______________________

5. Medicaid ______________________

6. Cuban Missile Crisis ______________________

7. Limited Test Ban Treaty ______________________

B. Identifying Main Ideas

Write the letter of the correct ending in the blank provided. (*33 points*)

_____ **8.** During the 1960 presidential campaign, John F. Kennedy promised to
a. win the Cold War against the Soviet Union.
b. cut back dramatically on military spending.
c. get the American economy moving again.
d. abolish the Electoral College.

_____ **9.** Kennedy won the 1960 election by a
a. landslide.
b. mandate.
c. very slim margin.
d. vote in the House of Representatives.

_____ **10.** In 1961, President Kennedy committed NASA and the nation to the goal of
a. expanding the nation's highway system.
b. landing a man on the moon within the decade.
c. replacing Fidel Castro with Fulgencio Batista as ruler of Cuba.
d. overhauling the nation's military forces.

_____ **11.** The Warren Commission declared that Kennedy's assassination was the work of a
a. large, organized conspiracy.
b. CIA-directed plot.
c. gang sent from Cuba.
d. lone assassin.

_____ **12.** Unlike Kennedy, President Lyndon B. Johnson
a. had a strong mandate.
b. was more concerned with foreign than domestic policy.
c. believed military commanders should use nuclear weapons.
d. opposed civil rights legislation.

_____ 13. Which of the following was a major part of Johnson's Great Society?
- a. a tax increase.
- b. aid to foreign countries.
- c. health care legislation.
- d. reductions in antipoverty programs.

_____ 14. Several of the important decisions of the Supreme Court under Chief Justice Earl Warren focused on
- a. protecting the constitutional rights of citizens accused of crimes.
- b. declaring Great Society legislation unconstitutional.
- c. continuing segregation policies in American public schools.
- d. medical care for the poor and the elderly.

_____ 15. Critics of the Great Society complained that it
- a. helped only the middle class.
- b. gave the federal government too much authority.
- c. spent too little money.
- d. gave local communities too much governmental power.

_____ 16. After Kennedy authorized a military buildup to show that the United States would not be bullied by the Soviet Union, the Soviets
- a. tried to invade West Germany.
- b. placed a blockade around West Berlin.
- c. began construction of the Berlin Wall.
- d. forced UN troops from East Germany.

_____ 17. As a result of the Cuban Missile Crisis,
- a. Fidel Castro was removed from power.
- b. the United States set up missile sites in Cuba.
- c. the United States increased investments in Cuba.
- d. the Soviets removed their missiles from Cuba.

_____ 18. Kennedy established the Alliance for Progress in the Western Hemisphere to
- a. replace the Monroe Doctrine.
- b. discourage the spread of communism.
- c. promote procommunist revolutionary movements in Latin America.
- d. end American involvement in South Vietnam.

C. Critical Thinking

Answer the following questions on the back of this paper or on a separate sheet of paper. (*22 points*)

19. Determining Relevance In what way was President Johnson's Great Society a continuation of President Kennedy's New Frontier?

20. Checking Consistency How was President Kennedy's foreign policy consistent with the United States' Cold War goal of containing communism?

D. Interpreting a Table

Use the table to answer questions 21-22. Write your answers on the back of this paper or on a separate sheet of paper. (*12 points*)

Social Welfare Expenditures in the United States, 1950–1975

	Expenditures per capita (in constant 1984 dollars)			Expenditures as percentage of GNP		
Fiscal Year	All social welfare programs	Social insurance	Public welfare	All social welfare programs	Social insurance	Public welfare
1950	630	133	75	8.2	1.7	1.0
1960	984	346	94	10.3	3.8	1.0
1965	1189	432	119	11.2	4.1	1.1
1970	1773	660	229	14.7	5.5	1.9
1975	2424	1026	389	19.0	8.1	2.9

Note: Social insurance includes all social security programs, including Medicare, public employee retirement, and unemployment insurance. Public welfare includes cash public assistance, Medicaid, food stamps, and public housing. Health and education expenditures are included in "All social welfare programs."

Source: Ann Kallman Bixby, "Public Welfare Expenditures, Fiscal Year 1984," *Social Security Bulletin* 50, no. 6 (June 1987).

21. President Johnson launched the "War on Poverty" in 1964. How did the program affect expenditures per capita for all social welfare programs from 1965-1975?

22. By 1975, how much greater was the percentage of GNP spent on social insurance programs than that spent on public welfare programs?

E. Analyzing a Document

The excerpt below comes from a speech that President Kennedy delivered in June 1963 dealing with relations between the United States and the Soviet Union. Read it and then answer questions 23-24 on the back of this paper or on a separate sheet of paper. (*12 points*)

> History teaches that enmities [conflicts] between nations, as between individuals, do not last forever. . . the tide of time and events will often bring surprising changes in the relations between nations and neighbors.
>
> …We are both devoting massive sums of money to weapons that could be better devoted to combating ignorance, poverty, and disease. We are both caught up in a vicious and dangerous cycle in which suspicion on one side breeds suspicion on the other and new weapons beget counterweapons….
>
> Agreements to this end [arms limitations] are in the interests of the Soviet Union as well as ours….

23. According to Kennedy, why do relations between countries change?

24. Why did he think that ending the Cold War would benefit both sides?

NAME ______________________ CLASS ______________ DATE ______________

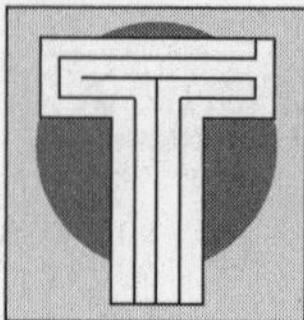

TEST FORM B

The Kennedy and Johnson Years (1960-1968)

CHAPTER 28

A. Identifying Key Terms, People, and Places

Use each key term in a sentence that shows the meaning of the term. *(21 points)*

1. New Frontier ______________________
2. Medicare ______________________
3. Miranda rule ______________________
4. Bay of Pigs invasion ______________________
5. Berlin Wall ______________________
6. Alliance for Progress ______________________
7. Peace Corps ______________________

B. Identifying Main Ideas

Write the letter of the correct answer in the blank provided. *(33 points)*

_____ **8.** Which best describes the state of the American economy in 1960?
- **a.** shrinking dramatically
- **b.** sluggish, with low GNP growth
- **c.** booming, with high GNP growth
- **d.** rapidly growing per capita income

_____ **9.** Which of the following was not a goal of the New Frontier program?
- **a.** to cut taxes
- **b.** to empower big business
- **c.** to provide aid to the poor
- **d.** to promote the space program

_____ **10.** Which of the following best describes Kennedy's domestic policy success?
- **a.** Congress supported nearly all his programs, but most were failures.
- **b.** He had won a popular mandate that made passage of his programs easy.
- **c.** He rarely succeeded in pushing legislation through Congress.
- **d.** He launched a remarkable reform program that altered American society.

_____ **11.** What did the Warren Commission decide about the Kennedy assassination?
- **a.** The assassination had been authorized by the CIA.
- **b.** Kennedy was killed by one man who had worked alone.
- **c.** Communist sympathizers had helped plan the assassination.
- **d.** Industrial leaders had plotted the murder.

_____ **12.** Which of the following best describes the Great Society?
- **a.** It won passage of several New Frontier goals and added to them.
- **b.** It threw out New Frontier measures and replaced them all.
- **c.** It lacked any support in Congress.
- **d.** It cut back considerably on federal government spending.

_____ 13. What was the effect of the tax-cut bill that Johnson got Congress to pass?
a. The unemployment rate increased. **b.** GNP rose steadily.
c. The federal deficit grew quickly. **d.** Inflation rose dramatically.

_____ 14. What was the intent of the Immigration Act of 1965, which was passed during the Johnson administration?
a. to increase the number of immigrants from northern and western Europe
b. to eliminate quotas restricting immigration from certain countries
c. to reduce the total annual number of immigrants to the United States
d. to stem the flow of political refugees to the United States

_____ 15. What effect did Supreme Court decisions on apportionment bring about?
a. People accused of a crime must be informed of their rights.
b. Low-cost health insurance must be provided for the poor.
c. Electoral districts had to be redrawn based on "one person, one vote."
d. Criminal suspects must be given legal aid free if they cannot afford it.

_____ 16. President Kennedy asked for a huge increase in military spending because
a. he was afraid that the Soviet Union planned to take over Europe.
b. the Soviet Union continually attacked American ships.
a. he wanted to compete with the Soviet Union's space program successes.
d. he wanted to attack Cuba.

_____ 17. Which of the following brought the United States and the Soviet Union to the brink of nuclear war?
a. the Cuban Missile Crisis **b.** the signing of the Limited Test Ban Treaty
c. the Panamanian riot **d.** the Bay of Pigs invasion

_____ 18. Which of the following best describes the major guiding principle behind the foreign policies of Kennedy and Johnson?
a. to keep European nations out of Latin American
b. to stifle Asian trade to benefit European trade
c. to make peace with the Soviet Union
d. to stop the spread of communism

C. Critical Thinking

Answer the following questions on the back of this paper or on a separate sheet of paper. (*22 points*)

19. Making Comparisons Why was President Johnson more successful than President Kennedy in pushing his measures through Congress?

20. Drawing Conclusions At the end of the Cuban Missile Crisis, Secretary of State Dean Rusk remarked to President Kennedy, "We have won a considerable victory. You and I are still alive." State in your own words what Rusk meant.

TEST FORM B *(continued)*

D. Interpreting a Table

Use the table to answer questions 21-22. Write your answers on the back of this paper or on a separate sheet of paper. (*12 points*)

Social Welfare Expenditures in the United States, 1950–1975

	Expenditures per capita (in constant 1984 dollars)			Expenditures as percentage of GNP		
Fiscal Year	All social welfare programs	Social insurance	Public welfare	All social welfare programs	Social insurance	Public welfare
1950	630	133	75	8.2	1.7	1.0
1960	984	346	94	10.3	3.8	1.0
1965	1189	432	119	11.2	4.1	1.1
1970	1773	660	229	14.7	5.5	1.9
1975	2424	1026	389	19.0	8.1	2.9

Note: Social insurance includes all social security programs, including Medicare, public employee retirement, and unemployment insurance. Public welfare includes cash public assistance, Medicaid, food stamps, and public housing. Health and education expenditures are included in "All social welfare programs."

Source: Ann Kallman Bixby, "Public Welfare Expenditures, Fiscal Year 1984," *Social Security Bulletin* 50, no. 6 (June 1987).

21. President Johnson launched the "War on Poverty" in 1964. How did this program affect expenditures on public welfare programs from 1965-1975?

22. What information from the table might some Americans have used to support their claim that social welfare programs were a drain on the economy?

E. Analyzing a Document

The excerpt below comes from a speech that President Kennedy delivered in June 1963 dealing with relations between the United States and the Soviet Union. Read it and then answer questions 23-24 on the back of this paper or on a separate sheet of paper. (*12 points*)

> History teaches that enmities [conflicts] between nations, as between individuals, do not last forever. . . the tide of time and events will often bring surprising changes in the relations between nations and neighbors.
>
> ...We are both devoting massive sums of money to weapons that could be better devoted to combating ignorance, poverty, and disease. We are both caught up in a vicious and dangerous cycle in which suspicion on one side breeds suspicion on the other and new weapons beget counterweapons....
>
> Agreements to this end [arms limitations] are in the interests of the Soviet Union as well as ours....

23. Did Kennedy believe that the Cold War led to a positive or a negative use of economic resources? Explain.

24. Was Kennedy correct about enmities between nations not lasting forever? Explain.

NAME _______________ CLASS _______________ DATE _______________

TEST FORM A

The Civil Rights Movement (1954–1968)

CHAPTER 29

A. Identifying Key Terms, People, and Places

Match the descriptions in Column I with the terms in Column II. Write the letter of the correct answers in the blank provided. You will not use all the terms. (*20 points*)

Column I

_____ **1.** civil rights organization founded in 1942 and dedicated to effecting change through peaceful confrontation

_____ **2.** civil rights organization founded by African American ministers in 1957

_____ **3.** protest technique in which African Americans occupied a segregated establishment and demanded service

_____ **4.** civil rights workers traveling on interstate buses to protest segregation at terminals

_____ **5.** a year-long campaign of protest marches against racial injustice in Georgia

_____ **6.** legislation that banned discrimination in all public facilities

_____ **7.** legislation that enabled more African Americans to register to vote

_____ **8.** actual, as opposed to legal, separation of whites and African Americans

_____ **9.** African American group founded by Elijah Muhammad that preached black separation and self-help

_____ **10.** the idea that African Americans should unite, take pride in their heritage, and control their own organizations

Column II

a. sit-in
b. de jure segregation
c. black power
d. Freedom Rides
e. March on Washington
f. Nation of Islam
g. Congress of Racial Equality (CORE)
h. Albany Movement
i. de facto segregation
j. Civil Rights Act of 1964
k. Southern Christian Leadership Conference (SCLC)
l. Voting Rights Act of 1965
m. Student Nonviolent Coordinating Committee (SNCC)

B. Identifying Main Ideas

Write the letter of the correct ending in the blank provided. (*32 points*)

_____ **11.** To achieve victory in the struggle for civil rights, Martin Luther King, Jr., and other members of the SCLC encouraged a policy of
a. armed confrontation. **b.** nonviolent protest.
c. lawsuits. **d.** national strikes.

_____ **12.** SNCC was formed to enable students to
a. use more peaceful tactics than the SCLC.
b. shift the civil rights movement to the North.
c. make their own decisions about priorities and tactics.
d. establish a more interracial organization.

CHAPTER 29

_____ 13. Martin Luther King, Jr., targeted Birmingham, Alabama, for demonstrations because he considered it
a. the most segregated city in the country.
b. a city with very little segregation.
c. a city that practiced de facto segregation.
d. a city that would welcome an end to segregation.

_____ 14. After watching television coverage of the brutal tactics used against protesters by the Birmingham police, even opponents of the civil rights movement were
a. appalled by the police violence.
b. angry with the peaceful protesters.
c. supportive of the actions of the police.
d. uninterested in the confrontation.

_____ 15. Participants in the 1963 March on Washington hoped to
a. get "Bull" Connor prosecuted for police brutality.
b. convince Congress to pass civil rights legislation.
c. prevent the reelection of President Kennedy.
d. do battle with the police of Washington, D.C.

_____ 16. After Congress passed the Voting Rights Act of 1965,
a. the civil rights movement slowly ended.
b. white Southerners still prevented most African Americans from voting.
c. many African Americans were elected to office at all levels.
d. the Supreme Court declared the law unconstitutional.

_____ 17. The black power movement taught that African Americans should
a. separate from white society and lead their own communities.
b. strive to end segregation.
c. emigrate to Africa.
d. use nonviolent protest to bring about change.

_____ 18. In his writings, James Baldwin warned Americans that
a. African Americans should not be allowed to vote.
b. desegregation would only lead to greater problems.
c. the Nation of Islam should be banned.
d. African Americans were angry and tired of promises.

C. Critical Thinking

Answer the following questions on the back of this paper or on a separate sheet of paper. (*24 points*)

19. Making Comparisons On the issue of segregation, compare the views of Martin Luther King, Jr., to those of Malcolm X.

20. Checking Consistency Explain how the Student Nonviolent Coordinating Committee (SNCC) changed between the early 1960s and the late 1960s.

CHAPTER 29

D. Interpreting Maps

Examine the maps below. Then write your answers to questions 21–22 on the back of this paper or on a separate sheet of paper. (*12 points*)

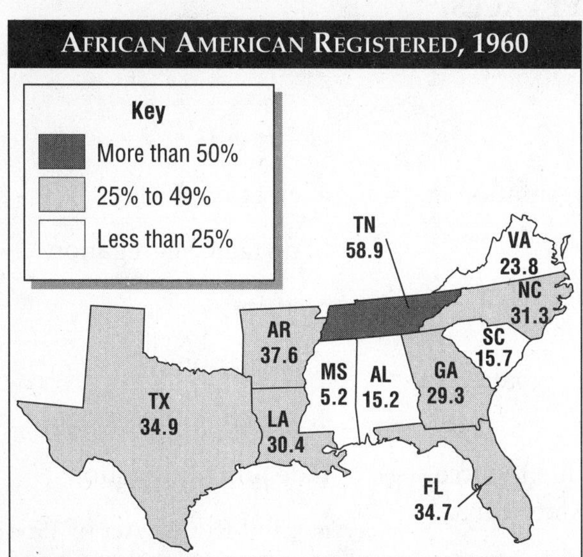

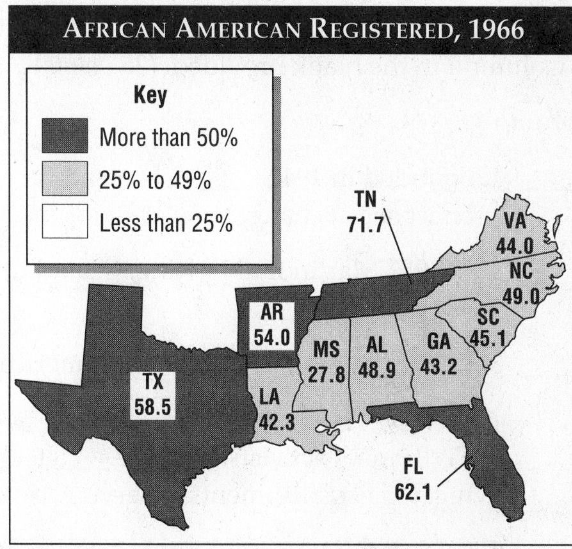

21. Which state had the lowest registration of African American voters in 1960?

22. Based on the maps, would you say that the civil rights movement was successful in the 1960s? Explain.

E. Analyzing a Document

This excerpt is taken from a speech that President Johnson delivered to Congress in support of the Voting Rights Act in March 1965. Read it and then answer questions 23-24 on the back of this paper or on a separate sheet of paper. (*12 points*)

> The Constitution says that no person shall be kept from voting because of his race or his color. We have all sworn an oath before God to support and defend that Constitution. We must now act in obedience to that oath... It is wrong—deadly wrong—to deny any of your fellow Americans the right to vote in this country. There is no issue of States' rights or National rights. There is only the struggle for human rights.

23. Why did Johnson urge members of Congress to support this bill?

24. Did Johnson believe the issue of State's rights was relevant to the voting rights debate? Explain.

NAME ______________________ CLASS ______________ DATE ______________

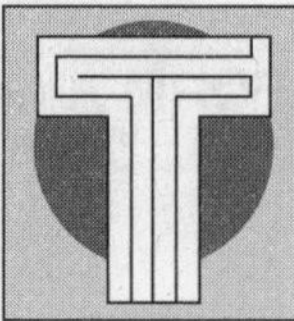

TEST FORM B

The Civil Rights Movement (1954–1968)

CHAPTER 29

A. Identifying Key Terms, People, and Places

Complete each sentence by writing the letter of the correct term from Column II in Column I in the blank provided. (*20 points*)

Column I

_____ **1.** Founded in 1942, ____ used peaceful confrontation to effect social change.

_____ **2.** In 1957 Martin Luther King, Jr., and other ministers founded the ____.

_____ **3.** The ____ gave young African Americans a greater voice in the civil rights movement.

_____ **4.** Civil rights activists used the ____ technique to force segregated establishments to serve African Americans.

_____ **5.** During the ____, civil rights activists used interstate buses to protest segregation at terminals.

_____ **6.** In August 1963, more than 200,000 joined the ____ in support of civil rights legislation.

_____ **7.** The ____ banned discrimination in all public facilities.

_____ **8.** As a result of the ____, the number of elected African American officials increased.

_____ **9.** The rigid pattern of separation dictated by law in the South was known as ____ .

_____ **10.** Stokely Carmichael called on African Americans to support ____ .

Column II

a. Freedom Rides

b. de facto segregation

c. sit-in

d. black power

e. March on Washington

f. de jure segregation

g. Civil Rights Act of 1964

h. Nation of Islam

i. Congress of Racial Equality (CORE)

j. Southern Christian Leadership Conference (SCLC)

k. Voting Rights Act of 1965

l. Albany Movement

m. Student Nonviolent Coordinating Committee (SNCC)

B. Identifying Main Ideas

Write the letter of the correct answer in the blank provided. (*32 points*)

_____ **11.** How did the National Urban League help African Americans?

a. by helping newcomers to large cities find homes and jobs
b. by providing legal support to defend them in court
c. by providing them with good medical care
d. by helping them to integrate lunch counters

_____ **12.** In what way were the SCLC and CORE alike?

a. Both relied on militant tactics.
b. Both were founded by church leaders.
c. Both promoted nonviolent protest.
d. Neither was interracial.

_____ **13.** In which state did Freedom Riders encounter violent resistance?
a. Michigan
b. California
c. Alabama
d. West Virginia

_____ **14.** How did President Kennedy respond to the riot over James Meredith's admission to the University of Mississippi?
a. He ignored the riot.
b. He blamed civil rights activists.
c. He condemned the university but did not interfere with local officials.
d. He sent army troops to restore order and protect Meredith.

_____ **15.** Which was a highlight of the March on Washington?
a. Martin Luther King, Jr.'s "I Have a Dream" speech
b. President Johnson's "Great Society" speech
c. President Kennedy's "New Frontier" speech
d. Stokely Carmichael's "Black Power" speech

_____ **16.** What was the goal of the Selma March?
a. to integrate bus terminal lunch counters
b. to get more low-cost housing built
c. to get voting rights legislation passed
d. to protest "Bull" Connor's tactics

_____ **17.** What did Malcolm X encourage African Americans to do?
a. to fight for greater integration with white society
b. to separate themselves from white society
c. to love and pray for white people
d. to abandon violent, militant tactics in favor of civil disobedience

_____ **18.** Which of the following was a result of the civil rights movement?
a. The federal government rebuilt the nation's ghettos.
b. De facto segregation ended in the North.
c. Racism in the South came to an end.
d. Thousands of African Americans could vote for the first time.

C. Critical Thinking

Answer the following questions on the back of this paper or on a separate sheet of paper. (*24 points*)

19. Recognizing Cause and Effect How did President Kennedy's policies on civil rights change between 1961 and 1963? What caused this change?

20. Testing Conclusions Your text states that the civil rights movement was "a grassroots effort of ordinary citizens determined to end racial injustice in the United States." What evidence would you give to support this statement?

TEST FORM B *(continued)*

CHAPTER 29

D. Interpreting Maps

Examine the maps below. Then write your answers to questions 21–22 on the back of this paper or on a separate sheet of paper. (*12 points*)

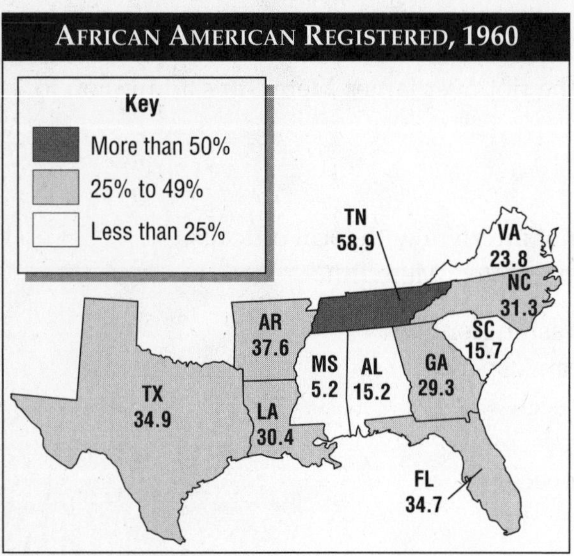

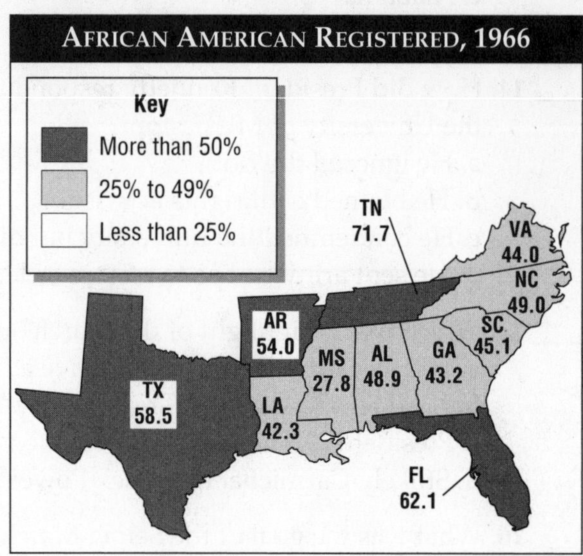

21. Which state had the highest registration of African American voters in 1960?

22. What evidence on the map supports the argument made by some African Americans that the civil rights movement did not make enough progress in the 1960s?

E. Analyzing a Document

This excerpt is taken from a speech that President Johnson delivered to Congress in support of the Voting Rights Act in March 1965. Read it and then answer questions 23–24 on the back of this paper or on a separate sheet of paper. (*12 points*)

> The Constitution says that no person shall be kept from voting because of his race or his color. We have all sworn an oath before God to support and defend that Constitution. We must now act in obedience to that oath… It is wrong—deadly wrong—to deny any of your fellow Americans the right to vote in this country. There is no issue of States' rights or National rights. There is only the struggle for human rights.

23. What does the Constitution say about voting rights?

24. Why did Johnson feel that Congress had to support the Voting Rights Act?

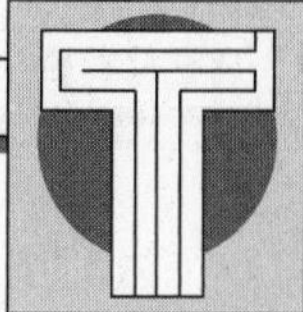

TEST FORM A

Other Social Movements (1960–1975)

A. Identifying Key Terms, People, and Places

Explain the main goal of each of the following. (*18 points*)

1. National Organization for Women (NOW)

____

____

2. Equal Rights Amendment (ERA)

____

____

3. United Farm Workers (UFW)

____

____

4. Japanese American Citizens League (JACL)

____

____

5. American Indian Movement (AIM)

____

____

6. Environmental Protection Agency (EPA)

____

____

B. Identifying Main Ideas

Write the letter of the correct ending in the blank provided. (*40 points*)

_____ **7.** Feminism describes the theory that
- **a.** women are better at doing most jobs than men.
- **b.** women and men should have political, economic, and social equality.
- **c.** the government should not involve itself in matters that concern women.
- **d.** women must occupy the roles of wife and homemaker.

_____ **8.** In the 1960s, the feminist movement grew in part as a result of
- **a.** the publication of *Ladies' Home Journal.*
- **b.** the *Roe* v. *Wade* decision.
- **c.** Betty Friedan's book *The Feminine Mystique.*
- **d.** the encouragement of Phyllis Schlafly.

_____ **9.** Many women rejected the women's movement because they
- **a.** thought it too weak to succeed.
- **b.** feared it was illegal.
- **c.** wanted to achieve equality on their own.
- **d.** preferred traditional roles.

CHAPTER 30

_____ 10. In the United States the Latino population is best described as made up
- **a.** only of Chicanos.
- **b.** of Spanish-speakers with origins in Latin America.
- **c.** only of people with origins in Puerto Rico and Cuba.
- **d.** of those Spanish-speakers who live in the Northeast.

_____ 11. To help improve conditions for migrant farm workers, César Chávez organized
- **a.** a march on Washington.
- **b.** a suit in the Supreme Court.
- **c.** consumer boycotts of produce picked on nonunion farms.
- **d.** the Mexican American Legal Defense and Education Fund.

_____ 12. Today, Native Americans are legally recognized citizens of
- **a.** their own or tribal groups only.
- **b.** their tribal groups and the United States.
- **c.** the United States only.
- **d.** North America.

_____ 13. Native American activism of the 1960s was driven by the desire to
- **a.** retain Native American lands and exercise self-government.
- **b.** make reservations part of mainstream American society.
- **c.** dissolve centuries-old treaties with the federal government.
- **d.** make new treaties with the federal government over unclaimed land.

_____ 14. The 1973 occupation of Wounded Knee by AIM activists was most successful in
- **a.** improving Native Americans' public image.
- **b.** gaining full citizenship rights for Native Americans.
- **c.** forcing the federal government to reexamine Native American treaty rights.
- **d.** encouraging industries to relocate to the Pine Ridge reservation.

_____ 15. Rachel Carson's *Silent Spring* focused national attention on the
- **a.** harmful effect of chemical pesticides.
- **b.** health hazards caused by air pollution.
- **c.** proper disposal of toxic wastes.
- **d.** problems of nuclear power plants.

_____ 16. In the 1960s, Ralph Nader became well known for
- **a.** setting up the Food and Drug Administration.
- **b.** pressuring car manufacturers to produce safer cars.
- **c.** blocking the ratification of the ERA.
- **d.** lobbying for conservation legislation in Washington, D.C.

C. Critical Thinking

Answer the following questions on the back of this paper or on a separate sheet of paper. (*22 points*)

17. Distinguishing False from Accurate Images In the 1960s, what kind of image of women did NOW activists consider "false"? What kind of image of women would NOW have considered "accurate"?

18. Recognizing Cause and Effect How did the civil rights movement influence the movements of other minorities and women?

D. Interpreting a Table

Examine the table below. Then write your answers to questions 21–22 on the back of this paper or on a separate sheet of paper. (*10 points*)

Median Earnings of Men and Women in the United States, 1960 to 1990

Year	Women	Men	Women's earnings as a percent of men's	Earnings gap in constant 1990 dollars
1960	$ 3,257	$ 5,368	60.7	$ 8,569
1970	5,323	8,966	59.4	11,529
1980	11,197	18,612	60.2	11,776
1990	19,822	27,678	71.6	7,856

Source: Bureau of the Census

19. How can you tell that women made little progress toward fair pay during the 1970s, despite the fact that their earnings more than doubled?

20. Which decade might equal rights activists label as the "best" decade for women's earnings? Explain.

E. Analyzing a Document

Shirley Chisholm was the first African American woman elected to the House of Representatives. Below is an excerpt from a 1969 speech she gave to Congress in support of the Equal Rights Amendment. Read it and then answer questions 21–22 on the back of this paper or on a separate sheet of paper. (*10 points*)

> Prejudice against blacks is becoming unacceptable although it will take years to eliminate it. But it is doomed because, slowly, white America is beginning to admit that it exists. Prejudice against women is still acceptable. There is very little understanding yet of the immorality involved in double pay scales and the classification of most of the better jobs as "for men only"....
>
> As in the field of equal rights for blacks, Spanish-Americans, the Indians, and other groups, laws will not change such deep-seated problems overnight. But they can be used to provide protection for those who are most abused, and to begin the process of evolutionary change by compelling the insensitive majority to reexamine its unconscious attitudes.

21. What did Representative Chisholm believe was the first step toward solving problems of prejudice?

22. Did she believe that the ERA would provide a quick solution to the problem of inequality? Explain.

NAME ______________________ CLASS ______________ DATE ______________

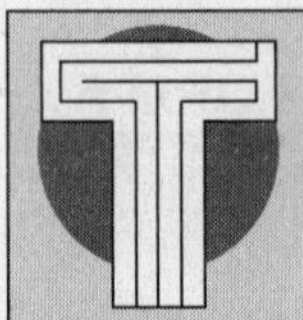

TEST FORM B

Other Social Movements (1960–1975)

CHAPTER 30

A. Identifying Key Terms, People, and Places

Match the descriptions in Column I with the names in Column II. Write the letter of the correct answer in each blank. You will not use all the names. (*16 points*)

Column I

_____ **1.** journalist who helped found *Ms.* magazine for women interested in feminist issues

_____ **2.** conservative political activist who led a national campaign to block ratification of the Equal Rights Amendment (ERA)

_____ **3.** Spanish-speaking Americans with origins in Latin America

_____ **4.** Mexican-Americans

_____ **5.** founder of the United Farm Workers (UFW)

_____ **6.** leader of the Native American activist movement in the late 1960s and early 1970s

_____ **7.** marine biologist who wrote *Silent Spring*

_____ **8.** attorney who attacked the auto industry in *Unsafe at Any Speed*

Column II

a. Gloria Steinem

b. César Chávez

c. Dennis Banks

d. Rachel Carson

e. Latinos

f. Phyllis Schlafly

g. Chicanos

h. feminists

i. Ralph Nader

j. Henry González

B. Identifying Main Ideas

Write the letter of the correct answer in the blank provided. (*40 points*)

_____ **9.** In what way did the civil rights movement help the women's movement in the 1960s?
a. It paved the way for ratification of the Equal Rights Amendment.
b. It inspired women and provided them with a model.
c. It encouraged women to maintain their traditional roles in society.
d. It gave the women's movement *Ms.* magazine.

_____ **10.** Which of the following was a main goal of the National Organization for Women (NOW) in the 1960s and 1970s?
a. to gain equal job opportunities for women
b. to overturn the *Roe* v. *Wade* decision
c. to promote traditional images of women
d. to exempt women from military combat

_____ **11.** Why was ratification of the Equal Rights Amendment (ERA) important to NOW members?
a. It would provide a legal guarantee of equal opportunities for women.
b. It would legalize "consciousness-raising" groups.
c. It would outlaw legal segregation.
d. It would prohibit discrimination based on race.

_____ 12. What tactic did the United Farm Workers (UFW) use in the fight for higher wages and improved working conditions?
a. They established their own "police" force.
b. They organized consumer boycotts.
c. They staged standoffs with the federal government.
d. They destroyed crops.

_____ 13. Which issue was a top priority for Japanese American activists after World War II?
a. citizenship rights
b. local control of public schools
c. compensation for losses during internment
d. integration into mainstream society

_____ 14. How did the demands of Native American activists differ from those of other minority groups?
a. Native Americans wanted citizenship rights.
b. Native Americans wanted autonomy over their lands.
c. Native Americans did not want government aid.
d. Native Americans wanted to dissolve all treaties with the federal government.

_____ 15. In what way was Native American occupation of Alcatraz a success?
a. It caused the federal government to grant the island to Native Americans.
b. It prevented any bloodshed at Wounded Knee.
c. It drew national attention to Native American grievances.
d. It won American citizenship for the Native Americans.

_____ 16. Which of the following was a direct result of the publication of *Silent Spring*?
a. opposition to nuclear power plants
b. conservation of farmlands
c. restrictions on the use of chemical pesticides
d. establishment of tree-planting programs

_____ 17. What was the chief goal of the Nuclear Regulatory Commission (NRC)?
a. to ensure that nuclear power plants were operated safely
b. to regulate the use of atomic weapons
c. to eliminate the use of nuclear power gradually
d. to outlaw the use of nuclear power

_____ 18. Which of the following is an example of legislation passed as a result of consumer movement activism?
a. the Civil Rights Act of 1964 **b.** the Equal Rights Amendment
c. the Clean Water Act **d.** the Wholesome Meat Act of 1967

C. Critical Thinking

Answer the following questions on the back of this paper or on a separate sheet of paper. (*24 points*)

19. Identifying Central Issues Which issues were central to the movements of women and minority groups in the 1960s?

20. Testing Conclusions Your text states that Native Americans faced "unique problems" in the United States. What unique problem did Native Americans face?

D. Interpreting a Table

Examine the table below. Then write your answers to questions 21-22 on the back of this paper or on a separate sheet of paper. (*10 points*)

Median Earnings of Men and Women in the United States, 1960 to 1990

Year	Women	Men	Women's earnings as a percent of men's	Earnings gap in constant 1990 dollars
1960	$ 3,257	$ 5,368	60.7	$ 8,569
1970	5,323	8,966	59.4	11,529
1980	11,197	18,612	60.2	11,776
1990	19,822	27,678	71.6	7,856

Source: Bureau of the Census

21. How did the income of working women compare with that of working men during the 1960s?

22. During which decade did women make the greatest strides toward equality in wages?

E. Analyzing a Document

Shirley Chisholm was the first African American woman elected to the House of Representatives. Below is an excerpt from a 1969 speech she gave to Congress in support of the Equal Rights Amendment. Read the excerpt and then answer questions 23-24 on the back of this paper or on a separate sheet of paper. (*10 points*)

> Prejudice against blacks is becoming unacceptable although it will take years to eliminate it. But it is doomed because, slowly, white America is beginning to admit that it exists. Prejudice against women is still acceptable. There is very little understanding yet of the immorality involved in double pay scales and the classification of most of the better jobs as "for men only"....
>
> As in the field of equal rights for blacks, Spanish-Americans, the Indians, and other groups, laws will not change such deep-seated problems overnight. But they can be used to provide protection for those who are most abused, and to begin the process of evolutionary change by compelling the insensitive majority to reexamine its unconscious attitudes.

23. Why did Representative Chisholm believe that prejudice against African Americans was doomed?

24. What did she believe the ERA could accomplish?

NAME ______________________ CLASS ______________ DATE ______________

TEST FORM A

The Vietnam War and American Society (1960–1975)

CHAPTER 31

A. IDENTIFYING KEY TERMS, PEOPLE, AND PLACES

Match the descriptions in Column I with the terms in Column II. Write the letter of the correct answer in the blank provided. You will not use all the terms. (*10 points*)

Column I

_____ **1.** congressional act giving the President nearly complete control over United States military actions in Vietnam

_____ **2.** major Viet Cong attack on towns, cities, and American bases throughout South Vietnam

_____ **3.** incident in which American troops killed from 175 to 400 Vietnamese villagers

_____ **4.** counterculture Music and Art Fair

_____ **5.** policy of replacing American forces with South Vietnamese soldiers

Column II

a. Tet Offensive

b. Geneva Conference

c. Vietnamization

d. New Left

e. Woodstock festival

f. Gulf of Tonkin Resolution

g. My Lai massacre

Complete each sentence in Column I by writing the letter of the correct term from Column II in the blank. You will not use all the terms. (*10 points*)

Column I

_____ **6.** In 1964, President Johnson began a military ____, or expansion of American involvement, in the Vietnam War.

_____ **7.** College professors held ____ in which they expressed opinions about the Vietnam War.

_____ **8.** Young men who opposed fighting in a war on moral or religious grounds were ____.

_____ **9.** College students could postpone being drafted into military service by getting a(n) ____.

_____ **10.** Like the Beat Generation of the 1950s, the ____ of the 1960s rejected conventional customs.

Column II

a. conscientious objectors

b. napalm

c. deferment

d. escalation

e. teach-ins

f. counterculture

TEST FORM A (continued)

CHAPTER 31

B. Identifying Main Ideas

Write the letter of the correct ending in the blank provided. (*32 points*)

_____ **11.** President Kennedy's policy in Vietnam was to
a. send 100,000 troops to South Vietnam.
b. increase the number of American military advisers.
c. gain the loyalty of the Viet Cong.
d. support the efforts of Ho Chi Minh.

_____ **12.** Escalation of the war in Vietnam began with the
a. My Lai massacre.
b. passage of the Gulf of Tonkin Resolution.
c. formation of the Viet Cong.
d. publication of the Pentagon Papers.

_____ **13.** American soldiers fighting in Vietnam had to cope with
a. lack of training.
b. tropical infections and booby traps.
c. a lack of sophisticated equipment.
d. working side by side with Communists.

_____ **14.** Civilians in both North Vietnam and South Vietnam had to suffer the effects of American efforts to destroy road and bridges through
a. Vietnamization.
b. guerrilla warfare.
c. saturation bombing.
d. sniper fire.

_____ **15.** In the United States, television was instrumental in
a. promoting understanding between Americans and the Vietnamese.
b. developing enthusiasm for the American war effort in Vietnam.
c. bringing the brutality of the war into people's living rooms.
d. revealing the contents of classified military documents.

_____ **16.** Some Americans questioned the fairness of the draft because
a. the government refused to draft African Americans.
b. only men between the ages of eighteen and twenty-six were drafted.
c. college students could easily avoid the draft.
d. women were drafted along with men.

_____ **17.** After Woodstock and Altamont, many conservative Americans
a. applauded the changes that hippies were trying to make in society.
b. adopted the new lifestyles they saw developing around them.
c. condemned the rejection of traditional morals and values.
d. offered their support for legalizing psychedelic drugs.

_____ **18.** The Vietnam War finally ended in 1975 when
a. North Vietnam surrendered.
b. U.S. forces invaded Cambodia.
c. Nixon signed a peace treaty with North Vietnam.
d. North Vietnam gained control over all of Vietnam.

C. Critical Thinking

Answer the following questions on the back of this paper or on a separate sheet of paper. (*24 points*)

19. Identifying Assumptions Before the Vietnam War, what assumptions did American leaders make about the ability of the United States to stop communism anywhere in the world? How did these assumptions change after the war?

20. Identifying Central Issues Identify one antiwar argument made by protesters of the Vietnam War, and one pro-war argument made by supporters of the war.

D. Reading a Chart

Use the chart to answer questions 21-23. (*12 points*)

21. In which year was there the greatest number of American troops in Vietnam?

______

22. How many additional military personnel were sent to Vietnam in 1966?

______

23. In which year did the policy of Vietnamization begin? How can you tell?

______

______

______

______

______

U.S. Military Personnel Assigned in Vietnam as of December 31

Year	Total	Net Change
1964	23,300	+7,000
1965	184,300	+161,000
1966	385,300	+201,000
1967	485,600	+100,300
1968	536,100	+50,500
1969	475,200	-68,200
1970	334,600	-140,600
1971	156,800	-177,800
1972	24,200	-132,600

Source: DOD/OASD

E. Analyzing a Document

Below is a statement by President Lyndon Johnson. Read it and then answer questions 24-25 on the back of this paper or on a separate sheet of paper. (*12 points*)

> The Communists' desire to dominate the world is just like the lawyer's desire to be the ultimate judge on the Supreme Court or the politician's desire to be President. You see, the Communists want to rule the world, and if we don't stand up to them, they will do it. And we'll be slaves. Now I'm not one of these folks seeing Communists under every bed. But I do know about the principles of power, and when one side is weak, the other steps in.

24. Why did Johnson believe it was important to "stand up" to Communists?

25. How does the above statement help explain American involvement in Vietnam?

NAME ______________________ CLASS ____________ DATE ____________

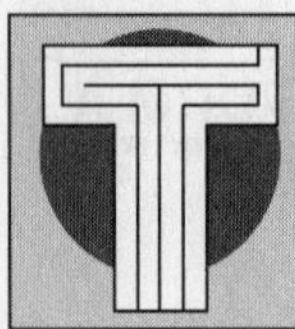

TEST FORM B

The Vietnam War and American Society (1960–1975)

CHAPTER 31

A. Identifying Key Terms, People, and Places

Complete each sentence in Column I by writing the letter of the correct term from Column II in the blank. You will not use all the terms. (*10 points*)

Column I

_____ **1.** Communist guerrillas called the ____ fought to gain control of South Vietnam.

_____ **2.** North Vietnamese troops and supplies poured into South Vietnam via the ____.

_____ **3.** During the ____, mounted during the Vietnamese New Year, many cities and military bases in South Vietnam were attacked by Communist forces.

_____ **4.** The brutality of the American soldiers who killed Vietnamese villagers during the ____ shocked many Americans.

_____ **5.** In 1969, about 400,000 people gathered to attend the ____, a Music and Art Fair in upstate New York.

Column II

a. Ho Chi Minh Trail

b. Geneva Conference

c. Viet Cong

d. My Lai massacre

e. Woodstock festival

f. Tet Offensive

Match the descriptions in Column I with the terms in Column II. Write the letter of the correct answer in the blank provided. You will not use all the terms. (*10 points*)

Column I

_____ **6.** expansion of the war effort

_____ **7.** political movement which believed that problems of racism and poverty called for radical changes in American society

_____ **8.** proceedings during which professors and others aired opinions about the Vietnam War

_____ **9.** person who resists fighting a war on moral or religious grounds

_____ **10.** 1960s social movement that rejected conventional customs and ways of life

Column II

a. napalm

b. New Left

c. teach-in

d. counterculture

e. conscientious objector

f. escalation

B. Identifying Main Ideas

Write the letter of the correct answer in the blank provided. (*32 points*)

_____ **11.** What did the United States fear would happen if it did not get involved in Vietnam?
a. Diem would be assassinated. **b.** The French would control the country.
c. Vietnam would invade China. **d.** Communists would take over the country.

_____ **12.** What congressional action gave President Johnson the authority to escalate the Vietnam War?
a. the Pentagon Papers
b. the Geneva Conference decision
c. the Gulf of Tonkin Resolution
d. a Joint Chiefs of Staff finding

_____ **13.** Which of the following conditions did Americans fighting in Vietnam experience?
a. an enemy with more advanced weapons
b. unqualified support from the home front
c. sniper fire and land mines
d. harsh cold

_____ **14.** Television coverage of the Vietnam War
a. encouraged support for the war.
b. built support for communism.
c. brought the brutality of the war into American homes.
d. showed how effective American weapons were in defeating the enemy.

_____ **15.** What was the primary focus of the protest movement of the 1960s?
a. to ban the use of Agent Orange
b. to demand U.S. withdrawal from Vietnam
c. to end segregation of the military
d. to build support for the draft

_____ **16.** Which of the following best describes the philosophy of the counterculture?
a. question traditions and experiment with new ways of living
b. support existing political parties
c. become members of the working-class
d. promote traditional American values and morals

_____ **17.** In 1970, President Nixon announced that American forces would invade which country?
a. China. **b.** Laos.
c. South Vietnam. **d.** Cambodia.

_____ **18.** How did the Vietnam War finally end in 1975?
a. with the defeat of North Vietnam
b. with the South Vietnamese takeover of Hanoi
c. with North Vietnam gaining control of all of Vietnam
d. with control of all of Vietnam being returned to France

CHAPTER 31

C. Critical Thinking

Answer the following questions on the back of this paper or on a separate sheet of paper. (*24 points*)

19. Determining Relevance Why was the Tet Offensive considered a "psychological" victory for the Viet Cong?

20. Making Comparisons Compare the reception given to American soldiers returning from the Vietnam War with that given to soldiers returning from World War II.

D. Reading a Chart

Use the chart to answer questions 21-23. (*12 points*)

21. During what year did the number of United States troops in Vietnam begin to fall?

____

22. During which year was there the greatest net increase in the number of troops in Vietnam?

____

23. How did the 1964 Gulf of Tonkin Resolution affect the number of personnel assigned in Vietnam?

____

____

____

____

____

U.S. Military Personnel Assigned in Vietnam as of December 31

Year	Total	Net Change
1964	23,300	+7,000
1965	184,300	+161,000
1966	385,300	+201,000
1967	485,600	+100,300
1968	536,100	+50,500
1969	475,200	-68,200
1970	334,600	-140,600
1971	156,800	-177,800
1972	24,200	-132,600

Source: DOD/OASD

E. Analyzing a Document

Below is a statement by President Lyndon Johnson. Read it and then answer questions 24-25 on the back of this paper or on a separate sheet of paper. (*12 points*)

> The Communists' desire to dominate the world is just like the lawyer's desire to be the ultimate judge on the Supreme Court or the politician's desire to be President. You see, the Communists want to rule the world, and if we don't stand up to them, they will do it. And we'll be slaves. Now I'm not one of these folks seeing Communists under every bed. But I do know about the principles of power, and when one side is weak, the other steps in.

24. What did Johnson believe would happen if the United States did not "stand up" to Communists?

25. When Johnson said "when one side is weak, the other steps in," what were the two sides he was referring to?

NAME ______________________ CLASS ____________ DATE ____________

TEST FORM A

The Nixon Years (1968–1974)

CHAPTER 32

A. Identifying Key Terms, People, and Places

Match the descriptions in Column I with the names in Column II. Write the letter of the correct answer in the blank provided. You will not use all the names. *(20 points)*

Column I

_____ **1.** "Plumber" hired by Nixon's administration to stop government leaks

_____ **2.** former attorney general and 1968 candidate for the Democratic presidential nomination

_____ **3.** FBI director

_____ **4.** Apollo 11 astronaut

_____ **5.** President Nixon's chief of staff

_____ **6.** Washington Post reporter who tried to investigate the Watergate coverup

_____ **7.** national security adviser and later secretary of state under President Nixon

_____ **8.** attorney general under President Nixon

_____ **9.** judge who sentenced the Watergate burglars

_____ **10.** Republican Vice President forced to resign in 1973

Column II

a. H. R. Haldeman
b. Robert F. Kennedy
c. Bob Woodward
d. J. Edgar Hoover
e. Spiro Agnew
f. Henry Kissinger
g. John Mitchell
h. Eugene McCarthy
i. Neil Armstrong
j. G. Gordon Liddy
k. John J. Sirica
l. Michael Collins

B. Identifying Main Ideas

Write the letter of the correct ending in the blank provided. *(32 points)*

_____ **11.** One result of the assassination of Martin Luther King, Jr., was
a. increased interest in the Poor People's Campaign.
b. an erosion of Americans' faith in the idea of nonviolent change.
c. increased political opposition to the Johnson administration.
d. a strong federal campaign to heal the rifts dividing the country.

_____ **12.** Violence erupted at the 1968 Democratic Convention in Chicago when
a. George C. Wallace was nominated.
b. Mayor Daly made a speech on TV.
c. Robert F. Kennedy was shot.
d. police moved in on demonstrators.

_____ **13.** OPEC's 1973 embargo on shipping oil to the United States resulted in
a. a flare-up of problems with the Soviet Union.
b. higher inflation and another recession at home.
c. a war between Israel and its Arab neighbors.
d. a British-American foreign policy offensive against Arab nations.

_____ **14.** President Nixon's "southern strategy" included
a. increasing the amount of money needed to enforce fair housing laws.
b. easing guidelines for desegregation.
c. encouraging the extension of the Voting Rights Act of 1965.
d. supporting busing of schoolchildren for purposes of integration.

_____ **15.** In foreign affairs, perhaps Nixon's greatest accomplishment was
a. abandoning *realpolitik,* or practical politics.
b. bringing about détente with the Soviet Union and with China.
c. establishing the People's Republic of China.
d. ending the Vietnam War with a resounding American victory.

_____ **16.** The SALT I treaty proved that
a. the United States could achieve nuclear superiority over the Soviet Union.
b. there was a basis for diplomatic ties between the United States and China.
c. the superpowers could reach agreements relating to arms control.
d. there were deep rifts within the communist world.

_____ **17.** The Plumbers and the Committee to Reelect the President were formed to
a. work with the FBI and CIA.
b. investigate illegal activities concerning the Watergate break-in.
c. befriend those on the "enemies list."
d. ensure an overwhelming victory for Nixon in 1972.

_____ **18.** One outcome of the Watergate scandal was the
a. impeachment of Nixon.
b. resignation of Gerald Ford.
c. conviction of Nixon by the Senate.
d. resignation of Richard Nixon.

C. Critical Thinking

Answer the following questions on the back of this paper or on a separate sheet of paper. *(24 points)*

19. Recognizing Ideologies How would you describe the political principle that lay behind President Nixon's handling of foreign policy?

20. Demonstrating Reasoned Judgment Do you think Nixon was justified in refusing to release the tapes of White House conversations until ordered to do so by the Supreme Court? Explain your reasons.

CHAPTER 32

D. Reading a Graph

Use the graph to answer questions 21–22. Write your answers on the lines provided. *(12 points)*

21. In which year was Nixon's popularity the highest during the period shown? What percentage of the people approved of Nixon's handling of his job as President at that time?

____

____

____

____

22. What was Nixon's approval rating when he took his trip to Russia?

____

____

Source: Gallup Poll Surveys 1969–1973

E. Analyzing a Document

This excerpt comes from a speech that President Nixon delivered to a joint session of Congress in 1972. Read it and then answer questions 23–24. *(12 points)*

> For decades, America has been locked in hostile confrontation with the two great Communist powers, the Soviet Union and the People's Republic of China. We were engaged with the one at many points and almost totally isolated from the other, but our relationships with both had reached a deadly impasse [standstill]. All three countries were victims of bondage about which George Washington long ago warned in these words: The nation which indulges toward another an habitual [constant] hatred is a slave to its own animosity [hatred].

23. With which nation was the United States "engaged at many points"? From which was it "almost totally isolated"?

24. Why is "an habitual hatred" of another nation such a bad thing, according to Washington and Nixon?

NAME ______________________ CLASS ______________ DATE ______________

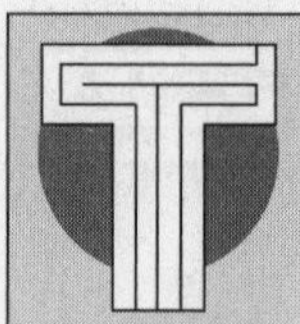

TEST FORM B

The Nixon Years (1968–1974)

CHAPTER 32

A. Identifying Key Terms, People, and Places

Complete each sentence in Column I by writing the letter of the correct name from Column II. You will not use all the names. (*20 points*)

Column I

____ **1.** ____ was a Washington Post reporter who tried to investigate the Watergate cover-up.

____ **2.** A former attorney general, ____ campaigned for the Democratic presidential nomination in 1968.

____ **3.** The Democrats chose Vice President ____ as their presidential candidate in 1968.

____ **4.** In 1968, the Republicans chose former Vice President ____ as their candidate for President.

____ **5.** Apollo 11 astronaut ____ said, "That's one small step for man, one giant step for mankind."

____ **6.** ____ was President Nixon's chief domestic advisor.

____ **7.** As national security adviser and secretary of state, ____ played a major role in shaping Nixon's foreign policy.

____ **8.** The attorney general who approved tapping phones at Democratic National Committee headquarters was ____.

____ **9.** Judge ____ sentenced the Watergate burglars.

____ **10.** The Republican Vice President who was forced to resign for illegal activities was ____.

Column II

a. Richard M. Nixon

b. Henry Kissinger

c. Carl Bernstein

d. Edwin E. "Buzz" Aldrin, Jr.

e. John J. Sirica

f. Robert F. Kennedy

g. Spiro Agnew

h. Hubert Humphrey

i. John Ehrlichman

j. John Mitchell

k. Neil Armstrong

l. George C. Wallace

B. Identifying Main Ideas

Write the letter of the correct answer in the blank provided. (*32 points*)

____ **11.** Why did Hubert Humphrey fail to win total support from the Democratic party?
a. He had ordered police to clear out protesters at a rally.
b. He had supported President Johnson's policies in Vietnam.
c. He had resisted Eugene McCarthy's support as too far from the mainstream.
d. He had failed to maintain law and order in Chicago.

____ **12.** To which groups did George Wallace target his campaign?
a. southerners and blue-collar voters
b. Republicans and left-leaning Democrats
c. campus radicals and antiwar forces
d. professors and editorial writers

_____ 13. What did President Nixon do to try to halt the inflation plaguing the country?
- **a.** He increased federal spending to provide jobs.
- **b.** He imposed an embargo on oil shipped from OPEC countries.
- **c.** He imposed a short-term freeze on wages, prices, and rents.
- **d.** He balanced the budget.

_____ 14. Whom did Nixon include in the silent majority?
- **a.** antiwar activists
- **b.** the counterculture
- **c.** quiet, respectful Americans
- **d.** students at Kent State University

_____ 15. What was the greatest foreign policy accomplishment during the Nixon years?
- **a.** keeping China's seat in the United Nations away from the People's Republic of China
- **b.** recognizing the Communist government of the Soviet Union
- **c.** bringing about American détente with the Soviet Union and China
- **d.** mending the rifts between China and the Soviet Union

_____ 16. What did SALT I prove to the world?
- **a.** that the policy of *realpolitik* could not work with the Soviet Union
- **b.** that the United States could not catch up to the Soviet Union militarily
- **c.** that the Soviet Union would no longer dominate Eastern Europe
- **d.** that the superpowers could reach agreements limiting nuclear arms.

_____ 17. Why did the Watergate break-in occur?
- **a.** The Nixon White House wanted to get Daniel Ellsberg's psychiatric records.
- **b.** The Committee to Reelect the President wanted to wiretap the Democratic National Committee.
- **c.** The Committee to Reelect the President needed money to carry on its work.
- **d.** The FBI and the CIA wanted information about the Democratic presidential campaign.

_____ 18. Why did Nixon resign?
- **a.** to avoid impeachment
- **b.** to prove his innocence
- **c.** to avoid turning over his tapes
- **d.** to prove his loyalty to his staff

C. Critical Thinking

Answer the following questions on the back of this paper or on a separate sheet of paper. (*24 points*)

19. Demonstrating Reasoned Judgment Do you think President Nixon made significant contributions to world peace with his foreign policy? Explain.

20. Predicting Consequences If Nixon had not chosen to resign, what do you think might have happened? Explain.

CHAPTER 32

D. Reading a Graph

Use the graph to answer questions 21–22. Write your answers on the lines provided. (*12 points*)

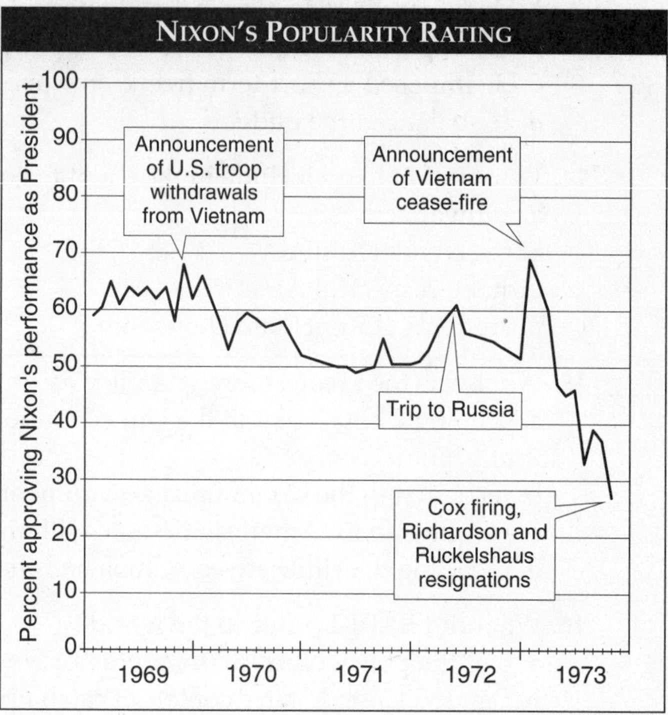

Source: Gallup Poll Surveys 1969–1973

21. What was Nixon's approval rating when he announced the Vietnam cease-fire?

____

22. When was Nixon's approval rating at its lowest during the period shown? What percentage of the people approved of the way he handled his job as President at that time?

____

____

____

E. Analyzing a Document

This excerpt comes from a speech that President Nixon delivered to a joint session of Congress in 1972. Read it and then answer questions 23–24. (*12 points*)

> For decades, America has been locked in hostile confrontation with the two great Communist powers, the Soviet Union and the People's Republic of China. We were engaged with the one at many points and almost totally isolated from the other, but our relationships with both had reached a deadly impasse [standstill]. All three countries were victims of bondage about which George Washington long ago warned in these words: The nation which indulges toward another an habitual [constant] hatred is a slave to its own animosity [hatred].

23. According to the passage, what was the situation between the United States and China and the United States and the Soviet Union?

24. Why did Washington and Nixon both believe that everyone was the loser in this situation?

NAME ________________ CLASS ________ DATE ________

TEST FORM A

CHAPTER 33

The Post-Watergate Period (1974–1980)

A. Identifying Key Terms, People, and Places

Match the descriptions in Column I with the terms in Column II. Write the letter of the correct answer in the blank provided. You will not use all the terms. (*10 points*)

Column I

____ **1.** condition in which unemployment and inflation rise while the economy stays flat

____ **2.** agreements reached by more than 30 nations to cooperate economically and promote human rights in the world

____ **3.** a person who already holds a political office

____ **4.** reduction or removal of government controls

____ **5.** general pardon, like the one President Carter granted to draft evaders of the Vietnam War

Column II

a. amnesty
b. Helsinki Accords
c. Camp David Accords
d. deregulation
e. incumbent
f. stagflation
g. recession

Complete each sentence in Column I by writing the letter of the correct name from Column II in the blank. You will not use all the names. (*10 points*)

Column I

____ **6.** ____, who had been appointed Vice President, inherited the presidency when Nixon resigned.

____ **7.** ____ had been the governor of Georgia before being elected President in 1976.

____ **8.** The Egyptian president who negotiated a peace treaty with the Israeli prime minister was ____.

____ **9.** ____ was the Israeli prime minister who negotiated a peace treaty with the Egyptian president.

____ **10.** ____ was an aggressively anti-Western leader who strove to make Iran a strict Islamic state.

Column II

a. Nelson Rockefeller
b. Menachem Begin
c. Ayatollah Khomeini
d. Anwar el-Sadat
e. James Earl Carter, Jr.
f. Gerald R. Ford
g. Shah Mohammad Reza Pahlavi

B. Identifying Main Ideas

Write the letter of the correct ending in the blank provided. (*32 points*)

____ **11.** One of Ford's first acts as President was to
a. deregulate several industries.
b. pardon Richard Nixon.
c. rescue the crew of the *Mayaquez*.
d. curb inflation and increase employment.

TEST FORM A *(continued)*

CHAPTER 33

_____ 12. The aim that Congress had in passing the War Powers Act was to
- **a.** give the President more power in using American forces overseas.
- **b.** forbid the President from ever sending American forces overseas.
- **c.** limit the President's emergency powers in sending troops overseas.
- **d.** order the President to bring American troops back from Iran.

_____ 13. A major reason for Jimmy Carter's winning the presidency in 1976 was
- **a.** his outstanding record in national politics.
- **b.** the public's distrust of the Washington establishment after Watergate.
- **c.** support for the pardon of Richard M. Nixon.
- **d.** the fact that he was the incumbent.

_____ 14. One of Carter's major problems as President was that he
- **a.** appointed many women and minorities to his staff.
- **b.** adopted a formal and highly dignified presidential style.
- **c.** did not support equal rights causes.
- **d.** lacked the ability to deal well with Congress.

_____ 15. As the cornerstone of his foreign policy, President Carter promoted
- **a.** anticommunism.
- **b.** human rights.
- **c.** more military involvement overseas.
- **d.** ending diplomatic relations with China.

_____ 16. Iranian students seized the U.S. embassy and took Americans hostage to protest
- **a.** Shah Mohammad Reza Pahlavi's return to power in Iran.
- **b.** Carter's letting the shah enter the United States for medical treatment.
- **c.** the failure of the United States to modernize Iran.
- **d.** the exile of their Islamic religious leader.

_____ 17. Like Ford before him, Carter faced the severe economic problems of
- **a.** too much lending to and borrowing from foreign countries.
- **b.** growing exports and shrinking imports.
- **c.** high inflation and high unemployment.
- **d.** shrinking federal spending and federal deficits.

_____ 18. Nuclear energy was dealt a severe blow in the United States when
- **a.** there was an accident at the nuclear plant at Three Mile Island, Pennsylvania.
- **b.** the Department of Energy was set up as a new Cabinet department.
- **c.** the Senate ratified SALT II.
- **d.** President Carter was defeated for reelection in 1980.

C. Critical Thinking

Answer the following questions on the back of this paper or on a separate sheet of paper. (*24 points*)

19. Testing Conclusions President Ford concluded that pardoning Nixon would heal the wounds caused by Watergate. Do you think his conclusion was valid? Explain.

20. **Determining Relevance** In what ways was the Iranian hostage crisis a critical point in Carter's presidency?

D. Reading a Table

Use the table below to answer questions 21-22. Write your answers on the back of this paper or on a separate sheet of paper. (*12 points*)

World Crude Oil Production

(Thousand Barrels Per Day)

Year	Total World Production	OPEC Production	OPEC Percentage
1974	56,088.4	30,729.2	54.8
1975	53,384.0	27,155.0	50.9
1976	57,883.2	30,737.7	53.1
1977	59,862.8	31,253.4	52.2
1978	60,396.8	29,805.3	49.3
1979	62,819.9	30,928.8	49.2
1980	59,826.0	26,879.2	44.9

Source: The Secretariat, Organization of Petroleum Exporting Countries

21. How much crude oil was produced in the world in 1976? Of this amount, what percentage was produced by the OPEC nations?

22. What overall trend do you observe in the percentage of the world's crude oil production supplied by the OPEC nations from 1974 to 1980?

E. Analyzing a Document

This excerpt comes from the keynote speech that Representative Barbara Jordan of Texas gave to the Democratic National Convention in 1975. Read it and answer questions 23–24. (*12 points*)

> We are a people in search of a national community, attempting to fulfill our national purpose, to create and sustain a society in which all of us are equal....We cannot improve on the system of government handed down to us by the founders of the Republic, but we can find new ways to implement the system and realize our destiny....[T]hose of us who are public servants must set examples. If we promise, we must produce. If we ask for sacrifice, we must be the first to give. If we make mistakes, we must be willing to admit them.

23. What "national purpose" did Representative Jordan refer to in her speech?

24. What standards does she set for those who are in politics?

NAME ______________________ CLASS ______________ DATE ______________

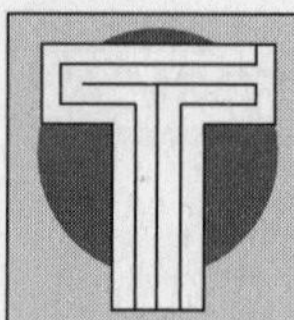

TEST FORM B

The Post-Watergate Period (1974–1980)

CHAPTER 33

A. Identifying Key Terms, People, and Places

Complete each sentence in Column I by writing the letter of the correct term from Column II in the blank. You will not use all the terms. (*10 points*)

Column I

_____ **1.** In the _____, more than 30 nations pledged themselves to cooperate economically and to promote human rights.

_____ **2.** The ____ resulted in a treaty defining a framework for peace between Israel and Egypt.

_____ **3.** President Carter's support of Soviet ____ led to a worsening of relations between the U.S. and the Soviet Union.

_____ **4.** The policy of ____ reduced or removed government controls in several industries.

_____ **5.** Carter granted ____ to draft evaders.

Column II

a. stagflation
b. Camp David Accords
c. amnesty
d. deregulation
e. Helsinki Accords
f. dissidents
g. fundamentalists

Match the descriptions in Column I with the names in Column II. Write the letter of the correct answer in the blank provided. You will not use all the names. (*10 points*)

Column I

_____ **6.** Vice President appointed by a nonelected President

_____ **7.** Egyptian president who negotiated peace terms with Israeli prime minister

_____ **8.** Israeli prime minister who negotiated peace terms with Egyptian president

_____ **9.** Iranian leader supported by the United States

_____ **10.** anti-Western Islamic leader in Iran

Column II

a. Anwar el-Sadat
b. Gerald R. Ford
c. Shah Mohammad Reza Pahlavi
d. Menachem Begin
e. Ayatollah Khomeini
f. Nelson Rockefeller
g. Cyrus Vance

B. Identifying Main Ideas

Write the answer to the question in the blank provided. (*32 points*)

_____ **11.** What was President Ford's program to overcome stagflation?
a. He tried to restore public confidence in the economy through the WIN campaign.
b. He increased the money supply.
c. He proposed a multibillion-dollar tax increase.
d. He provided financial incentives for people to save rather than spend.

_____ **12.** Which of the following statements characterizes Ford's foreign policy?
a. He thwarted congressional attempts to play a strong role in foreign affairs.
b. He followed the direction set by President Nixon and Henry Kissinger.
c. He initiated no foreign policy actions.
d. He refused to recognize the governments of newly independent African nations.

_____ **13.** What was an important theme in Jimmy Carter's election in 1976?
a. He believed the Soviet Union did not want to dominate Eastern Europe.
b. He was a Washington outsider stressing honesty and straightforwardness.
c. He was an experienced businessman.
d. He was an expert in nuclear energy.

_____ **14.** Which statement best describes Carter's presidency?
a. He used the presidency as a pulpit for his religious views.
b. He assumed a highly ceremonial style of presidency.
c. He was successful in both foreign policy and domestic issues.
d. He found it difficult to work with Congress and get legislation passed.

_____ **15.** What factor complicated President Carter's relations with the Soviet Union?
a. his commitment to human rights and support of dissidents
b. his program to build additional nuclear weapons
c. his move to close the Panama Canal to Soviet ships
d. his rejection of SALT II.

_____ **16.** What final step did Carter take to try to get the U.S. hostages released from Iran?
a. He encouraged U.S. banks to make loans to Iran.
b. He brought the shah to the United States for medical treatment.
c. He attempted a commando rescue of the hostages.
d. He sent Cyrus Vance to Tehran to talk with the Iranian captors.

_____ **17.** What did Carter characterize as "the moral equivalent of war"?
a. the need to conserve energy
b. the nuclear accident at Three Mile Island
c. ever-rising interest rates
d. draft evasion

_____ **18.** What effect did the *Bakke* decision have on affirmative action?
a. It legalized racial quotas for admission to medical schools.
b. It encouraged African Americans to apply to medical schools.
c. It signaled the start of a backlash against affirmative action.
d. It ruled out consideration of race as a factor in admissions decisions.

C. Critical Thinking

Answer the following questions on the back of this paper or on a separate sheet of paper. (*24 points*)

19. Expressing Problems Clearly What do you think was Gerald Ford's main problem as President? Support your answer.

20. **Determining Relevance** What effect do you think President Carter's strong religious beliefs had on his presidency?

D. Reading a Table

Use the table below to answer questions 21–22. Write your answers on the back of this paper or on a separate sheet of paper. (*12 points*)

World Crude Oil Production

(Thousand Barrels Per Day)

Year	Total World Production	OPEC Production	OPEC Percentage
1974	56,088.4	30,729.2	54.8
1975	53,384.0	27,155.0	50.9
1976	57,883.2	30,737.7	53.1
1977	59,862.8	31,253.4	52.2
1978	60,396.8	29,805.3	49.3
1979	62,819.9	30,928.8	49.2
1980	59,826.0	26,879.2	44.9

Source: The Secretariat, Organization of Petroleum Exporting Countries

21. In which year shown did OPEC countries produce the lowest percentage of world oil production? What percentage of the world's oil did OPEC countries produce that year?

22. What was the total world oil production in 1979?

E. Analyzing a Document

This excerpt comes from the keynote speech that Representative Barbara Jordan of Texas gave to the Democratic National Convention in 1976. Read it and answer questions 23–24. (*12 points*)

> We are a peopie in search of a national community, attempting to fulfill our national purpose, to create and sustain a society in which all of us are equal.…We cannot improve on the system of government handed down to us by the founders of the Republic, but we can find new ways to implement the system and realize our destiny.…[T]hose of us who are public servants must set examples. If we promise, we must produce. If we ask for sacrifice, we must be the first to give. If we make mistakes, we must be willing to admit them.

23. What high goal did Representative Jordan set for the American people?

24. What examples did she believe politicians should be able to set?

NAME ______________________ CLASS ____________ DATE ____________

TEST FORM A

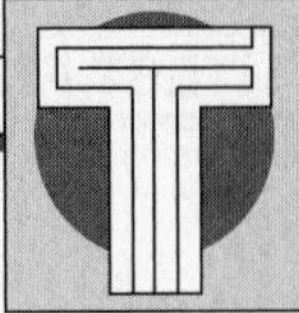

The Conservative Revolution (1980–1992)

CHAPTER 34

A. Identifying Key Terms, People, and Places

Match the descriptions in Column I with the terms in Column II. Write the letter of the correct answer in the blank provided. You will not use all the terms. (*10 points*)

Column I

_____ **1.** coalition of conservative groups in the 1980s

_____ **2.** plan to build a massive satellite shield to protect the United States from incoming missiles

_____ **3.** 1987 agreement calling for the destruction of 2,500 Soviet and American missiles in Europe

_____ **4.** secret operation to arm rebels in Nicaragua

_____ **5.** conflict in which Iraq was driven out of Kuwait

Column II

a. Strategic Defense Initiative (SDI)

b. New Federalism

c. Iran-contra affair

d. INF treaty

e. Persian Gulf War

f. New Right

Compete each sentence in Column I by writing the letter of the correct term from Column II in the blank. You will not use all the terms. (*10 points*)

Column I

_____ **6.** To focus the efforts of religious conservatives, Jerry Falwell and others used ____ to raise funds.

_____ **7.** According to the theory of ____, a cut in taxes would make the economy grow faster by putting more money into the hands of businesses.

_____ **8.** In 1981, a highly threatening disease of the immune system called ____ was discovered.

_____ **9.** Social Security, Medicare, and Medicaid are known as ____ programs.

_____ **10.** In the early 1990s, unemployment rose when companies engaged in ____ to cut costs.

Column II

a. supply-side economics

b. televangelism

c. Sandinista

d. downsizing

e. entitlement

f. contra

g. AIDS

B. Identifying Main Ideas

Write the letter of the correct ending in the blank provided. (*32 points*)

_____ **11.** Conservatives criticized the New Deal and the Great Society for having
a. succeeded in ending poverty in the United States.
b. expanded the size of the federal government.
c. put too much power into the hands of state governments.
d. encouraged the growth of big business.

NAME ______________________ CLASS ____________ DATE ____________

TEST FORM A *(continued)*

CHAPTER 34

_____ **12.** One major factor contributing to Ronald Reagan's defeat of President Carter in 1980 was
a. the Persian Gulf War.
b. the Camp David Accords.
c. the hostage crisis in Iran.
d. the decline of the New Right.

_____ **13.** One of President Reagan's main goals was to
a. keep tax hikes to a minimum.
b. cut back on government regulation of business and industry.
c. accelerate the growth of the federal government.
d. increase federal government spending for welfare.

_____ **14.** The Reagan administration rapidly increased spending on
a. social programs.
b. support of the Soviet Union.
c. the American military.
d. enlargement of the federal government.

_____ **15.** Critics charged that President Reagan's conservative policies led to
a. a larger gap between rich and poor.
b. the advancement of homosexual rights.
c. an expansion of government regulations.
d. a liberal Supreme Court.

_____ **16.** The savings and loan (S & L) scandal
a. cost American taxpayers billions of dollars.
b. cost Reagan his popularity with the American people.
c. grew out of an attempt to undermine the Sandinista government.
d. showed that federal regulation of banks is unnecessary.

_____ **17.** During Reagan's second term, United States relations with the Soviet Union
a. broke down completely.
b. improved.
c. grew increasingly cold.
d. did not change.

_____ **18.** To deal with the recession of the early 1990s, President Bush agreed to
a. vastly increase the federal bureaucracy.
b. raise new taxes as part of a deficit-reduction plan.
c. increase spending for social programs.
d. nominate Clarence Thomas to head the Department of the Treasury.

C. Critical Thinking

Answer the following questions on the back of this paper or on a separate sheet of paper. (*24 points*)

19. Recognizing Ideologies Identify two of the main policies that made up President Reagan's domestic program.

20. Making Comparisons How did Reagan's attitude toward the Soviet Union change during his eight years as President?

D. Reading a Table

Use the table to answer questions 21-22. Write your answers on the back of this paper or on a separate sheet of paper. (*12 points*)

Election Results, 1980–1988

Year	Candidates	Popular Vote	Percent of total vote	Electoral Vote
1980	Ronald Reagan (R)	43,899,248	52	489
	Jimmy Carter (D)	35,481,435	42	49
	John B. Anderson (Ind.)	5,719,437	6	0
1984	Ronald Reagan (R)	54,281,858	59	525
	Walter F. Mondale (D)	37,457,215	41	13
1988*	George Bush (R)	48,881,221	54	426
	Michael S. Dukakis (D)	41,805,422	46	111

*A majority of 270 electoral votes out of 538 are needed to win. In 1988, one vote was cast for Senator Lloyd Bentsen (D-TX).

21. In which election did the winning candidate receive the most popular votes?

22. In what ways does the table show that the Republican candidates received a huge mandate in the elections of 1980, 1984, and 1988?

E. Analyzing a Document

This excerpt is taken from a speech that President Ronald Reagan gave in 1987 as he stood near the Brandenberg Gate, a monument east of the Berlin Wall. Read it and then answer questions 23–24 on the back of the this paper or on a separate sheet of paper. (*12 points*)

> ...We believe that freedom and security go together, that the advance of human liberty can only strengthen the cause of world peace. There is one sign the Soviets can make that would be unmistakable, that would advance dramatically the cause of freedom and peace.
>
> General Secretary Gorbachev, if you seek peace, if you seek prosperity for the Soviet Union and Eastern Europe, if you seek liberalization: Come here to this gate! Mr. Gorbachev, open this gate! Mr. Gorbachev, tear down this wall!

23. What was Reagan asking Gorbachev to do?

24. According to Reagan, was it in the Soviet Union's interest to follow this advice? Explain.

NAME ______________________ CLASS ______________ DATE ______________

TEST FORM B

The Conservative Revolution (1980–1992)

CHAPTER 34

A. Identifying Key Terms, People, and Places

Complete each sentence in Column I by writing the letter of the correct term from Column II in the blank. You will not use all the terms. (*10 points*)

Column I

_____ **1.** Reagan called his plan for giving more responsibility to state and local governments the ____.

_____ **2.** The ____ was a plan for building a satellite shield in outer space.

_____ **3.** The ____ called for the reduction of strategic, long-range nuclear weapons.

_____ **4.** The ____ caused the most serious criticism that the Reagan administration ever faced.

_____ **5.** UN forces liberated Kuwait during the ____.

Column II

a. Strategic Defense Inititative (SDI)

b. Iran-contra affair

c. New Federalism

d. Persian Gulf War

e. New Right

f. Strategic Arms Reduction Treaty (START)

Match the descriptions in Column I with the terms in Column II. Write the letter of the correct answer in the blank provided. You will not use all the terms. (*10 points*)

Column I

_____ **6.** Nicaraguan guerrilla fighter

_____ **7.** theory that supporting business with tax breaks will help the economy grow faster

_____ **8.** a disease of the immune system

_____ **9.** guaranteed payments from the government like Social Security, Medicare, and Medicaid

_____ **10.** laying off workers to cut costs

Column II

a. coalition

b. AIDS

c. supply-side economics

d. contra

e. entitlements

f. downsizing

g. televangelism

B. Identifying Main Ideas

Write the letter of the correct answer in the blank provided. (*32 points*)

_____ **11.** Which aspect of the New Deal angered conservatives?

a. It aimed to end the Great Depression.
b. It expanded the size of the federal government.
c. It lowered taxes for the wealthy.
d. It was based on social Darwinism.

_____ **12.** What cause was promoted by some groups within the New Right?

a. women's rights **b.** homosexual rights
c. Christian values **d.** federal regulation

_____ 13. What were two major components of Ronald Reagan's economic plan?
a. expanding the government and reducing competition
b. increasing the demand for goods and cutting the supply of goods
c. encouraging business growth and discouraging investment
d. cutting taxes and cutting government regulations

_____ 14. Which best describes President Reagan's policy on military spending?
a. In order to balance the budget, spending must remain level.
b. In order to bring peace, spending must not increase.
c. In order to protect American interests, spending must increase.
d. In order to lower taxes, spending must decrease.

_____ 15. What distinction did Sandra Day O'Connor achieve in 1981?
a. She became the first woman American astronaut.
b. She became the first woman Republican candidate for vice president.
c. She became the first woman Speaker of the House.
d. She became the first woman justice of the U.S. Supreme Court.

_____ 16. What was the goal of Reagan's policy toward Nicaragua?
a. to prevent the government from being defeated by revolutionaries.
b. to overthrow the Marxist government
c. to build a large military base in Nicaragua
d. to remain neutral

_____ 17. How did the Soviet policies of perestroika and glasnost help bring an end to the Cold War?
a. They strengthened Eastern European support for the communist system.
b. They convinced the United States to end its military buildup.
c. They helped cause the fall of communist regimes in Eastern Europe.
d. They banned the demonstrations of Polish workers in the Gdansk shipyard.

_____ 18. What was a major reason that President George Bush responded forcefully to Iraq's invasion of Kuwait?
a. He wanted to protect the flow of oil to the West.
b. He wanted to keep the United Nations out of any conflict.
c. He feared that Iraq would invade the United States next.
d. He feared the spread of communism in the Middle East.

C. Critical Thinking

Answer the following questions on the back of this paper or on a separate sheet of paper. (*24 points*)

19. Testing Conclusions Your text states that Reagan's "hands-off" approach to running government led to several notable problems. Explain one of these problems.

20. Demonstrating Reasoned Judgement What do you think was President Bush's greatest foreign policy success? Explain.

NAME ______________________ CLASS ______________ DATE ______________

TEST FORM B *(continued)*

CHAPTER 34

D. Reading a Table

Use the table to answer questions 21–22. Write your answers on the back of this paper or on a separate sheet of paper. (*12 points*)

Election Results, 1980–1988

Year	Candidates	Popular Vote	Percent of total vote	Electoral Vote
1980	Ronald Reagan (R)	43,899,248	52	489
	Jimmy Carter (D)	35,481,435	42	49
	John B. Anderson (Ind.)	5,719,437	6	0
1984	Ronald Reagan (R)	54,281,858	59	525
	Walter F. Mondale (D)	37,457,215	41	13
1988*	George Bush (R)	48,881,221	54	426
	Michael S. Dukakis (D)	41,805,422	46	111

*A majority of 270 electoral votes out of 538 are needed to win. In 1988, one vote was cast for Senator Lloyd Bentsen (D-TX).

21. In which election did Reagan win his largest victory?

22. In the three elections listed, which Democratic candidate received the greatest number of electoral votes?

E. Analyzing a Document

This excerpt is taken from a speech that President Ronald Reagan gave in 1987 as he stood near the Brandenberg Gate, a monument east of the Berlin Wall in West Germany. Read it and then answer questions 23-24 on the back of the this paper or on a separate sheet of paper. (*12 points*)

> ...We believe that freedom and security go together, that the advance of human liberty can only strengthen the cause of world peace. There is one sign the Soviets can make that would be unmistakable, that would advance dramatically the cause of freedom and peace.
>
> General Secretary Gorbachev, if you seek peace, if you seek prosperity for the Soviet Union and Eastern Europe, if you seek liberalization: Come here to this gate! Mr. Gorbachev, open this gate! Mr. Gorbachev, tear down this wall!

23. According to Reagan, what actions should Gorbachev take?

24. According to Reagan, what benefits could the Soviets expect from "tearing down this wall"?

NAME ______________________ CLASS ______________ DATE ______________

TEST FORM A

CHAPTER 35

Entering a New Era (1992–Present)

A. Identify Key Terms, People, and Places

Match the descriptions in Column I with the names in Column II. Write the letter of the correct answer in the blank provided. You will not use all the names. (*20 points*)

Column I

_____ **1.** Former Arkansas governor who became President

_____ **2.** Vice President who cast a tie-breaking vote in the Senate to pass the President's 1994 budget

_____ **3.** Republican elected Speaker of the House after the 1994 congressional election

_____ **4.** Former Senate Majority Leader who ran for President in 1996

_____ **5.** Reform-minded president of Russia

_____ **6.** The first African American woman to win election to the Senate

_____ **7.** Anti-apartheid leader in South Africa

_____ **8.** Palestine Liberation Organization (PLO) leader who reached a peace agreement with Israel.

_____ **9.** Israeli prime minister who reached an agreement with the PLO

_____ **10.** Computer industry pioneer and billionaire

Column II

a. Boris Yeltsin

b. Newt Gingrich

c. Yasir Arafat

d. Nelson Mandela

e. Bill Clinton

f. Janet Reno

g. Al Gore

h. Benjamin Netanyahu

i. Bill Gates

j. Carol Moseley-Braun

k. Bob Dole

l. Yitzhak Rabin

B. Identifying Main Ideas

Write the letter of the correct ending in the blank provided. (*32 points*)

_____ **11.** The 1992 presidential election focused mainly on
- **a.** cultural issues.
- **b.** economic issues.
- **c.** military issues.
- **d.** character issues.

_____ **12.** President Clinton wanted to reform the health care system because
- **a.** few hospitals were making a profit.
- **b.** millions of Americans did not have health insurance.
- **c.** cities experienced a critical shortage of health care professionals.
- **d.** health insurance companies lobbied for more regulation of their industry.

CHAPTER 35

_____ **13.** In their 1994 Contract with America, Republicans pledged to
a. renew the "Star Wars" initiative.
b. end federal welfare spending entirely.
c. balance the budget.
d. increase taxes.

_____ **14.** American foreign policy in the post-Cold War era had to contend with
a. the military buildup in Russia.
b. brutal civil wars in the Balkans and Africa.
c. wars between the countries of Eastern and Western Europe.
d. the formation of the Warsaw Pact.

_____ **15.** An important world development of the 1990s was
a. rising tariffs and other trade barriers.
b. decreasing trade among world nations.
c. the collapse of the European Union.
d. the continuing growth of global trade.

_____ **16.** Starting in 1965, United States immigration policy
a. extended the bias favoring European immigrants.
b. aimed to limit the population of the United States.
c. contributed to the nation's increasing diversity.
d. banned immigration from communist countries.

_____ **17.** The movement for multiculturalism called for increased
a. attention to non-European cultures.
b. numerical targets for hiring women and minorities.
c. cuts in entitlement programs.
d. pressure on Americans to retire at age 65.

_____ **18.** In the 1990s, the fastest-growing age group in the United States was
a. teenagers.
b. women aged 15 to 30.
c. middle-aged immigrants from Latin America and Asia.
d. people over the age of 65.

C. Critical Thinking

Answer the following questions on the back of this paper or on a separate sheet of paper. (*24 points*)

19. Recognizing Cause and Effect Describe two effects of the surge in immigration to the United States in the 1990s.

20. Demonstrating Reasoned Judgment After the Cold War ended, what was the goal of American foreign policy concerning Russia? What steps did American leaders take to pursue this goal?

CHAPTER 35

D. Reading a Table

This table gives data about the Social Security trust fund, the government fund from which Social Security benefits are paid. Use it to answer questions 21–22. Write your answers on the back of this paper or on a separate sheet of paper. (*12 points*)

Social Security Trust Fund

Year	Amount in Social Security Trust Fund	Number of People Receiving benefits	Total Annual Payments
1980	$100.1 billion	35.5 million	$120.5 billion
1985	$179.9 billion	37.1 million	$186.2 billion
1990	$278.6 billion	39.8 million	$247.8 billion
1995	$326.1 billion	43.4 million	$332.6 billion

Source: U.S. Social Security Administration

21. What trend do you see in the number of people collecting Social Security during the period from 1980 to 1995?

22. Do you think this trend will continue into the future? Explain.

E. Analyzing a Document

Below is an excerpt from President Clinton's 1998 State of the Union Address, the President's annual report to Congress. Read it and then answer questions 23-24 on the back of this paper or on a separate sheet of paper. (*12 points*)

> ...As we enter the 21st century, the global economy requires us to seek opportunity not just at home, but in all the markets of the world. We must shape this global economy, not shrink from it. In the last five years, we have led the way in opening new markets, with 240 trade agreements that remove foreign barriers to products bearing the proud stamp "Made in the USA." Today, record high exports account for fully one-third of our economic growth. I want to keep them going, because that's the way to keep America growing and to advance a safer, more stable world.

23. According to Clinton, what actions has the government taken to expand global trade?

24. What are the benefits of expanding trade, according to Clinton?

NAME ______________________ CLASS ______________ DATE ______________

CHAPTER 35

TEST FORM B

Entering a New Era (1992 to Present)

A. Identifying Key Terms, People, and Places

Complete each sentence in Column I by writing the letter of the correct name from Column II. You will not use all the names. (*20 points*)

Column I

_____ **1.** ____, former governor of Arkansas, won the presidency in 1992 with 43 percent of the popular vote.

_____ **2.** In 1992 and 1996, ____, a successful businessman, ran as a third-party candidate for President.

_____ **3.** President Clinton appointed ____ Attorney General of the United States.

_____ **4.** Representative ____ of Georgia became Speaker of the House after the congressional election of 1994.

_____ **5.** Former Senate Majority Leader ____ of Kansas was the Republican candidate for President in 1996.

_____ **6.** In 1996, ____ won another term as Russia's president by defeating his communist rival.

_____ **7.** Imprisoned in South Africa for 27 years, ____ became that country's president after apartheid.

_____ **8.** Palestine Liberation Organization (PLO) leader ____ signed a historic peace agreement with Israel in 1993.

_____ **9.** Prime Minister ____ signed that same peace agreement for Israel.

_____ **10.** ____, elected prime minister of Israel in 1996, was more reluctant to grant concessions to the Palestinians than his predecessor had been.

Column II

a. Ross Perot

b. Nelson Mandela

c. Bill Gates

d. Janet Reno

e. Yitzhak Rabin

f. Bill Clinton

g. Yasir Arafat

h. Bob Dole

i. Benjamin Netanyahu

j. F. W. de Klerk

k. Newt Gingrich

l. Boris Yeltsin

B. Identifying Main Ideas

Write the letter of the correct answer in the blank provided. (*32 points*)

_____ **11.** What issue dominated the presidential campaign of 1992?

a. "gridlock" in Congress. **b.** foreign affairs
c. immigration **d.** the economy

_____ **12.** What was the main goal of Clinton's plan to reform the health care system?

a. health insurance for every American
b. increased profits for hospitals
c. loans for students in medical school
d. free health care for the elderly

_____ **13.** Which of the following describes the outcome of the 1994 congressional elections?
a. Democrats won a majority in both houses of Congress for the first time since World War II.
b. Democrats won control of the Senate, while Republicans gained a majority in the House of Representatives.
c. Republicans won a majority in both houses of Congress for the first time in over forty years.
d. Republicans won control of the Senate, while Republicans gained a majority in the House of Representatives.

_____ **14.** Which of the following best describes Russia's condition in the 1990s?
a. Russia went back to Soviet-style communism.
b. Russia faced severe difficulties as it tried to change to a market economy.
c. Russia prospered and was soon able to pay back all the loans it had taken.
d. Russians displayed strong and continued confidence in Boris Yeltsin's ability to govern.

_____ **15.** What led to the eruption of war in the Balkans in the early 1990s?
a. the Russian army's invasion of the region
b. civil wars in Rwanda and Zaire
c. the break-up of Yugoslavia
d. nuclear weapons tests in India and Pakistan

_____ **16.** What was the main purpose of the North American Free Trade Agreement (NAFTA)?
a. to reduce unemployment in the United States
b. to encourage immigration to the United States from Latin America
c. to promote free trade among Canada, Mexico, and the United States
d. to create a trading partnership with the European Union (EU).

_____ **17.** In 1992, Carol Moseley-Braun became the first African American woman to
a. run for Vice President.
b. be appointed to the Supreme Court.
c. be named Attorney General.
d. win election to the United States Senate.

_____ **18.** What has posed the greatest threat to Social Security and Medicare during the 1990s?
a. the refusal of younger workers to pay Social Security taxes
b. the rapidly growing number of Americans over 65 years old
c. congressional actions to end both Social Security and Medicare
d. opposition of health insurance companies to health care reform

C. Critical Thinking

Answer the following questions on the back of this paper or on a separate sheet of paper. (*24 points*)

19. Recognizing Ideologies Describe the main points of the Republicans' Contract with America.

CHAPTER 35

20. **Testing Conclusions** The United States played the role of peacemaker in the 1990s. Give two examples to support this conclusion.

D. Reading a Table

This table gives data about the Social Security trust fund, the government fund from which Social Security benefits are paid. Use it to answer questions 21–22. Write your answers on the back of this paper or on a separate sheet of paper. (*12 points*)

Social Security Trust Fund

Year	Amount in Social Security Trust Fund	Number of People Receiving benefits	Total Annual Payments
1980	$100.1 billion	35.5 million	$120.5 billion
1985	$179.9 billion	37.1 million	$186.2 billion
1990	$278.6 billion	39.8 million	$247.8 billion
1995	$326.1 billion	43.4 million	$332.6 billion

Source: U.S. Social Security Administration

21. By how much did total annual Social Security payments increase between 1980 and 1995?

22. Do you think these expanding payments could pose a problem in the future? Explain.

E. Analyzing a Document

Below is an excerpt from President Clinton's 1998 State of the Union Address, the President's annual report to Congress. Read it and then answer questions 23-24 on the back of this paper or on a separate sheet of paper. (*12 points*)

> …As we enter the 21st century, the global economy requires us to seek opportunity not just at home, but in all the markets of the world. We must shape this global economy, not shrink from it. In the last five years, we have led the way in opening new markets, with 240 trade agreements that remove foreign barriers to products bearing the proud stamp "Made in the USA." Today, record high exports account for fully one-third of our economic growth. I want to keep them going, because that's the way to keep America growing and to advance a safer, more stable world.

23. According to Clinton, what should be the nation's attitude toward trade?

24. Are exports important to the American economy? Explain using evidence from Clinton's speech.

NAME ______________________ CLASS ____________ DATE ____________

TEST FORM A

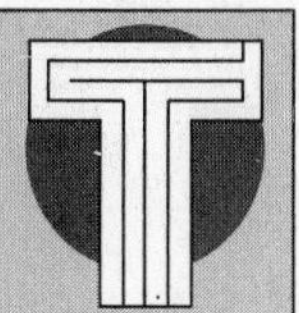

Immigration and the Golden Door

A. Identifying Key Terms, People, and Places

Match the descriptions in Column I with the terms in Column II. Write the letter of the correct answer in the blank provided. You will not use all the terms. *(20 points)*

Column I

_____ **1.** program to teach students in their native language as well as in English

_____ **2.** shelter offered by a country to people escaping persecution

_____ **3.** person living illegally in a country

_____ **4.** person who opposed immigration in the mid-1800s

Column II

a. nativist

b. undocumented immigrant

c. green card

d. political asylum

e. bilingual education

B. Identifying Main Ideas

Write the letter of the correct answer in the blank provided. *(60 points)*

_____ **5.** The main reason most immigrants come to the United States is that they
- **a.** fear for their lives.
- **b.** want to worship freely.
- **c.** have relatives who are American citizens.
- **d.** cannot find work elsewhere.

_____ **6.** The history of immigration to the United States can best be described as
- **a.** a series of spurts and slowdowns.
- **b.** a steady flow.
- **c.** a trickle.
- **d.** an overwhelming flood.

_____ **7.** A cultural argument for restricting immigration is that new immigrant groups
- **a.** settle mainly in urban areas.
- **b.** pay less in taxes.
- **c.** fragment American society.
- **d.** refuse to work at low-skill jobs.

_____ **8.** An economic argument in support of immigration is that immigrants
- **a.** take more than their share of welfare.
- **b.** are wealthier than native-born Americans.
- **c.** do not need job training.
- **d.** come to the United States highly motivated to work.

C. Critical Thinking

Answer the following question on the back of this paper or on a separate sheet of paper. *(20 points)*

9. Identifying Central Issues If immigration were severely restricted, what would be one possible gain for the United States? What would be one possible loss? Explain.

NAME ______________________ CLASS ____________ DATE ____________

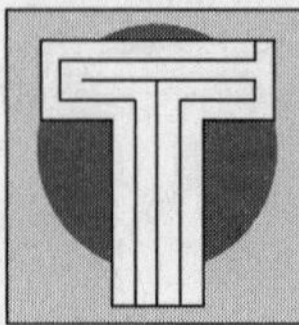

TEST FORM B

Immigration and the Golden Door

CHAPTER 36

A. Identifying Key Terms, People, and Places

Complete each sentence in Column I by writing the letter of the correct term from Column II in the blank. You will not use all the terms. (*20 points*)

Column I

_____ **1.** Refugees who want to escape persecution by their governments often seek _____.

_____ **2.** The Immigration Reform and Control Act of 1986 granted amnesty to some _____.

_____ **3.** ____ formed the Know-Nothing party in the mid-1800s to oppose immigration.

_____ **4.** Without a ____, foreigners are not permitted to work in the United States.

Column II

a. political asylum
b. undocumented immigrants
c. bilingual education
d. nativists
e. green card

B. Identifying Main Ideas

Write the letter of the correct answer in the blank provided. (*60 points*)

_____ **5.** Immigrants can legally enter the United States if
a. they will work for low pay. **b.** they have a small family.
c. they seek political office. **d.** they have needed job skills.

_____ **6.** The Gentlemen's Agreement of 1907 limited immigration from
a. Mexico. **b.** Japan.
c. Ireland. **d.** Germany.

_____ **7.** One argument against immigration is that
a. immigrants refuse to vote in national elections.
b. most people receiving public assistance are immigrants.
c. many state and local governments cannot afford to provide immigrants with social services.
d. immigrants do not want their children to attend school.

_____ **8.** Immigration supporters point out that most immigrants
a. leave the country within five years. **b.** are elderly.
c. are not interested in low-paying jobs. **d.** do not receive public assistance.

C. Critical Thinking

Answer this question on the back of this paper or on a separate sheet of paper. (*20 points*)

9. Formulating Questions Make up three questions that you think should be asked in any discussion of the immigration issue.

NAME ______________________ CLASS __________ DATE __________

TEST FORM A

Gun Control and Crime

CHAPTER 37

A. Identifying Key Terms, People, and Places

Define or identify each of the following. *(30 points)*

1. National Rifle Association (NRA)

____

____

2. homicide

____

____

3. Second Amendment

____

____

B. Identifying Main Ideas

Write the letter of the correct ending in the blank provided. *(50 points)*

_____ **4.** Statistics show that an overwhelming majority of violent crimes involve
a. militias. **b.** off-duty policemen.
c. traffic accidents. **d.** firearms.

_____ **5.** In colonial America, bands of citizens armed to defend themselves were called
a. colonists. **b.** monarchs.
c. loyalists. **d.** militias.

_____ **6.** Gun buyers must wait five days for a background check as a result of the
a. NRA. **b.** Brady law.
c. 1968 Gun Control Act. **d.** Second Amendment.

_____ **7.** Opponents of gun control believe that gun ownership by law-abiding citizens
a. helps to prevent crime. **b.** is unconstitutional.
c. should be mandatory. **d.** has no effect on crime.

_____ **8.** Gun control supporters claim that to reduce violent crime, we must
a. overturn the Brady law.
b. outlaw the NRA.
c. reduce production of Saturday-night specials.
d. restrict criminals' access to guns.

C. Critical Thinking

Answer this question on the back of this paper or on a separate sheet of paper. *(20 points)*

9. Testing Conclusions Your text states that "Guns have been part of the American way of life since the first Europeans came to North America." Support this conclusion.

NAME ______________________________ CLASS ______________ DATE ______________

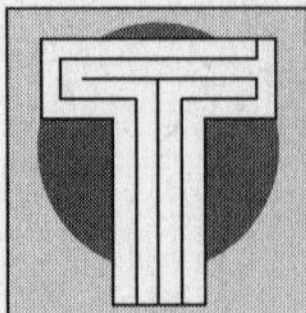

TEST FORM B

Gun Control and Crime

CHAPTER 37

A. Identifying Key Term, People, and Places

Complete each sentence by circling the correct term in parentheses. *(30 points)*

1. By 1974, the number of murders in the United States had risen so high that the (*homicide, handgun*) rate had doubled.

2. Opponents of gun control say the right to bear arms is guaranteed by the (*Brady law, Second Amendment*).

3. The (*FBI, NRA*) argues that gun control is not the answer to the crime problem.

B. Identifying Main Ideas

Write the letter of the correct ending in the blank provided. *(50 points)*

_____ **4.** On a line graph of the crime rate since 1950, what would the line look like?
- **a.** It would rise steadily.
- **b.** It would fall steadily.
- **c.** It would go up and down.
- **d.** It would go straight across.

_____ **5.** The "minutemen" who fought the British at Lexington and Concord in 1775 were an example of a
- **a.** militia.
- **b.** regular army.
- **c.** political party.
- **d.** national organization.

_____ **6.** What firearms issue emerged during the debate over ratification of the Constitution?
- **a.** James Brady called for a five-day waiting period before a handgun purchase.
- **b.** Many people demanded the right to bear arms.
- **c.** Soldiers wanted better rifles.
- **d.** Congress tried to ban handguns.

_____ **7.** How does the National Rifle Association describe a proposed ban on guns?
- **a.** It is the best answer to crime.
- **b.** It is a cause of violence.
- **c.** It is an American right.
- **d.** It is unconstitutional.

_____ **8.** According to gun control supporters, why is a gun in the home dangerous?
- **a.** It raises the risk of homicide in the home.
- **b.** It will probably be stolen by a criminal.
- **c.** A gun kept in a metal container can overheat and explode.
- **d.** Most gun owners do not know how to use a gun.

C. Critical Thinking

Answer this question on the back of this paper or on a separate sheet of paper. *(20 points)*

9. Making Comparisons On what issue or issues do you think opponents and supporters of gun control agree?

NAME ______________________ CLASS ______________ DATE ______________

TEST FORM A

The Minimum Wage

CHAPTER 38

A. Identifying Key Terms, People, and Places

Write a sentence that explains how each of the following relates to the minimum-wage issue. *(30 points)*

1. Triangle Shirtwaist Factory

____

____

2. progressives

____

____

3. New Deal

____

____

B. Identifying Main Ideas

Write the letter of the correct ending in the blank provided. *(40 points)*

_____ **4.** The majority of minimum-wage workers are
- **a.** teenagers.
- **b.** adults.
- **c.** restaurant employees.
- **d.** unemployed.

_____ **5.** The New Deal legislation that banned child labor and set a minimum wage was called the
- **a.** Works Progress Administration.
- **b.** Fair Labor Standard Act.
- **c.** Frances Perkins Labor Act.
- **d.** Minimum-Wage Protection Act.

_____ **6.** People who favor raising the minimum wage argue that
- **a.** a full-time worker earning minimum wage cannot support a family.
- **b.** teenagers earning minimum wage cannot afford a car.
- **c.** inflation is not a problem for the minimum-wager earner.
- **d.** raising the minimum wage will cause everyone's salary to rise.

_____ **7.** People who oppose raising the minimum wage argue that
- **a.** raising the minimum wage will hurt businesses, consumers, and workers.
- **b.** small business will profit from higher wages.
- **c.** the government should determine wages, not the marketplace.
- **d.** raising the minimum wage will cause everyone's salary to rise.

C. Critical Thinking

Answer this question on the back of this paper or on a separate sheet of paper. *(30 points)*

8. Testing Conclusions Your text states that "The majority of Americans favor increasing the minimum wage." Why do you think this is so?

NAME ______________________ CLASS ______________ DATE ______________

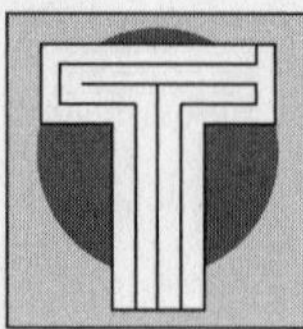

TEST FORM B

The Minimum Wage

CHAPTER 38

A. Identifying Key Terms, People, and Places

Define or identify each of the following. (*40 points*)

1. New Deal

____

2. work ethic

____

3. progressives

____

4. Triangle Shirtwaist Factory

____

B. Identifying Main Ideas

Write the letter of the correct ending in the blank provided. (*40 points*)

_____ **5.** Which job most likely pays minimum wage?
- **a.** selling insurance in Georgia
- **b.** assembling automobiles in Ohio
- **c.** fixing computers in Vermont
- **d.** picking lettuce in California

_____ **6.** How did the Fair Labor Standards Act help workers?
- **a.** It forced businesses to hire women.
- **b.** It gave child laborers paid vacations.
- **c.** It set a minimum wage.
- **d.** It set a minimum work week.

_____ **7.** People who favor raising the minimum wage argue that
- **a.** Americans must protect small businesses.
- **b.** the gap between rich and poor is too wide.
- **c.** the government should not interfere in the marketplace.
- **d.** businesses should lay off some employees in order to raise others' wages.

_____ **8.** People who oppose raising the minimum wage argue that
- **a.** Americans favor increasing the minimum wage.
- **b.** most minimum-wage workers do not want a raise.
- **c.** a wage increase will help only the rich.
- **d.** consumers suffer when the minimum wage is raised.

C. Critical Thinking

Answer this question on the back of this paper or on a separate sheet of paper. (*20 points*)

9. Distinguishing Fact from Opinion Representative John Lewis of Georgia said, "Raising the minimum wage is the right thing to do." Is this fact or opinion? Explain.

NAME ______________________ CLASS ______________ DATE ______________

TEST FORM A

Rethinking Entitlements

CHAPTER 39

A. Identifying Key Terms, People, and Places

Match the descriptions in Column I with the terms in Column II. Write the letter of the correct answer in each blank. You will not use all the terms. *(20 points)*

Column I

_____ **1.** all the money that the federal government owes

_____ **2.** federal health insurance program for the elderly and disabled

_____ **3.** social welfare programs for people of certain income levels and ages

_____ **4.** lump sum amounts sent by the federal government to the states

Column II

a. AFDC
b. block grants
c. federal deficit
d. national debt
e. entitlements
f. Medicare

B. Identifying Main Ideas

Write the letter of the correct answer in the blank provided. *(60 points)*

_____ **5.** Social Security provides
a. retirement pensions for workers over 65.
b. health insurance for people over 65.
c. slips of paper than can be used to purchase food.
d. job training for unemployed workers.

_____ **6.** Aid to Families with Dependent Children (AFDC) had its roots in the
a. New Deal. **b.** Great Society.
c. Reagan Revolution. **d.** New Frontier.

_____ **7.** People who favor deep cuts in welfare call for reducing
a. block grants to states.
b. Medicare premiums.
c. the amount of time people can receive assistance.
d. the use of Health Maintenance Organizations.

_____ **8.** People who oppose deep cuts in welfare point out that deep cuts will
a. lessen the need for food stamps.
b. make child care programs unnecessary.
c. balance the federal budget.
d. hurt children the most.

C. Critical Thinking

Answer this question on the back of this paper or on a separate sheet of paper. *(20 points)*

9. Testing Conclusions Consider the following statement: "Any long-term solution to the welfare crisis must include child care and job training." Do you think that conclusion makes sense? Explain your answer.

NAME ______________________ CLASS ____________ DATE ____________

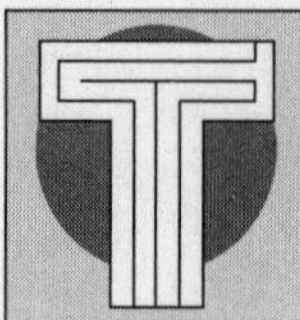

TEST FORM B

Rethinking Entitlements

CHAPTER 39

A. Identifying Key Terms, People, and Places

Complete each sentence in Column I by writing the letter of the correct term from Column II in the blank. You will not use all the terms. *(20 points)*

Column I

____ **1.** The total amount of money owed by the federal government is the ____.

____ **2.** Any year that the United States government spends more than it takes in from taxes there is a ____.

____ **3.** Some reformers want the states to administer welfare, using ____ from the federal government.

____ **4.** Through ____, older Americans are provided with health insurance.

Column II

a. Medicare
b. block grants
c. national debt
d. federal deficit
e. AFDC

B. Identifying Main Ideas

Write the letter of the correct answer in the blank provided. *(60 points)*

____ **5.** What characteristic was shared by most people receiving ADFC in 1996?
a. They were over 65. **b.** They were single mothers.
c. They were children. **d.** They were high school dropouts.

____ **6.** Which President promised to "end welfare as we have known it"?
a. Clinton **b.** Johnson
c. Roosevelt **d.** Reagan

____ **7.** What do people who favor deep cuts in welfare suggest?
a. Congress should create a constitutional amendment outlawing AFDC.
b. Congress should pass a law reducing Medicare payments by 50 percent.
c. Congress should force the states to spend block grants on job training.
d. Congress should budget a fixed amount of money for welfare each year.

____ **8.** What do those who favor moderate welfare reform point out?
a. Most people who receive welfare benefits want to work.
b. Privatizing Medicare is the best long-term solution.
c. The national debt is not a big problem.
d. Welfare programs will soon become unnecessary.

C. Critical Thinking

Answer this question on the back of this paper or on a separate sheet of paper. *(20 points)*

9. Identifying Assumptions What assumption about the poor lay behind the programs of the New Deal and the Great Society?

NAME ______________________ CLASS ______________ DATE ______________

TEST FORM A

The Debate over Trade

CHAPTER 40

A. Identifying Key Terms, People, and Places

Match the descriptions in Column I with the terms in Column II. Write the letter of the correct answer in the blank provided. You will not use all the terms. *(20 points)*

Column I

_____ **1.** the result of a nation's selling more than it buys

_____ **2.** a policy of promoting stability in Latin America by encouraging trade

_____ **3.** a Mexican border factory

_____ **4.** a free-trade agreement signed by the United States, Mexico, and Canada

Column II

a. tariff

b. Monroe Doctrine

c. maquiladora

d. Good Neighbor Policy

e. NAFTA

f. trade surplus

B. Identifying Main Ideas

Write the letter of the correct answer in the blank provided. *(60 points)*

_____ **5.** The goal of the Helms-Burton Act is to
- **a.** ensure that free trade does not harm the environment.
- **b.** promote trade with Canada.
- **c.** force Mexico to change its immigration policies.
- **d.** penalize foreign companies that do business with Cuba.

_____ **6.** The Monroe Doctrine helped the United States increase trade with Latin American nations by
- **a.** blocking the spread of communism.
- **b.** keeping European powers out of Latin America.
- **c.** lowering tariffs.
- **d.** creating new jobs.

_____ **7.** People who favor NAFTA claim that it will result in
- **a.** an increase in exports.
- **b.** an increase in tariffs.
- **c.** a decrease in jobs.
- **d.** a decrease in crime.

_____ **8.** According to opponents of NAFTA, nearly all the benefits of free trade go to
- **a.** large multinational corporations.
- **b.** American factory workers.
- **c.** Mexican farmers.
- **d.** small businesses.

C. Critical Thinking

Answer this question on the back of this paper or on a separate sheet of paper. *(20 points)*

9. Recognizing Cause and Effect NAFTA supporters say that free trade will help build political stability in Mexico. Explain this argument.

NAME ______________________ CLASS ____________ DATE ____________

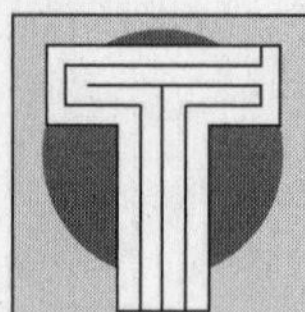

TEST FORM B

The Debate over Trade

CHAPTER 40

A. Identifying Key Terms, People, and Places

Complete each sentence in Column I by writing the letter of the correct term or name from Column II in the blank. You will not use all the terms and names. *(20 points)*

Column I

____ **1.** By signing NAFTA, Mexico, the United States, and Canada agreed to remove ____ and other barriers to trade.

____ **2.** ____ engaged in "gunboat diplomacy" to protect United States interests in Latin America.

____ **3.** In 1995, the United States had a ____ with Mexico because the United States imported more than it exported.

____ **4.** Many Mexicans have found jobs in the ____ that have been built along Mexico's northern border.

Column II

a. trade deficit

b. maquiladoras

c. tariffs

d. trade surplus

e. Theodore Roosevelt

f. Fidel Castro

B. Identifying Main Ideas

Write the letter of the correct ending in the blank provided. *(60 points)*

____ **5.** Which country is the United States' largest trading partner?
a. Britain
b. Japan
c. Canada
d. Mexico

____ **6.** Why did the United States make a $12.5 billion loan to Mexico in 1995?
a. to convince Mexico to close down factories
b. to help Mexico through a financial crisis
c. to invest in multinational corporations
d. to make Mexico less dependent on the United States

____ **7.** Which is an argument used by people who favor NAFTA?
a. Jobs are not an important aspect of NAFTA.
b. Trade is like a game—there is always a winner and a loser.
c. All three NAFTA members have increased their exports.
d. The key to a successful trade pact is border factories.

____ **8.** What point do people who oppose NAFTA make?
a. Canada is not a dependable trading partner.
b. NAFTA has hurt multinational corporations most.
c. Mexican workers are generally paid too much.
d. Mexico's instability could end up hurting the United States.

C. Critical Thinking

Answer this question on the back of this paper or on a separate sheet of paper. *(20 points)*

9. Predicting Consequences If you were a leader of a Latin American country, would you want to sign a free-trade pact with the United States? Explain your answer.

NAME ______________________ CLASS ____________ DATE ____________

TEST FORM A

Foreign Policy after the Cold War

CHAPTER 41

A. Identifying Key Terms, People and Places

Match the descriptions in column I with the terms and names in Column II. Write the letter of the correct answer in the blank provided. You will not use all the terms. *(20 points)*

Column I

____ **1.** Asian country in which the American military was involved from 1961 to 1973

____ **2.** Asian country in which American forces fought from 1950 to 1953

____ **3.** a policy that committed the United States to block the spread of communism

____ **4.** organization designed to defend Western Europe

Column II

a. Truman Doctrine
b. Cold War
c. Vietnam
d. NATO
e. Warsaw Pact
f. Korea

B. Identifying Main Ideas

Write the letter of the correct answer in the blank provided. *(60 points)*

____ **5.** When the Cold War ended, defense contractors were forced to
a. move their plants to Mexico. **b.** split up into smaller units.
c. increase production. **d.** lay off workers.

____ **6.** American foreign policy changed after World War II because the United States
a. could not afford any more wars.
b. decided to leave the United Nations.
c. had become a global power.
d. isolated itself from the rest of the world.

____ **7.** One argument for cutting the United States' foreign commitments is that
a. most NATO allies have joined the Warsaw Pact.
b. the American military is unwilling to fight.
c. the Soviet Union no longer exists.
d. Japan has become a military superpower.

____ **8.** One argument for maintaining foreign commitments is that
a. world domination should be the United States' primary goal.
b. reducing commitments would be dangerous and costly in the long run.
c. military spending is already too high.
d. abandoning North Korea would leave it open to invasion from the south.

C. Critical Thinking

Answer this question on the back of this paper or on a separate sheet of paper. *(20 points)*

9. Determining Relevance Is George Washington's advice about avoiding foreign entanglements as relevant today as it was in 1796? Why or why not?

NAME ______________________ CLASS ______________ DATE ______________

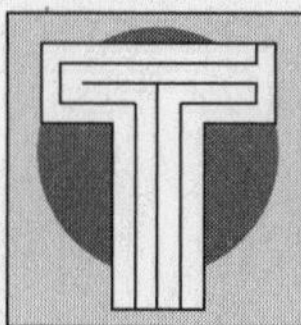

TEST FORM B

Foreign Policy after the Cold War

CHAPTER 41

A. Identifying Key Terms, People, and Places

Complete each sentence in Column I by writing the letter of the correct term or name from Column II in the blank. You will not use all the terms and names. *(20 points)*

Column I

_____ **1.** After World War I, ____ wanted the United States to join the League of Nations.

_____ **2.** Soviet leader ____ began reforms which quickened the pace of communism's decline.

_____ **3.** During the Cold War, Western Europe feared an attack by ____ forces.

_____ **4.** The ____ committed the United States to defending other nations against communism.

Column II

a. Joseph Stalin

b. Woodrow Wilson

c. Truman Doctrine

d. Monroe Doctrine

e. Warsaw Pact

f. Mikhail Gorbachev

B. Identifying Main Ideas

Write the letter of the correct answer in the blank provided. *(60 points)*

_____ **5.** How have post-Cold War military budgets affected defense contractors?
a. They have shifted into non-defense areas of production.
b. They have moved their operations to Russia.
c. They have hired more people and built more plants.
d. They have stopped selling military equipment to foreign countries.

_____ **6.** What approach did President Reagan take to foreign affairs?
a. a policy of isolation
b. a policy of colonization
c. a "keep the troops at home" policy
d. a stronger anti-Soviet policy

_____ **7.** Critics of foreign commitments say that the United States should cancel alliances such as NATO because
a. they are too expensive.
b. they do not work.
c. there will be no wars in the future.
d. the United States no longer needs an army.

_____ **8.** Why do some people say that the United States should keep its alliances?
a. Defending alliances is not expensive.
b. The future is sure to be peaceful.
c. Allies have their own armed forces.
d. A new enemy could appear at any time.

C. Critical Thinking

Answer this questions on the back of this paper or on a separate sheet of paper. *(20 points)*

9. Demonstrating Reasoned Judgement President Nixon argued that reducing foreign commitments would cost the United States even more money than maintaining them. Explain this belief.

NAME ________________ CLASS ________ DATE ________

TEST FORM A

Technology and You in the Next Century

CHAPTER 42

A. Identifying Key Terms, People, and Places

Match the descriptions in Column I with the terms in Column II. Write the letter of the correct answer in the blank provided. You will not use all the terms. *(20 points)*

Column I	Column II
_____ **1.** sending information over long distances	**a.** e-mail
_____ **2.** use of machines in place of human labor	**b.** productivity
_____ **3.** trend toward involving many countries in the production and sale of goods	**c.** globalization
	d. telecommunications
_____ **4.** electronic messages	**e.** modem
	f. automation

B. Identifying Main Ideas

Write the letter of the correct answer in the blank provided. (60 points)

_____ **5.** How has computer networking helped the globalization of production?
a. Friends can communicate with each other through e-mail.
b. Product information can travel around the globe in seconds.
c. Workers can use mass production methods to assemble a product.
d. Computers have become smaller and faster.

_____ **6.** What economic effect have automation and computerization had?
a. They have increased productivity.
b. They have increased labor costs.
c. They have decreased efficiency.
d. They have decreased supply.

_____ **7.** What point do supporters of educational technology make?
a. Computers are fun, and fun is what education is all about.
b. Computer skills help workers adapt to today's changing workplace.
c. Computers will replace teachers within two decades.
d. Computers help students do their work with having to think too much.

_____ **8.** What point do opponents of education technology make?
a. Technology is the answer to our nation's basic problems.
b. Computers are unnecessary in the workplace.
c. Students need thinking skills more than they need computer skills.
d. Teachers should be required to use e-mail.

C. Critical Thinking

Answer this question on the back of this paper or on a separate sheet of paper. *(20 points)*

9. **Testing Conclusions** Do you agree that the computer has had a profound effect on American life? Explain your answer.

NAME ______________________ CLASS ____________ DATE ____________

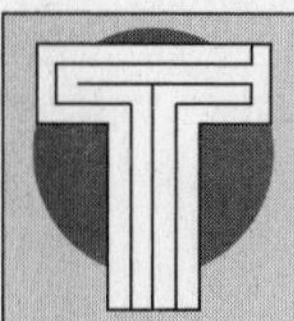

TEST FORM B

Technology and You in the Next Century

CHAPTER 42

A. Identifying Key Terms, People, and Places

Complete each sentence in Column I by writing the letter of the correct term or name from Column II in the blank. You will not use all the terms and names. *(20 points)*

Column I	Column II
_____ **1.** ____ allows people to tell their computers what to do.	**a.** software
_____ **2.** Students can browse the ____ to retrieve electronic files.	**b.** modem
_____ **3.** Mass production, automation, and computerization have all improved ____.	**c.** automation
	d. World Wide Web
_____ **4.** Without its ____, a computer cannot transmit data to a phone line.	**e.** productivity
	f. globalization

B. Identifying Main Ideas

Write the letter of the correct ending in the blank provided. *(60 points)*

_____ **5.** Computer networks have helped service industries prosper by
- **a.** eliminating workers.
- **b.** encouraging thinking skills.
- **c.** introducing the practice of automation.
- **d.** making it easier to manage information.

_____ **6.** Because of automation and computerization, more and more workers
- **a.** left the service sector.
- **b.** left manufacturing jobs.
- **c.** worked behind conveyor belts.
- **d.** were hired by Henry Ford.

_____ **7.** People who support computer use in schools say that
- **a.** computer skills are essential in the workplace.
- **b.** students using computers must work at a faster pace.
- **c.** computers help students dress up their information in a flashy package.
- **d.** without e-mail, student cannot receive a proper education.

_____ **8.** People who oppose a computer-based approach to education say that
- **a.** computer skills are unnecessary in the workplace.
- **b.** thinking skills are more important in the workplace than computer skills.
- **c.** more school assignments should require a high-tech delivery.
- **d.** good computers beat good teaching any day.

C. Critical Thinking

Answer this question on the back of this paper or on a separate sheet of paper. *(20 points)*

9. Identifying Alternatives What kind of compromise can you suggest that should satisfy both supporters and opponents of computers in schools?

Chapter 1

Test Form A

A. Identifying Key Terms, People, and Places

1. e	6. c
2. i	7. d
3. j	8. a
4. h	9. f
5. g	10. b

B. Identifying Main Ideas

11. c	15. a
12. b	16. d
13. c	17. c
14. c	18. a

C. Critical Thinking

Possible answers:

19. Europeans, who lived where land was scarce, greatly valued land and considered it part of personal wealth. African rulers, who lived where land was plentiful, were more concerned with control over people than with land ownership. Native Americans believed that no one could own the land because it belonged only to the one who created it.
20. The voyages of Columbus established a permanent exchange among Native Americans, Europeans, and Africans and brought tremendous changes to these cultures. The diseases that Europeans brought to the Americas decimated Native American populations. Gold and silver from the Americas caused Europe's economy to increase eight times over. Millions of Africans were abducted from their homelands and enslaved.

D. Interpreting a Chart

21. smallpox, measles, typhus
22. a. maize and beans

E. Analyzing a Document

23. Columbus was curious about Native Americans. He also seemed to believe that he had a right to seize the Native Americans by force, whether they accepted it or not.
24. Possible answers might include wonderment at these strangely dressed, different-looking people in their unfamiliar ships; fear of their power and weapons; and curiosity about who they were, where they came from, and what they would want.

Test Form B

A. Identifying Key Terms, People, and Places

1. d	6. k
2. f	7. b
3. h	8. g
4. j	9. i
5. a	10. l

B. Identifying Main Ideas

11. b	15. c
12. c	16. b
13. d	17. d
14. a	18. c

C. Critical Thinking

19. Native Americans, Europeans, and West Africans all had extensive trading networks, which were well traveled, whether by land, river, or sea. Europeans and Africans carried out trade primarily as an economic activity, while Native Americans often traded to demonstrate hospitality and friendliness, and they never traded land.
20. Native Americans might have successfully resisted the European invasion, or at least held off the conquering Europeans for a longer time.

D. Interpreting a Chart

21. Any four of the following: horse, pig, cattle, goat, sheep, chicken, guinea hen, mule.
22. c. wheat and rice

E. Analyzing a Document

23. He wanted both to learn what they could tell them about their lands and to explain to them who he and his men were and where they came from.
24. They adopted a kind of "charades," using signs and gestures and sometimes words to give information and explain ideas.

Chapter 2

Test Form A

A. Identifying Key Terms, People, and Places

1. c	6. m
2. f	7. b
3. l	8. o
4. a	9. i
5. e	10. d

B. Identifying Main Ideas

11. b	15. b
12. a	16. c
13. c	17. d
14. d	18. b

C. Critical Thinking

19. Any two: British privateers wanted a base in the Americas from which to attack Spanish ships and cities; the British

wanted to find a Northwest Passage to the Indies; British merchants wanted new markets for their goods; England was becoming crowded.

20. William Penn wanted the people of his colony to practice religious tolerance, and he welcomed many faiths. The Puritans wanted the people of their colony to practice only the faith of the Puritans and to support it with taxes.

D. Interpreting A Graph

21. about 120,000 pounds
22. between 1620 and 1622

E. Analyzing A Document

23. Since the pamphlet is printed in London and can be purchased there, it seems to be appealing to people in London.
24. It promises excellent farming and offers them the excitement of finding it in Virginia.

Test Form B

A. Identifying Key Terms, People, and Places

1. f	6. n
2. j	7. b
3. h	8. m
4. a	9. i
5. o	10. c

B. Identifying Main Ideas

11. c	15. b
12. a	16. a
13. c	17. c
14. d	18. a

C. Critical Thinking

Possible answers:

19. The French fur trade led to rivalries between many Native American groups, igniting an increase in warfare among them. English farming methods, which destroyed valuable hunting grounds, brought Native Americans into conflict with the English colonists.
20. Anne Hutchinson's ideology of allowing people to think for themselves about religious ideas and obedience to God came into direct conflict with the Puritan idea that Puritan authority was to be accepted unquestioningly in all matters of religion—as well as other areas of life.

D. Interpreting A Graph

21. about 60,000 pounds
22. 1622-1624 and 1624-1626, at about 140,000 pounds in each period

E. Analyzing A Document

23. Virginia offers the "most excellent fruites by Planting," which should excite all who want such opportunity.
24. Since it concentrates on "Planting," its major appeal would probably be to people who wanted to make their lives in farming.

Chapter 3

Test Form A

A. Identifying Key Terms, People, and Places

1. mercantilism
2. balance of trade
3. duty
4. gentry
5. apprentice
6. tobacco
7. self-sufficient
8. Middle Passage
9. Stono Rebellion
10. dissent

B. Identifying Main Ideas

11. c	15. b
12. d	16. d
13. b	17. b
14. b	18. d

C. Critical Thinking

Possible answers:

19. Colonial legislatures created and passed laws regarding taxes and defense. They set the salaries for royal officials. They influenced the appointment of judges and other officials.
20. Under English law, a woman was under her husband's control. Women had no legal or political standing of their own. Women could not own property, vote, or hold public office.

D. Interpreting A Map

21. Europe, Africa, and North America
22. The colonies obtained enslaved Africans to cultivate tobacco and other cash crops; England obtained raw materials from the colonies in exchange for manufactured goods. Merchants in both places profited from the trade.

E. Analyzing A Document

23. 14
24. Ravel would be free after fourteen years of labor. Enslaved Africans were slaves for life.

Test Form B

A. Identifying Key Terms, People, and Places

1. i	6. l
2. m	7. c
3. a	8. j
4. k	9. f
5. d	10. g

B. Identifying Main Ideas

11. c
12. c
13. b
14. a
15. a
16. b
17. b
18. d

C. Critical Thinking

19. White colonists ate better, lived longer, and had more children to help them with their work. They also had more opportunities to advance in wealth and social rank.

20. Enslaved Africans who lived in South Carolina and Georgia usually farmed large plantations, maintained strong kinship networks, and preserved many cultural traditions. By contrast, enslaved African Americans in Maryland, Virginia, and the Middle and Northern colonies blended their cultures with European culture and performed a wider variety of tasks, including shipbuilding, lumbering, and domestic service. In all colonies, enslaved Africans were the victims of harsh laws and brutal treatment.

D. Interpreting A Map

21. England, Africa, the British Colonies, and the West Indies
22. Enslaved Africans were transported to the West Indies to work on sugar plantations and to the Southern Colonies to work on tobacco and cotton plantations.

E. Analyzing A Document

23. Two.
24. He was sold to a new owner.

Chapter 4

Test Form A

A. Identifying Key Terms, People, and Places

1. c
2. g
3. e
4. l
5. n
6. a
7. m
8. k
9. f
10. h

B. Identifying Main Ideas

11. c
12. b
13. b
14. b
15. c
16. d
17. b
18. c

C. Critical Thinking

Possible answers:

19. Unlike many writers of his time, Paine used simple and direct language. He argued that any person could understand the issues behind the conflict between Britain and the colonies. He made clear and powerful arguments for independence.
20. British advantages: the British had a well-equipped, well-trained army and the world's finest navy. Britain also had help from Loyalists, some Native Americans, and 30,000 mercenaries. British disadvantages: the war was unpopular in Britain. British soldiers had to fight in hostile territory and British commanders did not adapt their tactics to conditions in North America. American advantages: the Americans were on familiar ground and had a strong leader in George Washington. American disadvantages: throughout much of the war, the American army lacked experienced soldiers and military supplies.

D. Interpreting A Political Cartoon

21. rebellious Americans, or Patriots
22. The snake is saying that it has room in its stomach for more British armies, meaning the Americans are prepared to continue defeating the British on the battlefield.

E. Analyzing A Document

23. the colonial boycott of tea
24. to gain support for the boycott of British tea

Test Form B

A. Identifying Key Terms, People, and Places

1. d
2. h
3. f
4. j
5. l
6. a
7. m
8. k
9. c
10. n

B. Identifying Main Ideas

11. b
12. b
13. d
14. b
15. c
16. a
17. c
18. d

C. Critical Thinking

Possible answers:

19. These protesters believed that a person should not be taxed without consent. In other words, a government can not tax people unless the people have representatives in that government. Colonists had no representatives in the British government, so they believed the British could not legally tax them.
20. Most students will probably agree, citing that sheer persistence and determination enabled the Patriots to outlast

the British and finally win the war.

D. Interpreting a Political Cartoon

21. Britain
22. Like the rattlesnake, the Americans are powerful and dangerous.

E. Analyzing a Document

23. She is giving up tea. To protest the tax on tea put in place by the Townshend Acts, she is supporting the boycott of British tea.
24. Liberty, in the form of freedom from British taxation and authority

Chapter 5

Test Form A

A. Identifying Key Terms, People, and Places

1. i	6. n
2. o	7. g
3. e	8. j
4. k	9. l
5. d	10. a

B. Identifying Main Ideas

11. d	15. a
12. c	16. c
13. a	17. a
14. a	18. b

C. Critical Thinking

Possible answers:

19. Nationalists felt the national government created by the Articles of Confederation was ineffective. They made the following objections: weak national government; lawmakers did not attend sessions; no national court system; no national economic policies; too much possibility for chaos in citizens' challenging governmental authority; the United States did not command the respect of outside world.
20. If enslaved persons were counted in the population, southern states would gain greater power in the House of Representatives. The debate was settled by the Three-Fifths Compromise, which stated that three fifths of the enslaved people in each state would be counted when determining that state's population.

D. Interpreting a Political Map

21. Virginia (with 21 electors); Delaware and Vermont (each with 3 electors)
22. Under such a plan, Virginia would have the most voting power, as it had the largest population.

E. Analyzing a Document

23. Each person brings his own passions, prejudices, and personal interests.
24. No. He believed it was as good an agreement as could be expected from a diverse group of people.

Test Form B

A. Identifying Key Terms, People, and Places

1. m	6. j
2. f	7. i
3. b	8. a
4. k	9. o
5. e	10. c

B. Identifying Main Ideas

11. c	15. d
12. b	16. a
13. c	17. b
14. a	18. b

C. Critical Thinking

Possible answers:

19. Antifederalists argued that the Constitution would give the federal government too much power. Specific objections included: the Constitution is a betrayal of the Revolution; a President would be nothing but a king; the new court system will endanger people's liberties; local and state governments will be crushed by the federal government.
20. As the country's first President, Washington knew that his actions would set precedents and he wanted to set a good example for future leaders. Also, he knew that the world was watching the United States, and he wanted to win respect for the new country.

D. Interpreting a Political Map

21. New York had two representatives in the Senate and ten in the House of Representatives.
22. A candidate would campaign hardest in Virginia, Massachusetts, and Pennsylvania because those states had the greatest number of electoral votes.

E. Analyzing a Document

23. Each man also brings his own prejudices, selfish views, and personal interests.
24. Franklin felt that the diverse group of delegates could not have produced a better Constitution.

Chapter 6

Test Form A

A. Identifying Key Terms, People, and Places

1. g
2. k
3. n
4. f
5. l
6. c
7. b
8. a
9. h
10. d

B. Identifying Main Ideas

11. c
12. b
13. d
14. a
15. b
16. a
17. d
18. d

C. Critical Thinking

Possible answers:

19. Federalists thought the Constitution should be interpreted loosely. They felt it was intended as a general guide to how the government should be run. The Jeffersonian Republicans thought it should be interpreted strictly. They felt the government was limited to those powers that were specified in the Constitution.

20. Impressment is the act of forcing people into military service. For years, the American government had protested the British practice of impressing American citizens into British military service. The British ignored these protests. This became one of the main causes of the war.

D. Interpreting A Graph

21. 1807; 1814

22. The War of 1812

E. Analyzing A Document

23. Hamilton felt that people change their minds easily and rarely make the right decisions.

24. Jefferson. Unlike Hamilton, he had faith in people and believed they were capable of governing themselves.

Test Form B

A. Identifying Key Terms, People, and Places

1. e
2. f
3. d
4. b
5. k
6. i
7. c
8. n
9. l
10. a

B. Identifying Main Ideas

11. d
12. c
13. d
14. c
15. c
16. c
17. b
18. b

C. Critical Thinking

Possible answers:

19. It set a pattern for the peaceful transfer of power from one party to another. This was very rare in the world at that time.

20. The westward expansion worsened relations with Native Americans and resulted in organized Native American resistance. Also, the issue of slavery in the western territories increased tensions between the North and South.

D. Interpreting A Graph

21. The embargo caused exports to drop sharply.

22. They began to rise.

E. Analyzing A Document

23. Hamilton viewed the common people as having poor judgment. Jefferson had more confidence in the common people.

24. Hamilton felt the voice of the people was not the voice of God. He had little confidence in the people's ability to make wise choices.

Chapter 7

Test Form A

A. Identifying Key Terms, People, and Places

1. i
2. h
3. j
4. a
5. d
6. f
7. b

B. Identifying Main Ideas

8. b
9. c
10. a
11. d
12. c
13. b
14. a
15. b
16. d
17. c

C. Critical Thinking

Possible answers:

18. Young people wanted new lands to settle on, and many of them had the energy, strength, and desire to find and settle western lands. As a result, the American population of these regions increased dramatically.

19. Many white settlers feared that free African Americans would compete for land and jobs. They passed discriminatory laws to discourage blacks from settling in the territories.

D. Reading A Table

20. Population grew substantially in all of the regions.

21. There was a greater increase in population in the Middle Atlantic region.

22. The North Central region

E. Analyzing A Document

23. children of wealthy families

24. The government was in the hands of the people, Webster argued, therefore it was important that the people be well informed.

Test Form B

A. Identifying Key Terms, People, and Places

1. j	5. e
2. c	6. g
3. h	7. b
4. a	

B. Identifying Main Ideas

8. d	13. b
9. a	14. a
10. b	15. a
11. c	16. d
12. c	17. b

C. Critical Thinking

Possible answers:

18. 1. People often moved from place to place; 2. People were able to move upward in society from one social class to another.
19. The cotton gin made cotton production more efficient and profitable. More planters began to rely on cotton and cotton soon became the most important product in the southern economy. Demand for slave labor to cultivate cotton increased.

D. Reading a Table

20. South Atlantic; South Atlantic
21. The Middle Atlantic
22. Nearly three times as many people lived in the regions east of the Appalachian mountains (9.2 million) as in the North and South Central regions (3.3 million).

E. Analyzing a Document

23. Yes. He argued that since government is in the hands of the people, it is important to society that the people be educated.
24. The legislatures, or governments of the states.

Chapter 8

Test Form A

A. Identifying Key Terms, People, and Places

1. f	6. h
2. a	7. m
3. j	8. i
4. e	9. g
5. b	10. k

B. Identifying Main Ideas

11. c	15. b
12. a	16. b
13. b	17. c
14. b	18. a

C. Critical Thinking

Possible answers:

19. The Market Revolution seemed to improve life for many, since goods that once needed to be made by hand could now be purchased in stores. For those who owned successful businesses, large fortunes could be made. However, life for factory workers was difficult, as many had to live in dirty, crowded cities, working long hours for low wages.
20. Any two: the North's economy was becoming more and more industrial, while the South's remained based on agriculture; the North relied on free laborers while the South relied on slave labor; the North was growing increasingly urban while the South remained rural.

D. Interpreting a Political Cartoon

21. the paper marked "VETO" in his hand.
22. his kingly crown and robes, and his trampling on the Constitution
23. probably the National Democrats, since they were the opposition party and therefore would want to weaken Jackson's popularity

E. Analyzing a Document

24. Bibb lived as a free man and earned a living by his labor.
25. that he did not escape sooner

Test Form B

A. Identifying Key Terms, People, and Places

1. h	6. d
2. i	7. a
3. l	8. c
4. g	9. k
5. b	10. f

B. Identifying Main Ideas

11. a	15. b
12. b	16. a
13. b	17. a
14. d	18. b

C. Critical Thinking

Possible answers:

19. A middle-class businessman was more likely to benefit. During the Market Revolution, a businessman could borrow money from a bank to start or expand a business, make profits, and live well. On the other hand, an urban factory worker was likely to live in a dirty, overcrowded tenement and to work for low wages under poor working conditions.
20. The goal of the Monroe Doctrine was to prevent European powers from seeking new colonies in the Americas. Yes, the policy has been followed to some degree by every President since Monroe.

D. Interpreting a Political Cartoon

21. Jackson is holding a bill marked "VETO" in his hand.
22. No, the cartoonists portrays him as a king, not as a common man.
23. The National Democrats, the party that opposed Jackson, most likely promoted this cartoon to explain their opposition to Jackson.

E. Analyzing a Document

24. Bibb was seen as a free man
25. that he did not escape sooner from slavery

Chapter 9

Test Form A

A. Identifying Key Terms, People, and Places

1. h	6. j
2. b	7. d
3. a	8. f
4. c	9. k
5. m	10. i

B. Identifying Main Ideas

11. d	15. a
12. a	16. b
13. d	17. d
14. d	18. b

C. Critical Thinking

Possible answers:

19. In Beecher's view, women played very important roles in society. As wives, mothers, and teachers, they set an example for the entire family. A proper education could help women have a positive influence on society.
20. Most white southerners enjoyed their traditional way of life. They resented northern reform groups telling them they had to change. They were particularly bitter toward abolitionists. Also, much of the South was not touched by the social turmoil that came with the growth of cities and industry of the North. Thus, southerners saw no reason to reform their society.

D. Interpreting a Graph

21. 1851-1855; about 650,000
22. German immigration increased from about 100,000 to over 650,000.

E. Analyzing a Document

23. 500 looms were all operating at once
24. Yes. The air was full of cotton filaments and dust, which was dangerous for the workers' lungs.

Test Form B

A. Identifying Key Terms, People, and Places

1. c	6. i
2. j	7. h
3. k	8. a
4. g	9. e
5. m	10. d

B. Identifying Main Ideas

11. a	15. a
12. c	16. d
13. b	17. c
14. c	18. b

C. Critical Thinking

Possible answers:

19. Urbanization and the Industrial Revolution brought many problems to the North. These included poverty, alcoholism, overcrowded housing and poor health care. These problems inspired the reform movements of the early 1800s.
20. Any two: Some people disapproved of the immigrants' culture; immigrants competed for jobs and often worked for low wages; immigrants were predominantly Catholic and many American-born Protestants disapproved of this religion.

D. Interpreting a Graph

21. Irish immigration grew from under 200,000 to 600,000, an increase of about three times.
22. German immigration grew from about 330,000 to about 670,000, more than doubling.

E. Analyzing a Document

23. The passage states that they worked 13 hours a day and went to sleep right after dinner. Also, they had to work three looms at the same time, which required a lot of concentration.
24. The work room was very loud and the air was filled with cotton and dust.

Chapter 10

Test Form A

A. Identifying Key Terms, People, and Places

1. j	6. c
2. k	7. h
3. a	8. e
4. i	9. l
5. d	10. f

B. Identifying Main Ideas

11. b
12. b
13. a
14. b
15. d
16. b
17. c
18. b

C. Critical Thinking

Possible answers:

19. Through trade, the United States developed strong economic relations with Texas, New Mexico, and California long before it gained political control of these areas. These close ties encouraged many Americans to settle in northern Mexico.
20. Any one: the war left many Mexicans bitter toward the United States and led to many years of poor relations; the war led to new debates over the question of slavery in United States territories; the war opened the door to more western migration, leading to increased tensions with Native Americans in the West.

D. Reading A Table

21. It sank from 5,000 to 1,000; the Mexican War
22. 1849 and 1850; the discovery of gold in California

E. Analyzing A Document

23. His army was besieged by a much larger Mexican army. The Texans would be defeated if they did not receive aid.
24. He appealed to their patriotism and love of liberty. He also made it clear that he would be killed if help did not arrive quickly.

Test Form B

A. Identifying Key Terms, People, and Places

1. c
2. j
3. h
4. i
5. f
6. k
7. l
8. b
9. a
10. d

B. Identifying Main Ideas

11. d
12. c
13. b
14. b
15. a
16. b
17. a
18. c

C. Critical Thinking

Possible answers:

19. Nomadic Native Americans were accustomed to living in different areas and could adapt more easily when pushed from one territory to another. Also, nomadic Native Americans were skilled warriors.
20. For: it was a chance for the United States to greatly expand its territory; southerners looked forward to adding another slave state. Against: northerners opposed the addition of a new slave state; annexation would lead to war with Mexico.

D. Reading A Table

21. 1841; 1850
22. It caused a dramatic increase in western migration.

E. Analyzing A Document

23. Travis and the Texans were surrounded by a large Mexican army under General Santa Anna.
24. He expected to fight as long as possible, and die with honor.

Chapter 11

Test Form A

A. Identifying Key Terms, People, and Places

1. i
2. f
3. a
4. e
5. h
6. k
7. g
8. c
9. j
10. d

B. Identifying Main Ideas

11. c
12. a
13. c
14. b
15. b
16. d
17. a
18. d

C. Critical Thinking

Possible answers:

19. Northern whites who opposed slavery thought it violated the liberty of the enslaved people. Southern whites believed that abolishing slavery would violate their liberty by denying them the right to own property.
20. Lincoln believed secession was illegal. He also opposed the expansion of slavery.

D. Interpreting A Graph

21. the North; the North
22. The North had substantially more farmland.
23. The North had the advantage. The North had a larger population, more wealth, more factories, and more miles of railroads.

E. Analyzing A Document

24. to free slaves
25. No. He felt he was justified in using force to oppose slavery.

Test Form B

A. Identifying Key Terms, People, and Places

1. f	6. a
2. l	7. k
3. b	8. j
4. i	9. h
5. g	10. e

B. Identifying Main Ideas

11. d	15. b
12. a	16. a
13. d	17. b
14. c	18. a

C. Critical Thinking

Possible answers:

19. Northern abolitionists believed that the Constitution guaranteed freedom for all people, including enslaved African Americans. Southern slaveholders believed that the abolition of slavery violated their constitutional right to own property.
20. Lincoln was elected without winning a single electoral vote in the South. This angered many southerners, who felt they no longer had any power in the federal government. Also, they did not want a President who opposed slavery. These feelings led to the formation of the Confederacy and the outbreak of the Civil War.

D. Interpreting a Graph

21. The population of the North was about double that of the South.
22. the North; the North
23. The North had substantially more farm machinery, railroads, and factories.

E. Analyzing a Document

24. allowing slavery to exist
25. because he felt the government, in allowing slavery, was guilty of a great wrong against God and human beings

Chapter 12

Test Form A

A. Identifying Key Terms, People, and Places

1. d	5. i
2. f	6. h
3. a	7. b
4. j	8. g

B. Identifying Main Ideas

9. c	14. b
10. c	15. a
11. b	16. b
12. c	17. b
13. d	18. b

C. Critical Thinking

Possible answers:

19. The textile mills of Britain and France relied on Southern cotton. Southern leaders assumed that European industrial leaders would pressure their governments into supporting the Confederacy. The assumption was incorrect. The Europeans turned to India and Egypt for cotton.
20. The North was better prepared for a major war. The North had more miles of railroad track, twice as many factories, a much larger population, a balanced economy, and a functioning government already in place.

D. Interpreting a Map

21. Mississippi, Cumberland, and Tennessee Rivers
22. Vicksburg

E. Analyzing a Document

23. 1776, the year the United States declared its independence from Britain.
24. to dedicate a portion of the Gettysburg battlefield to the soldiers who died there

Test Form B

A. Identifying Key Terms, People, and Places

1. g	5. h
2. c	6. f
3. a	7. j
4. i	8. d

B. Identifying Main Ideas

9. d	14. a
10. a	15. b
11. c	16. b
12. a	17. c
13. b	18. b

C. Critical Thinking

Possible answers:

19. Northern advantages: double the miles of railroad tracks, for shipment of troops and goods; twice as many factories; an economy balanced between farming and industry; more money to spend on war production; a functioning government; an existing army and navy; a larger population. Southern advantages: more trained military leaders; ability to fight a defensive war; the emotional advantage of fighting to preserve way of life.
20. In July 1863, for the first time, a Northern victory was in sight. Lee had just lost a third of his army at Gettysburg and was retreating into Virginia. Grant had just captured Vicksburg, giving the Union control of the entire Mississippi River.

D. Interpreting a Map

21. New Orleans and Port Hudson

22. The western region of the Confederacy would be cut off from the eastern region, and the South would lose the ability to ship goods and military supplies along the river.

E. Analyzing a Document

23. whether any nation dedicated to liberty could survive

24. as men who gave their lives so their nation could live

Chapter 13

Test Form A

A. Identifying Key Terms, People, and Places

1. a	**5.** d
2. i	**6.** f
3. b	**7.** h
4. j	**8.** g

B. Identifying Main Ideas

9. b	**14.** b
10. c	**15.** c
11. c	**16.** a
12. a	**17.** a
13. d	**18.** b

C. Critical Thinking

Possible answers:

19. Planters had a hard time finding workers, while former slaves had no land of their own. As a result, many people became sharecroppers or tenant farmers. Because these farmers produced cash crops, the South had to begin importing much of its food.

20. Successes: the Union was restored; the South began to recover from war; 14th and 15th Amendments gave rights to African Americans; the South adopted system of public education. Failures: Most blacks in the South remained poor; state governments and racist groups denied rights to African Americans; lasting bitterness between North and South.

D. Interpreting a Cartoon

21. to ensure that the government remained in the hands of white men

22. either one: lynching African Americans; burning down their schoolhouses

E. Analyzing a Document

23. It ended slavery in the United States.

24. as punishment for a crime

Test Form B

A. Identifying Key Terms, People, and Places

1. h	**5.** i
2. g	**6.** b
3. e	**7.** d
4. c	**8.** a

B. Identifying Main Ideas

9. d	**14.** b
10. a	**15.** b
11. a	**16.** c
12. c	**17.** b
13. c	**18.** c

C. Critical Thinking

Possible answers:

19. Former slaves had no money, no work, and were often homeless. They were also the victims of racial violence. Plantation owners lost their workforce with the abolition of slavery. Many could not afford to hire new workers. Poor whites had to compete with freedmen for the few available jobs. Unable to find work, many chose to migrate.

20. Students may choose to write about any one: 13th Amendment; Freedmen's Bureau; Reconstruction Acts; 14th Amendment; 15th Amendment; Civil Rights Act of 1866.

D. Interpreting a Cartoon

21. white men

22. Conditions were worse than they had been during slavery. Blacks were lynched and schools were burned.

E. Analyzing a Document

23. to abolish slavery everywhere in the United States

24. the Legislature, or Congress.

Chapter 14

Test Form A

A. Identifying Key Terms, People, and Places

1. b	**5.** h
2. a	**6.** f
3. e	**7.** c
4. d	**8.** g

B. Identifying Main Ideas

9. b	**14.** a
10. c	**15.** d
11. b	**16.** c
12. c	**17.** c
13. b	**18.** c

C. Critical Thinking

Possible answers:

19. Large numbers of immigrants were coming to the United States in search of work in American cities. At the same time, poor economic conditions on the nation's farms caused many Americans to move to cities.

20. The term "robber barons" reflects a belief that industrialists built their fortunes by stealing from the public. They abused the law and mistreated their workers. The term "captains of industry" reflects the belief that business leaders served their country in a positive way. They built businesses, provided jobs, and founded museums and universities.

D. Reading a Cross-Sectional Map

21. Omaha
22. 1,800 miles

E. Analyzing a Document

23. Workers suffered from the powerful smell of tobacco. Children and women were especially vulnerable to the effects of the odor.
24. winter, when the factories shut the windows, trapping the tobacco odors inside

Test Form B

A. Identifying Key Terms, People, and Places

1. b	5. h
2. k	6. a
3. i	7. f
4. e	8. g

B. Identifying Main Ideas

9. b	14. c
10. c	15. b
11. a	16. c
12. c	17. c
13. a	18. a

C. Critical Thinking

Possible answers:

19. Social Darwinism applied Darwin's "survival of the fittest" theory of evolution to the struggle between workers and employers. The theory stated that, if the government does not interfere, the smartest and strongest members of society will succeed, and society as a whole will benefit.
20. The federal government consistently sided with factory owners. Federal troops were often used to break up strikes. The government also denied unions recognition as legally protected organizations.

D. Reading a Cross-Sectional Map

21. The Sierra Nevada Mountains
22. 7,000 feet

E. Analyzing a Document

23. Student answers will probably focus on the overpowering tobacco terrible odor, and the health hazards that resulted from it.
24. people who are not used to the smell, along with women and children

Chapter 15

Test Form A

A. Identifying Key Terms, People, and Places

1. f	5. a
2. b	6. d
3. e	7. g
4. j	8. i

B. Identifying Main Ideas

9. a	14. d
10. d	15. b
11. a	16. c
12. a	17. b
13. c	18. b

C. Critical Thinking

Possible answers:

19. Questions might include: How much does the land cost? What is the climate like? What farming equipment will I need? What challenges will I face? What kinds of crops grow well there?
20. Native Americans and homesteaders both lived off the land, but in different ways. Native Americans mainly lived off the buffalo that roamed the plains, and did little to change the land. Homesteaders grew crops and raised domestic livestock, both of which changed the land.

D. Interpreting a Graphic

21. The white man seems to be disrespectful to the Native American. The Native American is being told to leave the land that he has always lived on.
22. The graphic shows the buffalo herds of the Great Plains. Eventually, the buffalo were nearly wiped out by settlers and railroad workers.

E. Analyzing a Document

23. The song tells people to give up their jobs and move to California to search for gold.
24. No. The song makes it sound like there is gold everywhere, and can be easily found. In reality, life was hard for prospectors and very few ever "struck it rich."

Test Form B

A. Identifying Key Terms, People, and Places

1. d	5. g
2. j	6. b
3. f	7. a
4. c	8. h

B. Identifying Main Ideas

9. c	14. a
10. b	15. b
11. c	16. b
12. c	17. a
13. b	18. b

C. Critical Thinking

Possible answers:

19. Answers should focus on any of the following categories—building housing, difficulty getting water, dangers of unsafe drinking water, plowing the tough prairie sod, earning money while waiting for crops to come in, having to make their own necessities like clothing and soap.
20. The railroads had several negative effects on life for Native Americans. Railroads brought settlers, who then began taking over Native American lands. Railroad workers also contributed to the slaughter of the buffalo herds of the Great Plains. The railroads had positive effects for white settlers. Farmers and ranchers relied on the railroads to transport their goods to market.

D. Interpreting A Graphic

21. The white settler wants the Native American to move off of the land. The settler wants to use the land himself.
22. In the Great Plains. The land is flat and mostly treeless, and a herd of buffalo runs in the background.

E. Analyzing A Document

23. because it would be easier to get rich by finding gold in California
24. No. According to the song, gold could be found almost everywhere: on mountains and plains, beneath trees, and among flowers.

Chapter 16

Test Form A

A. Identifying Key Terms, People, and Places

1. e	5. j
2. g	6. b
3. k	7. c
4. a	8. d

B. Identifying Main Ideas

9. b	14. c
10. c	15. a
11. b	16. b
12. d	17. d
13. c	18. a

C. Critical Thinking

Possible answers:

19. Life was difficult for most immigrants. They were likely to live in dirty, overcrowded tenements. Many worked long hours for low wages in poor working conditions. On the other hand, most immigrants enjoyed more personal and political freedom than they had at home.
20. Mark Twain's "thin layer of glitter" referred to the prosperity enjoyed by only a small segment of society. His "cheap base" referred to problems throughout society, including corruption in government, unfair business practices, the increasing gap between rich and poor, discrimination against immigrants, poor living conditions, and unsafe working conditions.

D. Reading A Table

21. rural: 45,835,000; urban: 30,160,000
22. The urban population began to grow larger than the rural population.

E. Analyzing A Document

23. Riis said that gangs began in the tenements and reflected the characteristics of tenement life.
24. American-born sons of immigrants from Europe

Test Form B

A. Identifying Key Terms, People, and Places

1. b	5. i
2. e	6. k
3. g	7. c
4. j	8. f

B. Identifying Main Ideas

9. b	14. a
10. c	15. c
11. d	16. d
12. a	17. c
13. b	18. b

C. Critical Thinking

Possible answers:

19. Any two: she will enjoy personal and political freedoms; with hard work, she may achieve a better life than she had back home; expect to find low wages; be prepared for hostility and discrimination; be prepared for overcrowded living conditions.
20. Nativists believed that immigrants were bad for the country. They sought to restrict immigration. Settlement house workers believed that poor immigrants should be made to feel welcome in the community and should be helped to adapt to American life and culture.

D. Reading A Table

21. rural: 25,227,00; urban: 6,217,000
22. 1910–1920; Immigrants were flooding into America's cities and people from rural areas were moving to cities.

E. Analyzing a Document

23. Riis said gangs were made up of American-born sons of European immigrants living in tenements.

24. living conditions in the tenement houses of New York

Chapter 17

Test Form A

A. Identifying Key Terms, People, and Places

1. h	**5.** j
2. e	**6.** f
3. b	**7.** i
4. d	**8.** c

B. Identifying Main Ideas

9. d	**14.** a
10. b	**15.** b
11. c	**16.** a
12. b	**17.** b
13. c	**18.** a

C. Critical Thinking

Possible answers:

19. Du Bois wanted the brightest African Americans to pursue advanced liberal arts education. He felt they should prepare themselves to lead the fight for equal rights. Washington believed that vocational education would train African Americans to achieve economic success, and help them gain white acceptance.

20. Students may explain any two: discrimination in higher education; no right to vote; limited control over property and income; denial of access to public roles; limited access to the professions.

D. Interpreting a Bar Graph

21. about 15 percent; about 85 percent

22. Between 1890 and 1910, the percentage of single women in the labor force decreased while the percentage of married women increased.

E. Analyzing a Document

23. He hoped that she would get a good education, allowing her to enjoy a good life in the United States.

24. He was very proud. He had very high hopes for his daughter.

Test Form B

A. Identifying Key Terms, People, and Places

1. d	**5.** l
2. b	**6.** g
3. m	**7.** c
4. f	**8.** i

B. Identifying Main Ideas

9. b	**14.** b
10. a	**15.** c
11. b	**16.** a
12. b	**17.** d
13. c	**18.** a

C. Critical Thinking

Possible answers:

19. Women began by establishing small clubs where members shared information and ideas. Some clubs worked for social and political causes. As club membership grew, women formed national organizations. Through these groups, women worked for reforms and suffrage.

20. Bias in the South was expressed through Jim Crow laws and violent acts such as lynching. In the North, African Americans faced bias, though it was not backed by law. Most northern schools and housing were effectively segregated. Racial fears led to race riots in several northern cities.

D. Interpreting a Bar Graph

21. It increased from about 15 percent to about 25 percent.

22. Based on the trend developing, married women will form a continually larger percentage of women in the labor force, and single women will form a decreasing percentage.

E. Analyzing a Document

23. He saw it as a key to success in the United States.

24. Possible answer: Education is not a physical item that can be stolen. Once you have an education, no one can take it away.

Chapter 18

Test Form A

A. Identifying Key Terms, People, and Places

1. c	**6.** c
2. f	**7.** b
3. a	**8.** a
4. b	**9.** d
5. g	**10.** e

B. Identifying Main Ideas

11. a	**15.** b
12. c	**16.** d
13. a	**17.** c
14. b	**18.** c

C. Critical Thinking

Possible answers:

19. Arguments included that imperialism violated the American idea of "liberty for all" upon which the nation was founded. In addition, defending American interests abroad might require a large standing army, which could then be used to crush dissent at home.

20. "Dollar diplomacy" was not always profitable for investors in the United States, because of revolutionary activities or interference from other nations. Dollar diplomacy also damaged U.S. relations with many countries, especially in the Caribbean and Central America, where U.S. influence was often resented.

D. Interpreting a Map

Possible answers:

21. Cuba is located close to the United States, just off the Florida coast. United States businesses had established plantations in Cuba, and many Cuban exiles lived in the United States.
22. Panama is located on the narrowest part of Central America. The narrow isthmus divides the Pacific and Atlantic Oceans.

E. Analyzing a Document

Possible answers:

23. The Monroe Doctrine "coops up" European countries and keeps them from hurting the countries of Latin America.
24. The rooster representing the U.S. is much larger than the other roosters, suggesting it is the most powerful in the Western Hemisphere. Its posture and plumage indicate pride, confidence, and control.

Test Form B

A. Identifying Key Terms, People, and Places

1. b	**5.** e
2. i	**6.** f
3. g	**7.** h
4. d	**8.** a

B. Identifying Main Ideas

9. d	**14.** a
10. b	**15.** c
11. b	**16.** c
12. b	**17.** c
13. d	**18.** d

C. Critical Thinking

Possible answers:

19. Roosevelt and Taft both promoted expansionism and intervened in the affairs of weaker countries to safeguard American interests. However, Roosevelt relied on military force to preserve stability and order in neighboring countries, while Taft promoted U.S. investment in foreign economies.
20. Some imperialists drew on the doctrine of Social Darwinism to justify the takeover of new territories. They believed in the superiority of the Anglo-Saxon and Teutonic peoples and thought it was in the best interest of other peoples to be introduced to Christianity and "modern civilization." At the same time, some anti-imperialists opposed expansionism because they feared it would encourage immigrants of different racial backgrounds to come to the United States.

D. Interpreting a Map

Possible answers:

21. Panama was narrower than Nicaragua and so offered a shorter route between the Pacific and the Atlantic.
22. The United States probably feared that Europeans would establish naval bases in Central America or the Caribbean and might interfere with U.S. trade and shipping.

E. Analyzing a Document

Possible answers:

23. The coop represents the Monroe Doctrine. It prevents the 'European' roosters from running in the 'American' field, just as the Monroe Doctrine kept European powers from intervening in Latin America.
24. The U.S. rooster is much larger and stronger-looking than the others. It appears as though the United States is proud, powerful, and in control as it protects nearby countries.

Chapter 19

Test Form A

A. Identifying Key Terms, People, and Places

1. h	**5.** e
2. f	**6.** i
3. j	**7.** b
4. a	**8.** c

B. Identifying Main Ideas

9. b	**14.** b
10. c	**15.** c
11. a	**16.** a
12. b	**17.** c
13. d	**18.** b

C. Critical Thinking

Possible answers:

19. Progressivism encouraged the federal government to take a more active role in regulating business and preserving the environment. Inspired by

Progressive ideas, the government enforced antitrust legislation, regulated the railroad and food and drug industries, enacted legislation protecting women and children, and created national parks.

20. Roosevelt and Wilson supported many of the same reforms, such as lower tariffs and antitrust laws, and other forms of federal regulation of big business. However, unlike Roosevelt, Wilson also criticized "big government." In campaigning for office, Wilson promised to preserve free economic competition.

D. Interpreting a Map

21. Wyoming, Colorado, Idaho, Utah
22. The movement was most successful in the West. Possible reasons: Survival on the frontier required the combined efforts of men and women, which encouraged a sense of equality.

E. Analyzing a Document

23. poverty and unemployment.
24. Possible answer: It is likely there were many unemployed men who sought jobs at the factory, that there was competition among them, and that they had to wait outside in very cold weather. However, some of the expressions, such as "all day long," "penniless," "made no difference," and "froze all together" may be exaggerations for effect.

Test Form B

A. Identifying Key Terms, People, and Places

1. d	**5.** h
2. e	**6.** f
3. j	**7.** a
4. b	**8.** g

B. Identifying Main Ideas

9. d	**14.** c
10. d	**15.** b
11. a	**16.** c
12. b	**17.** a
13. c	**18.** b

C. Critical Thinking

Possible answers:

19. Progressives might ask for candidates' opinions about antitrust laws, tariff reduction, unfair business practices, workplace conditions, or the environment. They would likely vote for candidates who supported controlling the trusts, ending unfair business practices, improving workplace conditions, and preserving the environment.
20. One suffragist strategy was to convince individual states to grant voting rights to women. The other strategy was to push for a federal amendment to the Constitution. Ultimately, the political force of the states that did grant suffrage combined with the continuing work of suffragists convinced Congress. The Nineteenth Amendment was ratified in 1920.

D. Interpreting a Map

21. Wyoming, 1890
22. in the West. Possible reason: Survival on the frontier required the combined efforts of men and women, which encouraged a sense of equality.

E. Analyzing a Document

Possible answers:

23. Sinclair probably wishes to create sympathy for the plight of the unemployed men, in order to convince the reader that change is necessary.
24. The passage is an example of muckraking in that it is the product of investigation into an issue of concern to reformers, and it uses specific details to move the reader to action.

Chapter 20

Test Form A

A. Identifying Key Terms, People, and Places

1. c	**5.** h
2. a	**6.** d
3. i	**7.** f
4. j	**8.** e

B. Identifying Main Ideas

9. d	**14.** d
10. a	**15.** d
11. b	**16.** b
12. b	**17.** a
13. c	**18.** c

C. Critical Thinking

Possible answers:

19. Public opinion played a large role in the United States' decision to enter the war. At first, business people with strong commercial ties to Great Britain urged preparedness for war, while various other groups called for continued neutrality. However, public outrage at Germany grew, in response to Germany's continued submarine warfare and the Zimmerman Note. By April 1917, public opinion was

strongly behind the war resolution passed by Congress.

20. Sacrifices at home included conserving food and fuel. For example, households voluntarily cut down on use of wheat, butter, and meat. Fuel was saved by voluntary "gasless days" as well as by instituting daylight saving time. Other sacrifices included having civil liberties restricted, buying Liberty Bonds, and the passage of the Prohibition Amendment, in part to preserve grain.

D. Interpreting a Table

21. Allied countries
22. Commercial relations between the United States and the Central Powers deteriorated rapidly in the early years of the war. Trade dropped from over 169 million dollars in 1914 to a little over a million dollars in 1916.

E. Analyzing a Document

23. The Imperial German Embassy placed the notice to warn American travelers that if they traveled on ships belonging to Great Britain or other Allies, they would face possible attack.
24. The warning did apply to the *Lusitania*, as it was a British ship and was sailing in "waters adjacent to the British Isles." In early May, 1915, the ship was attacked by a German U-boat and sunk in the Irish Sea.

Test Form B

A. Identifying Key Terms, People, and Places

1. e	5. b
2. d	6. i
3. c	7. g
4. a	8. f

B. Identifying Main Ideas

9. c	14. d
10. b	15. c
11. c	16. d
12. a	17. b
13. c	18. a

C. Critical Thinking

Possible answers:

19. Americans with roots in Germany and Ireland tended to be biased against Great Britain because of ongoing conflicts. However, most Americans were biased toward the Allies and against the Central Powers. The press portrayed Germans as extremely militaristic. Anti-German sentiment was encouraged by the British, who controlled the news that reached the United States from the European front. Commercial interests also biased many business leaders toward the Allies.
20. The Espionage Act of 1917 made it illegal to interfere with the draft. The Sedition Act of 1918 made it illegal to speak out against the government, Constitution, or armed forces. Some Americans, including socialists and radical labor leaders, continued to criticize the war, although they faced possible jail sentences for doing so. Others took it upon themselves to attack people who appeared disloyal.

D. Interpreting a Table

21. with the Allied countries, because its greatest volume of trade was with them
22. Support: U.S. trade with the Central Powers dwindled from nearly $170 million in 1914 to just over $1 million by 1916.

E. Analyzing a Document

23. The notice addresses American travelers and warns them not to travel on British ships.
24. The ship advertised on the right, the British *Lusitania*, was sunk by a German U-boat about two weeks after the date on the notice, as per the warning.

Chapter 21

Test Form A

A. Identifying Key Terms, People, and Places

1. e	6. e
2. a	7. a
3. g	8. b
4. b	9. f
5. d	10. d

B. Identifying Main Ideas

11. b	15. a
12. c	16. c
13. d	17. c
14. b	18. b

C. Critical Thinking

Possible answers:

19. Communist ideology was hostile to capitalism. Many Americans feared that communism would undermine American values such as private ownership of land and business and First Amendment freedoms.

20. The boom in the automobile industry stimulated the American economy both directly and indirectly. It employed many people and increased the demand for materials such as steel, rubber, glass, and leather. Suddenly ordinary people could afford cars. New businesses were created to serve automobile travel. These included motels, restaurants, and gas stations. New roads were built, and highways were lined with billboards advertising new products.

D. Interpreting a Bar Graph

21. (a) Southern Europe; (b) almost 300,000
22. Northwestern Europe
23. Immigration was greatly curtailed. It went down for all groups shown. In 1921 and 1924 laws were passed restricting immigration.

E. Analyzing a Document

24. He claimed that true prohibition never really existed, because the rules were never enforced.
25. He pointed out that speakeasies, or illegal bars, were widespread and flourishing.

Test Form B

A. Identifying Key Terms, People, and Places

1. d	6. b
2. b	7. a
3. e	8. f
4. a	9. e
5. c	10. d

B. Identifying Main Ideas

11. a	15. a
12. b	16. b
13. c	17. b
14. b	18. c

C. Critical Thinking

Possible answers:

19. The Soviet Union was a communist dictatorship in which the government owned all land and property. In contrast, the United States was a multi-party democracy in which most land and businesses were privately owned.
20. Supporters of Prohibition assumed that outlawing alcohol would limit or end its consumption and would solve related social problems. Their assumption was partly accurate, in that consumption of alcohol did decrease in some parts of the country. However, it was mostly inaccurate, as drinking did not end. Rather than solving urban problems, Prohibition led to new ones, including the rise of organized crime.

D. Interpreting a Bar Graph

21. Southern Europeans
22. (a) Northwestern Europe (b) about 75,000
23. Possible answer: Many Americans were suspicious of immigrants in the 1920s. A nativist reaction following World War I led to the setting of quotas limiting immigration.

E. Analyzing a Document

Possible answers:

24. La Guardia argued that Prohibition never truly existed as the law was neither obeyed nor enforced.
25. Speakeasies sold alcohol illegally, supporting La Guardia's point that the sale and consumption of alcohol continued despite Prohibition.

Chapter 22

Test Form A

A. Identifying Key Terms, People, and Places

1. c	6. a
2. b	7. d
3. e	8. c
4. f	9. b
5. a	10. e

B. Identifying Main Ideas

11. b	15. a
12. a	16. b
13. d	17. a
14. c	18. c

C. Critical Thinking

Possible answers:

19. Students will probably argue that Hoover painted a false image. For example, in trying to boost the country's confidence he made the inaccurate claims that people were protected from hunger and cold, and that the causes of the Depression were global rather than domestic.
20. A survivor of the Depression might counsel younger adults to save regularly, to limit installment buying, to pay off debts as quickly as possible, and not to speculate in the stock market.

D. Interpreting a Line Graph

21. about $40 billion
22. They appear to rise and fall together.
23. By 1939, the GNP and personal income were climbing and had almost reached 1929 levels.

E. Analyzing a Document

24. Hoover believed that action freely taken by individuals would lead to an economic solution.
25. Roosevelt believed government should take an active role in the nation's economic life in times of crisis.

Test Form B

A. Identifying Key Terms, People, and Places

1. c	**6.** g
2. f	**7.** d
3. d	**8.** b
4. b	**9.** e
5. g	**10.** f

B. Identifying Main Ideas

11. c	**15.** c
12. b	**16.** b
13. c	**17.** d
14. c	**18.** b

C. Critical Thinking

Possible answers:

19. The maxim is inconsistent with attitudes of many Americans of the 1920s who eagerly invested their savings in the stock market, many with borrowed money. A common attitude of the time was that one should get rich through high returns, rather than simply get by on hard work. Spending and borrowing, whether to buy stocks, automobiles or appliances, were common and socially acceptable practices.
20. Students may cite the way in which the Depression altered Americans' perception of the federal government. Or they may cite a change in the economic behavior and the attitude toward spending and saving among Depression survivors. Accept any well reasoned argument.

D. Interpreting a Line Graph

21. 1933; the Gross National Product and personal income were at their lowest.
22. Roosevelt might have used the data to argue that both GNP and personal income had dropped by about $40 billion during Hoover's presidency.
23. It would also increase.

E. Analyzing a Document

24. Hoover believed that the American system was based on individual freedoms and opportunities, and the idea that these would lead to progress.
25. He was arguing against the federal government's taking a very active role in relieving the Depression.

Chapter 23

Test Form A

A. Identifying Key Terms, People, and Places

1. d	**5.** i
2. f	**6.** j
3. c	**7.** e
4. g	**8.** a

B. Identifying Main Ideas

9. c	**14.** c
10. b	**15.** a
11. b	**16.** c
12. d	**17.** b
13. a	**18.** c

C. Critical Thinking

Possible answers:

19. A priority of the New Deal was to create jobs so that people could earn their own money and get back their self-esteem. Hopkins himself headed the Federal Emergency Relief Administration which put money into public works programs. These programs created jobs for the unemployed.
20. Some critics of the New Deal felt that the government was taking too much control over the economy. They objected to limitations on individual freedoms, and equated programs such as compulsory unemployment insurance with the philosophy of the Soviet Union. Some feared that the assignment of Social Security numbers was the first step in transforming the country into a militaristic, regimented society.

D. Interpreting a Line Graph

21. (a) 1937 (b) about 8 million
22. Roosevelt could argue based on the graph that unemployment went down during his administration, particularly in the period from 1933 to 1937.

E. Analyzing a Document

Possible answers:

23. The cartoonist was hinting that the Supreme Court was behind the nine valentines.
24. Such messages as "Faithful Unto Death!" and "Your Idea of a Chief Justice" accompanied by a picture of a baby show resentment toward FDR's claim that he wanted to appoint younger judges to ease the burden on older ones. Other cards with images of Roosevelt as king or dictator show anger at Roosevelt's attempt to strengthen the pres-

idency at the expense of the Supreme Court.

Test Form B

A. Identifying Key Terms, People, and Places

1. c **5.** a
2. b **6.** i
3. h **7.** j
4. e **8.** f

B. Identifying Main Ideas

9. c **14.** a
10. b **15.** c
11. a **16.** c
12. c **17.** a
13. d **18.** c

C. Critical Thinking

Possible answers:

19. A common belief at the time was that men were responsible for supporting their families financially. For this reason men tended to receive available jobs, and New Deal legislation and codes permitted lower wages to be paid to women.

20. New Deal programs were often carried out in a discriminatory way, but they did offer some help to African Americans, and so were probably viewed by many as better than no programs at all. Also, FDR appointed African Americans to policy-making positions in his administration in much greater numbers than his predecessors did.

D. Interpreting A Line Graph

21. (a)1933; (b) about 13 million

22. Possible answer: The graph suggests that New Deal programs were working, as unemployment went down, especially in Roosevelt's' first term. After spending was cut back in 1937 unemployment rose again.(Accept well-reasoned answers supporting different interpretations.)

E. Analyzing A Document

Possible answers:

23. There are nine valentines, just as there are nine justices on the Supreme Court; the Supreme Court building appears in the background.

24. Cards such as "Faithful Unto Death!" and "Your Idea of a Chief Justice" relate to FDR's claim that he wanted to appoint younger justices to lighten the burden of those over 70. Cards with images of FDR as king or dictator imply that FDR wants to control the Court so that he can have unchecked powers. "Now Ruin All" plays on the acronym for the National Recovery Administration.

Chapter 24

Test Form A

A. Identifying Key Terms, People, and Places

1. h **5.** i
2. b **6.** e
3. c **7.** a
4. g **8.** f

B. Identifying Main Ideas

9. c **14.** b
10. c **15.** c
11. b **16.** d
12. d **17.** b
13. d **18.** d

C. Critical Thinking

Possible answers:

19. Many Germans and Italians resented the terms of the Treaty of Versailles. Germans felt humiliated by the treaty's harsh terms, and Italians felt they had been shortchanged. Japanese military leaders resented their dependence on other nations for resources such as petroleum and iron. In addition, all three nations viewed aggression as a means to solving economic problems.

20. Students will probably answer that the Allies would have lost the war without the United States since the Axis Powers had conquered much of Europe by the time the United States entered the war. Britain, though still unconquered, had suffered heavy damage, and might have been isolated by Germany without the actions of American warships. American forces helped turn the tide in North Africa and were instrumental in reclaiming both Europe and the Pacific islands. Students may also argue that Americans were responsible for the atomic bomb, which forced the surrender of Japan.

D. Interpreting A Map

21. Ireland, Portugal, Spain, Switzerland, Sweden, and Turkey

22. Because Great Britain is an island, it could not be invaded by land.

23. By attacking the Soviet Union, Germany had to fight a war on both an eastern and a western front.

E. Analyzing A Document

24. It is being changed for the sake of efficiency—to make better use of the training personnel and other resources available.

25. probably to ideas that people grew up with about segregation of the races

Test Form B

A. Identifying Key Terms, People, and Places

1. f
2. c
3. h
4. g
5. e
6. b
7. d
8. a

B. Identifying Main Ideas

9. b
10. c
11. b
12. a
13. c
14. a
15. b
16. d
17. b
18. a

C. Critical Thinking

Possible answers:

19. Leaders in Germany, Italy, and Japan transformed their nations into strong national powers by building up the military and by invading, occupying, or annexing neighboring lands. All used aggression to bolster national pride and to improve their economies.
20. Alternatives included launching a massive invasion of Japan, using a naval blockade or continued conventional bombing, softening insistence that Japan's surrender be unconditional, and demonstrating the bomb's power on a deserted island. Students who think the bomb was a better alternative to any of these will probably argue that it quickly and definitively ended the war and the killing of Americans, and that it may have taken fewer Japanese lives than continued conventional warfare. Others may argue that dropping the bomb on Japanese cities was not the best strategy because it resulted in the deaths of many thousands of civilians, or that the second bomb was unnecessary. Accept any well-reasoned argument.

D. Interpreting a Map

21. With the exception of Britain and six neutral countries, the Axis Powers controlled all of Europe, from France to the western Soviet Union.
22. Because Britain is an island, the Axis Powers could not invade it by land.
23. They were all neutral.

E. Analyzing a Document

24. The letter suggests that not everyone will welcome the change, as it goes against "some individual ideas and attitudes."
25. intelligent and forceful planning and leadership

Chapter 25

Test Form A

A. Identifying Key Terms, People, and Places

1. j
2. e
3. b
4. f
5. h
6. i
7. d
8. a

B. Identifying Main Ideas

9. b
10. c
11. d
12. a
13. c
14. d
15. a
16. a
17. c
18. a

C. Critical Thinking

Possible answers:

19. The decision seemed to assume that Japanese Americans were more likely to be spies for the Japanese than were other Americans. A related assumption was that at least some Japanese Americans might side with their country of ancestry. The same assumption did not seem to be made of other groups to the same degree. German and Italian Americans, for example, were not sent to internment camps.
20. Students may argue that the image was accurate in depicting a woman in a defense-related job while men were away in the military. Others may argue the image was misleading in depicting Rosie the Riveter as young and white, when in reality, women of all ages, ethnic, and economic groups worked in the defense industry.

D. Interpreting Graphs

21. 1941 and 1942
22. about 95,000
23. During the war, consumer industries converted to war production. As passenger car production went down, military aircraft production went up.

E. Analyzing a Document

24. Farmers, like soldiers, have an important role to play in the war effort.
25. Both symbolized patriotic duty during wartime.

Test Form B

A. Identifying Key Terms, People, and Places

1. c
2. i
3. e
4. h
5. f
6. a
7. g
8. b

B. Identifying Main Ideas

9. b
10. c
11. b
12. d
13. b
14. a
15. c
16. b
17. b
18. d

C. Critical Thinking

Possible answers:

19. Because so many American women worked in defense-related jobs during World War II, they may have thought of themselves as capable, adaptable, and successful in a wider field than was previously available to them. Many women found new satisfactions in these jobs, including that of earning their own money. While some women wanted to continue working outside the home after the war, others thought of these jobs as temporary emergency measures.

20. Students may argue that the country's goals were inconsistent, as the military was fighting the injustices and racial policies of the Axis Powers overseas, while ignoring social injustices and racial discrimination at home.

D. Interpreting Graphs

21. 1943

22. about 85,000

23. During the war, consumer industries converted to war production. As passenger car production went down, military aircraft production went up.

E. Analyzing a Document

24. The poster suggests that farming is a patriotic duty, analogous to serving in the military. The slogan "Food for Freedom" also relates agricultural work to the war effort. Indeed, great amounts of food were needed to support military forces overseas as well as people at home.

25. Possible answers: The artist might have assumed that young farmers would prefer to be fighting overseas; that many farmers were young, white, and male; or that depicting a farmer as such would elicit a patriotic response.

Chapter 26

Test Form A

A. Identifying Key Terms, People, and Places

1. Winston Churchill
2. Josip Broz (Tito)
3. George C. Marshall
4. Douglas MacArthur
5. Mao Zedong
6. Ethel and Julius Rosenberg
7. Fidel Castro
8. John Foster Dulles

B. Identifying Main Ideas

9. c	**14.** a
10. d	**15.** d
11. a	**16.** c
12. b	**17.** a
13. c	**18.** b

C. Critical Thinking

Possible answers:

19. The Soviet leaders probably viewed the Marshall Plan and NATO as direct threats to Soviet security. Soviet leaders felt the United States was using its wealth to buy influence and power in Europe. They feared that strong, rebuilt Western European nations would be a threat to its satellite nations in Eastern Europe.

20. In all these regions, the United States pursued the policy of containment. Asian examples: Korean War, aid to anti-Communist South Vietnam. Middle Eastern examples: support for Israel, restoring pro-American government in Iran, Eisenhower Doctrine. Latin American examples: overthrow of leftist Guatemalan government, opposition to Castro in Cuba.

D. Using Map Skills

21. Any three: Ireland, Spain, Switzerland, Austria, Sweden, Finland, Yugoslavia

22. Any four: Albania, Bulgaria, Czechoslovakia, East Germany, Hungary, Poland, Romania.

E. Analyzing a Document

23. One way of life was based on capitalism and democracy, while the other was based on the communist system.

24. Truman meant that the Soviet Union was using pressure and intimidation to spread communism to other nations.

Test Form B

A. Identifying Key Terms, People, and Places

1. m	**6.** g
2. d	**7.** j
3. k	**8.** f
4. h	**9.** e
5. b	**10.** c

B. Identifying Main Ideas

11. b	**15.** b
12. a	**16.** a
13. a	**17.** d
14. c	**18.** c

C. Critical Thinking

Possible answers:

19. Both helped to carry out the American policy of containment of communism. The Truman Doctrine advocated direct aid to countries resisting Soviet domination. The Marshall Plan helped European nations rebuild after

World War II, with the belief that countries with strong economies would not be tempted by communist ideas.

20. The United States and the Soviet Union had very different goals for the post-war period. The U.S. wanted to help spread democracy and free enterprise. The Soviets wanted to protect themselves from attack and help spread communism. Due to these differing views, the U.S. and Soviet Union began debating the future of Europe even before World War II ended. After the war, these tensions quickly developed into the Cold War.

D. Using Map Skills

21. members of NATO and members of the Warsaw Pact
22. Germany was divided into West and East. West Germany was a member of NATO, while East Germany was a member of the Warsaw Pact.

E. Analyzing a Document

23. The United States supported the way of life based on the "will of the majority."
24. Truman declared that it must be the policy of the United States to support peoples in their struggle for freedom and self-determination.

Chapter 27

Test Form A

A. Identifying Key Terms, People, and Places

1. d	**5.** f
2. h	**6.** g
3. b	**7.** e
4. a	**8.** j

B. Identifying Main Ideas

9. a	**14.** a
10. c	**15.** d
11. b	**16.** d
12. a	**17.** c
13. d	**18.** a

C. Critical Thinking

Possible answers:

19. Someone with a franchise had the backing of a million-dollar parent company that could promote and popularize a product or service nationwide and thus put many lesser known providers out of business.
20. Modern republicanism was consistent with traditional Republican ideology in that it favored decreasing the power of the federal government and limiting government interference in big business. Unlike his Republican predecessors, however, Eisenhower accepted the New Deal principle of government responsibility for the social welfare of its citizens.

D. Reading a Table

21. In the previous year, 1946, 4.6 million workers went out on strike, more than 10 percent of the work force. The Taft-Hartley Act was an attempt to restrict strikes in industries affecting the national interest.
22. The act appears to have been successful; the work stoppages in the early 1950s involved fewer workers and a lower percentage of the total work force than did the 1946 strikes.

E. Analyzing a Document

23. Students will probably choose one from among the following: being good and informed citizens, learning cultural values, professional training, and life success. Accept any reasonable choice and well-reasoned explanation for it.
24. The Court felt that to separate people solely on the basis of their race will invariably make them feel inferior—a feeling that will affect them throughout their lives.

Test Form B

A. Identifying Key Terms, People, and Places

1. g	**5.** b
2. c	**6.** a
3. f	**7.** d
4. e	**8.** i

B. Identifying Main Ideas

9. c	**14.** d
10. c	**15.** a
11. c	**16.** b
12. b	**17.** b
13. a	**18.** a

C. Critical Thinking

Possible answers:

19. President Truman probably assumed that the American people wanted to extend the New Deal of the 1930s even further, by passing more social legislation having to do with working conditions and pay, living conditions, and health insurance.
20. Technological advances created more white-collar jobs and introduced coomputers into the workplace and television into the home. Innovations such as affordable mass-produced housing, an interstate highway system, and affordable automobiles encouraged Americans to settle in the suburbs.

D. Reading a Table

21. The high figures for work stoppages and percentage of workers striking in the previous

year, 1946, might have been used to build up support for the Taft-Hartley Act, which was designed to limit strikes.

22. Students who agree may cite the table's information that during Eisenhower's first term no more than 2,650,000 workers, or 5.2 percent of workers, were on strike in any one year. This percentage was exceeded four times during the Truman years. Students who disagree might state that the number of work stoppages during the two periods was not very different.

E. Analyzing a Document

23. According to the excerpt, people who are denied an education would be unlikely to succeed since education is the foundation of good citizenship, cultural values, and preparation for a career.
24. "Separate" solely on the basis of race cannot be "equal." Therefore, students separated for reasons of race would feel inferior, and this feeling of inferiority would affect them throughout their lives.

Chapter 28

Test Form A

A. Identifying Key Terms, People, and Places

1. A mandate is a set of wishes expressed to a candidate by his or her voters.
2. The Great Society was President Johnson's domestic program that included educational aid, medical care for the elderly, and programs to fight poverty.
3. VISTA, established during Johnson's presidency, was a domestic version of the Peace Corps, made up of volunteers who helped the nation's poor communities.
4. The Immigration Act of 1965 eliminated quotas for immigrants from individual countries, replacing the quotas with more flexible limits on immigration.
5. Medicaid provided low-cost health insurance for poor Americans.
6. The Cuban Missile Crisis occurred in 1962, during Kennedy's presidency, when the United States and the Soviet Union confronted each other over the Soviets' building of missile bases in Cuba.
7. The Limited Test Ban Treaty, signed in 1963, banned nuclear testing above the ground.

B. Identifying Main Ideas

8. c
9. c
10. b
11. d
12. a
13. c
14. a
15. b
16. c
17. d
18. b

C. Critical Thinking

Possible answers:

19. The Great Society advanced many of the New Frontier's policy goals, including a tax cut, aid to the poor, fighting inequality, aid to education, and medical care for the aged.
20. Accept answers that cite one or more stands that Kennedy took in an effort to contain communism: the Bay of Pigs invasion, the stand on Berlin, the stand against missiles in Cuba, the Alliance for Progress, the Peace Corps, sending help to South Vietnam.

D. Interpreting a Table

21. Expenditures for all social welfare programs increased significantly from 1965 to 1975.
22. The percentage of GNP spent for social insurance programs was more than double that spent on public welfare programs, 8.1 percent as compared to 2.9 percent.

E. Analyzing a Document

23. Kennedy believed that time inevitably brought change, expected or unexpected.
24. Both sides could divert funds from military spending to programs that improved people's lives.

Test Form B

A. Identifying Key Terms, People, and Places

1. The New Frontier was the name given to Kennedy's proposals to improve the economy, give aid to the poor, and strengthen the space program.
2. The Medicare program provided hospital and low-cost medical insurance for most Americans ages 65 and older.
3. The Miranda rule stated that criminal suspects must be read their rights to remain silent and to receive legal aid.
4. The Bay of Pigs invasion was an unsuccessful attempt by Cuban rebels, backed by the United States, to overthrow Cuba's Fidel Castro.
5. The Soviets built the Berlin Wall to keep East Germans from escaping to West Germany.
6. The Alliance for Progress was a Kennedy program to prevent

the spread of communism by giving aid to developing countries.

7. The Peace Corps sent volunteers to developing countries to work as teachers, health workers, and technicians.

B. Identifying Main Ideas

8. b	14. b
9. b	15. c
10. c	16. a
11. b	17. a
12. a	18. d
13. b	

C. Critical Thinking

Possible answers:

19. President Johnson's landslide election in 1964 gave him a strong mandate and his experience in Congress made him highly skillful in getting legislation passed. Also, Congress realized that the American people needed some swift action to heal the wound caused by Kennedy's assassination.

20. Rusk's words indicated that a nuclear war might have caused the destruction of entire nations, including the United States. The fact that Rusk and Kennedy were still alive was a major victory in itself, even though no actual nuclear war took place.

D. Interpreting a Table

21. It more than tripled expenditures per capita, from $119 to $389, and nearly doubled expenditures as a percentage of GNP, from 1.1 percent to 2.9 percent.

22. Expenditures as a percentage of GNP had more than doubled, from 8.2 percent to 19.0 percent, indicating that a greater amount of the economy's resources was flowing into social welfare programs.

E. Analyzing a Document

23. Kennedy believed that the Cold War led to a negative use of economic resources. The Cold War spent massive amounts of money on weapons that could have been better spent on other projects that contributed to the public good.

24. Students will probably say that Kennedy was right, citing examples from history of enemies in one war becoming allies in another. For instance, Britain and the United States fought each other in the Revolutionary War and the War of 1812, but became allies in World Wars I and II. They might also cite that the Cold War is over and the Soviet Union no longer exists.

Chapter 29

Test Form A

A. Identifying Key Terms, People, and Places

1. g	6. j
2. k	7. l
3. a	8. i
4. d	9. f
5. h	10. c

B. Identifying Main Ideas

11. b	15. b
12. c	16. c
13. a	17. a
14. a	18. d

C. Critical Thinking

Possible answers:

19. Martin Luther King, Jr., wanted to achieve an end to segregation in the United States. He dreamed of a day when blacks and whites would be truly integrated. Malcolm X was a black nationalist who opposed the idea of desegregation. He believed that true integration in American society was impossible.

20. When the group was first founded, SNCC was interracial. Using nonviolent protest, SNCC worked to end discrimination against African Americans. Toward the later 1960s, SNCC became more militant. SNCC adopted the idea of "black power." One leader, Stokely Carmichael, wanted SNCC to exclude white activists.

D. Interpreting Maps

21. Mississippi

22. Possible answers: Yes, many more African Americans had registered to vote in 1966 than in 1960. No, in most southern states less than 50 percent of African Americans were registered to vote by 1966.

E. Analyzing a Document

23. Johnson felt that Congress should support voting rights because voting rights were guaranteed in the Constitution, and members of Congress had sworn to uphold the Constitution.

24. No, Johnson said there was no issue of states' rights. He argued that the voting rights struggle was a human rights struggle, and that voting rights were guaranteed in the Constitution.

TEST FORM B

A. IDENTIFYING KEY TERMS, PEOPLE, AND PLACES

1. i	6. e
2. j	7. g
3. m	8. k
4. c	9. f
5. a	10. d

B. IDENTIFYING MAIN IDEAS

11. a	15. a
12. c	16. c
13. c	17. b
14. d	18. d

C. CRITICAL THINKING

Possible answers:

19. During his early months in office, Kennedy moved slowly on civil rights issues. He did not want to lose the support of southern members of Congress. Later in his term, Kennedy became a much stronger supporter of civil rights. He wanted American society to put into practice the principles of freedom that U.S. leaders preached to the world. He decided it was time for the government to take action in support of civil rights.
20. The civil rights movement was led, not by the government, but by individuals and organizations. Through actions like the March on Washington, people of all ages protested against segregation and racism. In response, the government began passing new civil rights laws.

D. INTERPRETING MAPS

21. Tennessee
22. Even after passage of the Voting Rights Act of 1965, registration of African American voters was still under fifty percent in seven southern states.

E. ANALYZING A DOCUMENT

23. The Constitution says that no person shall be kept from voting because of his race or his color.
24. Johnson argued that Congress must obey the Constitution. Since voting rights are guaranteed in the Constitution, Congress must support voting rights.

CHAPTER 30

TEST FORM A

A. IDENTIFYING KEY TERMS, PEOPLE, AND PLACES

1. to gain economic, political and social equality for women
2. to declare discrimination based on sex illegal
3. to improve pay and conditions for migrant farm workers
4. to gain compensation for Japanese Americans who were interned during World War II
5. to gain self-government of Native American lands
6. to set and enforce national pollution-control standards

B. IDENTIFYING MAIN IDEAS

7. b	12. b
8. c	13. a
9. d	14. c
10. b	15. a
11. c	16. b

C. CRITICAL THINKING

Possible answers:

17. NOW considered the image of women solely as happy housewives "false." The image NOW might have considered more "accurate" was of women as well-educated, qualified, capable, and politically and socially motivated.
18. The civil rights movement inspired women and minorities to seek equality. It also demonstrated that tactics such an nonviolent action, political pressure, and publicity could bring about change. The civil rights movement also produced the Civil Rights Act of 1964, which helped many groups fight discrimination.

D. INTERPRETING A TABLE

19. Women still earned only about 60 percent of what men earned.
20. Probably the 1980s, since women's earnings rose to nearly 72 percent of men's.

E. ANALYZING A DOCUMENT

21. admitting that the problem exists
22. No, but she felt the ERA could protect some women, while encouraging society to examine its prejudicial attitudes.

TEST FORM B

A. IDENTIFYING KEY TERMS, PEOPLE, AND PLACES

1. a	5. b
2. f	6. c
3. e	7. d
4. g	8. i

B. IDENTIFYING MAIN IDEAS

9. b	14. b
10. a	15. c
11. a	16. c
12. b	17. a
13. c	18. d

C. CRITICAL THINKING

Possible answers:

19. Women and minority groups all sought equal opportunity and equality before the law. They all hoped to end discrimi-

nation by changing the attitudes of people in American society.

20. The loss of traditional homelands was a problem unique to Native Americans. The Native American way of life has always been based on close ties to the land. Yet, many years after the first settlers had moved into Native American territory, state and federal governments continued to take over traditional tribal lands.

D. Interpreting a Table

21. During the 1960s, women continued to earn about 60 percent of what men earned. In 1990 dollars, the gap increased significantly, from $8,569 to $11,529.

22. Women made the greatest strides during the 1980s, when their median earnings increased by more than $8,000 and the gap between men's and women's earnings decreased by more than 11 percentage points.

E. Analyzing a Document

23. because white Americans were beginning to admit that this prejudice existed in American society

24. She felt the ERA could protect women who most needed it, while helping to start the slow process of change.

Chapter 31

Test Form A

A. Identifying Key Terms, People, and Places

1. f **6.** d
2. a **7.** e
3. g **8.** a
4. e **9.** c
5. c **10.** f

B. Identifying Main Ideas

11. b **15.** c
12. b **16.** c
13. b **17.** c
14. c **18.** d

C. Critical Thinking

Possible answers:

19. Before the war, American leaders assumed that American weapons, money, and technology could bring victory over communism anywhere, at any time. After the war, Americans realized this assumption was false.

20. Antiwar: the conflict was a civil war which should be resolved by the Vietnamese alone; American involvement in Vietnam was an act of imperialism; the draft was unfair because men who could afford to go to college could avoid serving in the war; the conflict was a racist war in which thousands of African American and Latino soldiers were used against a nonwhite enemy. Pro-war: the United States was fighting to support freedom in Vietnam; if Vietnam fell to communism, other Asian nations would soon follow.

D. Reading a Chart

21. 1968

22. 201,000

23. 1969; this is the first year there was a net decrease in the number of American troops in Vietnam.

E. Analyzing a Document

24. It was important to stand up to Communists, Johnson argued, because they wanted to rule the world – and they would if the United States didn't stop them.

25. Johnson and many other American leaders believed that the Vietnam War was a necessary part of the struggle to stop Communists from taking over the world.

Test Form B

A. Identifying Key Terms, People, and Places

1. c **6.** f
2. a **7.** b
3. f **8.** c
4. d **9.** e
5. e **10.** d

B. Identifying Main Ideas

11. d **15.** b
12. c **16.** a
13. c **17.** d
14. c **18.** c

C. Critical Thinking

Possible answers:

19. With the Tet Offensive, the Viet Cong demonstrated that they could launch a massive attack on targets all over South Vietnam. Up until this point, many Americans had believed that U.S. forces were defeating the Communists. After Tet, many Americans were discouraged, and began to express doubts about American involvement in Vietnam.

20. Unlike soldiers returning from World War II, Vietnam veterans were not given welcoming parades. Many Vietnam veterans felt that Americans did not appreciate what the veterans had gone through in Vietnam.

D. Reading a Chart

21. 1969

22. 1966

23. It caused the number of troops to increase sharply. The next year, 161,000 more troops were sent to Vietnam.

E. Analyzing a Document

24. Johnson argued that if the United States didn't stand up to communism, Communists would be able to take over the world.

25. Johnson was referring to the two sides in the cold war – the United States and its allies, and the Soviet Union and other communist nations.

Chapter 32

Test Form A

A. Identifying Key Terms, People, and Places

1. j **6.** c
2. b **7.** f
3. d **8.** g
4. i **9.** k
5. a **10.** e

B. Identifying Main Ideas

11. b **15.** b
12. d **16.** c
13. b **17.** d
14. b **18.** d

C. Critical Thinking

Possible answers:

19. Perhaps the guiding principle behind Nixon's foreign policy was *realpolitik*, or practical politics. This idea, advanced by Nixon's advisor Henry Kissinger, held that decisions should be based on what is best for the nation rather than on rigid moral principles that say what is definitely right and what is definitely wrong.

20. Students who argue that Nixon was justified in refusing to release the tapes may cite rights to privacy, presidential privilege, or the constitutional right not to incriminate oneself. Students who argue he was not justified may cite obedience to the law (in this case, the law upheld by the Supreme Court), which is demanded from everyone, both Presidents and private citizens.

D. Reading a Graph

21. 1973; about 70 percent

22. about 60 percent

E. Analyzing a Document

23. the Soviet Union; China

24. Such a hatred enslaves the nation that holds the hatred; the necessity to spend vast sums on weaponry rather than on more socially rewarding purposes.

Test Form B

A. Identifying Key Terms, People, and Places

1. c **6.** i
2. f **7.** b
3. h **8.** j
4. a **9.** e
5. k **10.** g

B. Identifying Main Ideas

11. b **15.** c
12. a **16.** d
13. c **17.** b
14. c **18.** a

C. Critical Thinking

Possible answers:

19. Students are likely to answer yes, that Nixon's policies opened the door to establishing relations with China, reduced tensions between the United States and the Soviet Union, and established the first steps toward nuclear disarmament.

20. He would probably have been impeached. The House Judiciary Committee had already voted for impeachment and chances were good that the full House and Senate would have voted for impeachment also. Students might add that an impeachment hearing would have intensified political divisions in the country and further eroded public morale.

D. Reading a Graph

21. about 70 percent

22. 1973, with the Cox firing; about 28 percent

E. Analyzing a Document

23. The United States was actively "engaged at many points" with the Soviet Union, meaning there was constant conflict between the two nations. The United States was "almost totally isolated" from China, which led to fear and suspicion. There was a "deadly impasse" (meaning a standstill or inaction) with both nations.

24. Nations that continue to hold national hatreds are themselves enslaved by such hatreds.

CHAPTER 33

TEST FORM A

A. IDENTIFYING KEY TERMS, PEOPLE, AND PLACES

1. f	**6.** f
2. b	**7.** e
3. e	**8.** d
4. d	**9.** b
5. a	**10.** c

B. IDENTIFYING MAIN IDEAS

11. b	**15.** b
12. c	**16.** b
13. b	**17.** c
14. d	**18.** a

C. CRITICAL THINKING

Possible answers:

19. Students who answer no might argue that it clouded the facts that should have been made public. They might add that most Americans could not understand why Nixon had paid no penalty for his involvement in Watergate. Voters were angry enough over the pardon that they booed Ford, voted a number of Republicans out in 1974, and voted him out in 1976. Students who answer yes might argue that the pardon saved the nation from the continuing trauma of an impeachment trial. They would in effect be agreeing with Ford's comment that "someone must write the end" to the Watergate scandal.

20. Nightly newscasts turned the hostage crisis into a national debate, and the public became frustrated and impatient. President Carter's inability to secure the hostages' freedom lowered his popularity. When a commando rescue mission that he authorized ended in disaster, his administration was further humiliated. Carter's chance for reelection was severely damaged.

D. READING A TABLE

21. 57,883.2 thousand barrels per day; 53.1

22. In general, with the exception of 1976 and 1977, there was a downward trend.

E. ANALYZING A DOCUMENT

23. to create and sustain a society in which all people are equal

24. They must act as good role models, show integrity, be willing to make sacrifices, and be willing to admit their mistakes.

TEST FORM B

A. IDENTIFYING KEY TERMS, PEOPLE, AND PLACES

1. e	**6.** f
2. b	**7.** a
3. f	**8.** d
4. d	**9.** c
5. c	**10.** e

B. IDENTIFYING MAIN IDEAS

11. a	**15.** a
12. b	**16.** c
13. b	**17.** a
14. d	**18.** c

C. CRITICAL THINKING

Possible answers:

19. Some students might argue that Ford's ideological leanings did not suit the times. For example, he believed in a limited role for government at a time of serious difficulties. Other students might cite Ford's lack of administrative or foreign experience. Still other students might argue that Ford was a good leader who was plagued by difficult problems: the public disillusionment over Watergate, stagflation and recession, and a hostile Congress that would have hurt any President.

20. Some students might say that Carter's strong religious beliefs raised the standards of the Presidency to a higher level. For instance, Carter's support of human rights was a cornerstone of his Presidency. Because of Carter's high standards, the United States stopped helping regimes that seriously abused human rights. Other students might say that Carter's beliefs and principles were stumbling blocks to his effectiveness as President. They affected his ability to "wheel and deal" with Congress to get his legislative program passed. In foreign affairs, his commitment to finding ethical solutions to complex issues undermined efforts to improve relations between the United States and the Soviet Union.

D. READING A TABLE

21. 1980; 44.9 percent

22. 62,819.9 thousand barrels per day

E. ANALYZING A DOCUMENT

23. to create a society in which all are equal, to find new ways to implement the system the founders handed down

24. honesty and follow-through, willingness to show the way through example, willingness to admit mistakes

Chapter 34

Test Form A

A. Identifying Key Terms, People, and Places

1. g	**6.** b
2. a	**7.** a
3. d	**8.** g
4. c	**9.** e
5. e	**10.** d

B. Identifying Main Ideas

11. b	**15.** a
12. c	**16.** a
13. b	**17.** b
14. c	**18.** b

C. Critical Thinking

Possible answers:

19. Any two: cut taxes to stimulate economic growth; eliminate government regulation of American business and industry; cut spending on social welfare programs; give more responsibility to state and local governments.

20. When Reagan first came into office he adopted a "get tough" policy toward the Soviet Union, which he called the "evil empire." He supported the rapid buildup of military forces and nuclear weapons. During his second term, Reagan developed a close relationship with the new Soviet leader, Mikhail Gorbachev. In 1987, the two leaders signed an important nuclear arms reduction treaty.

D. Interpreting a Table

21. the election of 1984, when Reagan received more than 54 million votes

22. In each election, the Republican candidate received a clear majority of the popular vote and an overwhelming majority of electoral votes.

E. Analyzing a Document

23. Reagan was calling for Gorbachev to come to Berlin and order the destruction of the Berlin Wall.

24. Yes. Reagan argued that the expansion of freedom in the Soviet Union and Eastern Europe would lead to peace and greater prosperity.

Test Form B

A. Identifying Key Terms, People, and Places

1. c	**6.** d
2. a	**7.** c
3. f	**8.** b
4. b	**9.** e
5. d	**10.** f

B. Identifying Main Ideas

11. b	**15.** d
12. c	**16.** b
13. d	**17.** c
14. c	**18.** a

C. Critical Thinking

Possible answers:

19. Any one: The S & L scandal—After Reagan pressed for deregulation of the banking industry, many S & Ls made risky investments, eventually losing $2.6 billion in depositors' savings. The Iran-Contra affair—Disregarding Congress, administration officials secretly funded the contras, a military group working to overthrow the Marxist government of Nicaragua. These actions were against the will of Congress. Reagan claimed to have no knowledge of the operation.

20. Some students may cite the end of the Cold War as Bush's greatest foreign policy success. During Bush's presidency, communism collapsed in Eastern Europe and the Soviet Union, and the Soviet Union broke apart. The United States became the world's only superpower. Others may say the Persian Gulf War was Bush's greatest success. Under Bush's leadership, 28 nations came together to drive Iraqi forces out of Kuwait in 1991.

D. Interpreting a Table

21. the election of 1984

22. Michael Dukakis in 1988

E. Analyzing a Document

23. Reagan argued that Gorbachev should come to Berlin and destroy the wall that restricted travel between East and West Berlin.

24. By tearing down the Berlin Wall, Soviet leaders could expect an expansion of peace and prosperity throughout the Soviet Union and Eastern Europe.

Chapter 35

Test Form A

A. Identifying Key Terms, People, and Places

1. e	**6.** j
2. g	**7.** d
3. b	**8.** c
4. k	**9.** l
5. a	**10.** i

B. Identifying Main Ideas

11. b	**15.** d
12. b	**16.** c
13. c	**17.** a
14. b	**18.** d

C. Critical Thinking

Possible answers:

19. Any two: the surge in immigration contributed to the nation's growing diversity; it helped increase the population of the Sunbelt and urban areas; it led to a debate over how many immigrants should be allowed into the United States, and whether or not immigration was good for the American economy.
20. After the Cold War, the United States tried to help Russia make the transition to democracy and a free market economy. U.S. leaders supported the newly-elected president of Russia, Boris Yeltsin. The U.S. also offered Russia a $2.5 billion aid package.

D. Reading a Table

21. The number of people receiving benefits grew at a rapid pace.
22. Yes. Americans over the age of 65 make up the fastest-growing age group in the country. This means more and more people will qualify for social security benefits.

E. Analyzing a Document

23. In its first five years, the Clinton administration made 240 trade agreements. These agreements removed barriers to American exports.
24. According to Clinton, trade leads to economic growth in the United States, and helps build a safer, more stable world.

Test Form B

A. Identifying Key Terms, People, and Places

1. f	6. l
2. a	7. b
3. d	8. g
4. k	9. e
5. h	10. i

B. Identifying Main Ideas

11. d	15. c
12. a	16. c
13. c	17. d
14. b	18. b

C. Critical Thinking

Possible answers:

19. The main points were to scale back the size of the federal government, to eliminate regulations, to cut taxes, and to balance the budget.
20. Any two: the U.S. used economic sanctions to help bring an end to apartheid in South Africa and bring a peaceful transition to black majority rule; the U.S. helped the PLO and Israel reach a peace agreement; U.S. troops intervened in Haiti, helping to restore democracy; U.S. negotiators helped Protestants and Catholics in Northern Ireland reach a peace agreement; U.S. hosted peace talks among the combatants in the Bosnian conflict, and sent troops to Bosnia to help keep the peace; U.S. troops tried to stop starvation and civil war in Somalia.

D. Reading a Table

21. by about $212 billion
22. Yes. If the trend shown in this table continues, costs will continue to surge. The huge baby boom generation will begin retiring in the twenty-first century. The cost of Social Security will rise even more quickly, putting a strain on the nation's ability to pay for the program.

E. Analyzing a Document

23. According to Clinton, the United States should welcome trade, and work to expand trade with nations around the world.
24. Yes. Exports account for one-third of the nation's economic growth.

Chapter 36

Test Form A

A. Identifying Key Terms, People, and Places

1. e
2. d
3. b
4. a

B. Identifying Main Ideas

5. c
6. a
7. c
8. d

C. Critical Thinking

9. Possible gains: the level of wages might rise; unemployment might fall; the cost of social services might fall; American culture might be more unified. Possible losses: fewer new small businesses might be created; taxpayer rolls might get shrunk; certain jobs might not be filled; the nation would become less diverse.

Test Form B

A. Identifying Key Terms, People, and Places

1. a
2. b
3. d
4. e

B. Identifying Main Ideas

5. d
6. b
7. c
8. d

C. Critical Thinking

9. Possible questions: Does immigration help or hurt the economy? Should the government lower the number of immigrants allowed to enter the country? Should immigrants have to know English before entering the country? Should the government provide social services for immigrants? Should the children of illegal immigrants be welcome in public schools?

Chapter 37

Test Form A

A. Identifying Key Terms, People, and Places

1. an organization which strongly opposes gun control
2. murder
3. amendment to the Constitution which deals with the question of gun ownership

B. Identifying Main Ideas

4. d
5. d
6. b
7. a
8. d

C. Critical Thinking

9. Possible answer: English colonists brought to the American colonies their belief in the right to own guns. Then, during the American Revolution, Americans used their own guns to defeat the British. When the Constitution was written, many people demanded that the right to bear arms be included in the Bill of Rights. In the 1800s, armed pioneers and cowboys became symbols of American freedom.

Test Form B

A. Identifying Key Terms, People, and Places

1. homicide
2. Second Amendment
3. NRA

B. Identifying Main Ideas

4. c
5. a
6. b
7. d
8. a

C. Critical Thinking

9. Possible answer: They will probably agree that violent crime is a problem across the nation. They will perhaps also agree that violent criminals should not be allowed to own guns.

Chapter 38

Test Form A

A. Identifying Key Terms, People, and Places

1. The death of 140 workers when the Triangle Shirtwaist Factory burned led to legislation on worker safety and minimum wages.
2. As part of their campaign to improve working conditions for the poor, progressives pushed for state laws setting minimum wages.
3. The New Deal's Fair Labor Standards Act included a minimum wage.

B. Identifying Main Ideas

4. b
5. b
6. a
7. a

C. Critical Thinking

8. Possible answer: Many Americans believe that a person who works hard should earn enough money to support a decent life. Without raises in the minimum wage, workers earning this wage can not keep up with rising costs.

Test Form B

A. Identifying Key Terms, People, and Places

1. President Franklin Delano Roosevelt's plan to help the country through the Depression
2. the idea that hard work will produce a decent life
3. social reformers who worked to improve the living and working conditions of the poor

4. New York City factory at which a fire killed 140 workers in 1911

B. Identifying Main Ideas

5. d
6. c
7. b
8. d

C. Critical Thinking

9. Possible answer: The statement is an opinion. Lewis can't prove that it is the right thing to do, but he believes it is. He offers evidence to support his view, but others offer evidence to support the opposing view.

Chapter 39

Test Form A

A. Identifying Key Terms, People, and Places

1. d
2. f
3. e
4. b

B. Identifying Main Ideas

5. a
6. a
7. c
8. d

C. Critical Thinking

9. Possible answers: Yes: Job training will allow people to leave welfare and find decent jobs. Child care is also necessary because parents need a safe place to leave their children while they work. No: Job training and child care are important, but it is not the government's responsibility to provide these services.

Test Form B

A. Identifying Key Terms, People, and Places

1. c
2. d
3. b
4. a

B. Identifying Main Ideas

5. c
6. a
7. d
8. a

C. Critical Thinking

9. Possible answer: The assumption that the government should take responsibility for helping poor people through hard times.

Chapter 40

Test Form A

A. Identifying Key Terms, People, and Places

1. f
2. d
3. c
4. e

B. Identifying Main Ideas

5. d
6. b
7. a
8. a

C. Critical Thinking

9. Possible answer: NAFTA supporters predict that free trade will help the Mexican economy improve over time. A healthy economy, supporters argue, is the best way to build political stability.

Test Form B

A. Identifying Key Terms, People, and Places

1. c
2. e
3. a
4. b

B. Identifying Main Ideas

5. c
6. b
7. c
8. d

C. Critical Thinking

9. Possible answers: Yes: Free trade is the wave of the future. I would not want my country to be left out of the expanding global trade. Access to the huge American market will be good for the businesses of my country. Also, free trade will help our economy improve, leading to greater political stability. No: Free trade benefits huge American corporations, while exploiting our workers and damaging our environment. Small businesses in my country will not be able to compete with large international corporations.

Chapter 41

Test Form A

A. Identifying Key Terms, People, and Places

1. c
2. f
3. a
4. d

B. Identifying Main Ideas

5. d
6. c
7. c
8. b

C. Critical Thinking

9. Possible answers: Yes: As in Washington's time, foreign entanglements are dangerous and costly. Soldiers die, and money is spent on weapons, when it should be spent on domestic programs such as education. No: The world has changed since then. In the long run, American security, freedom, and prosperity depend on upon international stability. For its own good and the good of the world, the United States must maintain close ties with other nations.

Test Form B

A. Identifying Key Terms, People, and Places

1. b
2. f
3. e
4. c

B. Identifying Main Ideas

5. a
6. d
7. a
8. d

C. Critical Thinking

9. According to this view, reducing foreign commitments would be dangerous. Other countries might try to gain world power. This could lead to global conflicts, as it did in World War II. Wars are far more costly than foreign commitments.

Chapter 42

Test Form A

A. Identifying Key Terms, People, and Places

1. d
2. f
3. c
4. a

B. Identifying Main Ideas

5. b
6. a
7. b
8. c

C. Critical Thinking

9. Possible answer: Yes. Computers have changed the way Americans work and study. Nearly all businesses now use computers to improve their productivity. In schools, students use computers to conduct research and communicate with other students around the world.

Test Form B

A. Identifying Key Terms, People, and Places

1. a
2. d
3. e
4. b

B. Identifying Main Ideas

5. d
6. b
7. a
8. b

C. Critical Thinking

9. Answers will vary. Some students might suggest that schools teach both computers skills and traditional academic skills. Others might suggest ways in which computers can be used to develop students' communication and problem solving skills.

TEACHER'S NOTES

TEACHER'S NOTES

TEACHER'S NOTES